Maud's Memoirs,
Peter's Portrait,
Sarah's Story

Maud's Memoirs, Peter's Portrait, Sarah's Story

Sarah Friars

To order additional copies of this book, contact:
Xlibris Corporation
1-888-795-4274
www.Xlibris.com
Orders@Xlibris.com
53645

Contents

Chapter 1: "The Orphanage" 7

Chapter 2: "The Situation Girl" 19

Chapter 3: "To Catch a Bus" 37

Chapter 4: "Jobs, Jobs and More Jobs" 40

Chapter 5: "Unforbidden Territory" 46

Chapter 6: "Mom, Where Are You?" 50

Chapter 7: "A Nurse Overnight" 54

Chapter 8: "What is a Vocation? Did I have the Call to Religious Life?" 57

Chapter 9: "Simple Adoption" 61

Chapter 10: "Big Decisions" 63

Chapter 11: "One More Try" 65

Chapter 12: "A Trunk in Passageway" 69

Chapter 13: "On the English train as it pulled along my thoughts were of Belfast and Ireland" 73

Chapter 14: "A Postulant in Training" 75

Chapter 15: "Doubts and Temptation to Leave" 83

Chapter 16: "I'll Try Again" 86

Chapter 17: "Free Again" 92

Chapter 18: "The Novice" 94

Chapter 19: "A Practical Nurse Again" 100

Chapter 20: "The Vows" 103

Chapter 21: "I Became a Teacher Overnight" 108

Chapter 22: "Preparation for Africa" 118

Chapter 23: "Out on the High Seas" 120

Chapter 24: "Some Introspection on Life" 126

Chapter 25: Arrival in Durban, South Africa 129

Chapter 26: My First Day in the Classroom.................................133

Chapter 27: First Train Ride in South Africa..............................136

Chapter 28: Birthday Dip in the Indian Ocean...........................140

Chapter 29: Another Transfer Where I Would Learn
to Toe the Line...144

Chapter 30: Déjà Vu!..157

Chapter 31: To Durban for Nursing Training 164

Chapter 32: General Nursing..167

Chapter 33: The Sound of Music—My First Movie........................174

Chapter 34: Scary Times...180

Chapter 35: Baby Found at Doorstep 182

Chapter 36: Happy Birthday 187

Chapter 37: Tragic Events Thrown in with Happy Events................189

Chapter 38: African Hospital...192

Chapter 39: Transferred Again 204

Chapter 40: Big Changes and Surprises....................................206

Chapter 41: Habit Changes—the Good and the Bad....................210

Chapter 42: Home Leave..213

Chapter 43: Back in Belfast..216

Chapter 44: To the Orphanage Twenty-first Birthday Party 218

Chapter 45: Belfast Had Changed 220

Chapter 46: Back to Africa into a Ten-day Silence Retreat 226

Chapter 47: Back to Hospital Life Again...................................231

Chapter 48: Big Changes in the Convent..................................241

Chapter 49: Off to California 252

Chapter 50: Exclaustration while Living in America 255

Chapter 51: "Nurse Becomes a Patient" 268

Chapter 52: In 1950s Technology Stepped In 271

Chapter 53: Back to Visit the Orphanage in Belfast....................273

Chapter 1

"The Orphanage"

I grew up in an orphanage in Belfast, Northern Ireland had no recollection of being put there in 1936. I was among a large number of children; I did hear that we were about two-hundred to three-hundred children, the numbers varied at different times. World War II orphans helped to swell the numbers.

The Bishop of Ballynafeigh, Northern Ireland, Bishop Dorrian, handed over his own house to the Sisters of Nazareth on May ___, 1876. It was known as Nazareth House. It was situated on the Ormeau Road, Ballynafeigh, Belfast. Over the years the house was expanded to accommodate a convent for the nuns, and homes for the people with diseases, the elderly, orphans, and the or, who would come knocking at their doors. I believe that the first two people admitted to Nazareth House were an incurable child and a Presbyterian woman. As the need for beds grew, the Sisters slept on the floor and gave up their beds to the poor.

The Nazareth Sisters depended on the charity of the laity to assist them in providing for those in their care. The people were poor in those days. It was a case of the poor helping the poor. Everyday, I would see the Sisters walking through the front door of the convent, to go out to beg, which was the term that we children used. They went to different areas of the city of Belfast, to collect alms. They did not go alone but always two by two to the private homes. It was pennies from the HAVE-NOTS of Belfast that helped to keep the house in existence. It was the poor outside who helped the poor orphan children inside.

As a child in the orphanage, I was not aware of course, of what responsibilities these nuns had. I recall, many children were deformed, and we'd make fun of their behavior and imitated their distorted faces. Many children would throw fits and have convulsions. I remember one child who had uncontrollable fits of laughter. We had a child in the class below me who would throw a fit, and lie on the floor, frothing at the mouth. We all had different chores and were told to clean up after these children's outbursts; we had to take our turn of taking care of these children. They really scared me and I was afraid to go near any of them. I can't forget one girl who had some kind of episode periodically. We were all responsible, at least as many of us as possible, to get her up immediately during the episodes and stand her against a wall, so that she would stop her contortions.

The orphanage was a huge monumental building. When I lived there, it housed different sections of the population. The elderly were divided into different sections for the men and women. They would come together for meals and in the chapel for Church Services in the morning. Generally mass was at seven in the morning. The men went to the top part of the chapel, and women were further back, but all were on the same side. We, children, who occupied the largest section of the building, would be in pews on the opposite side of the elderly folks. The nuns had a wing at the front entrance of the convent to the chapel.

The convent was kind of sacrosanct and located away, though still connected to the rest of the building. We never saw inside the convent or even went anywhere near their place. Part of the chapel was cordoned off, set aside for the nuns, and they had a direct view of the altar in the chapel. We children occupied the largest section of the main building, which housed the classrooms, dormitories, refectories, kitchens and laundry. There was a closed-in area for younger children, and part of that is where the babies were kept. I thought, as I think many of us did, that we were put in the orphanage as babies and that we came from the nursery, and progressed from there up to six or seven years, then moved into the bigger dormitories and moved up into the different classrooms.

All our teachers were nuns, with the exception of a wonderful lay teacher who taught us in Standard Four and Standard Five, when we were about nine or ten years old. The lay teacher was Miss O'Donnell. There were two classes in every classroom.

Down the road, about twenty minutes walk from the Girl's Orphanage on the Ormeau Road, was a Boy's Orphanage. It was run on the same lines as ours, by the same nuns. It was situated on the Ravenhill Road. The only time that we ever went down the road to visit that orphanage was when a nun from the Boys' Orphanage died, and we had to go to help swell the singing. I'm sure the boy's choir would not have needed any help from us girls! I recall that we would walk down the road, four abreast, holding hands all the way. I'm not sure how often I was down at the Boys' Orphanage, but I recall two times. I certainly remember being sent outside to play in the fields after the funeral, and walking right into the cow dung that was soft and mushy after the "Soft Irish Rains". We all hated that, but we still walked into it. We walked all the way home and we had to clean our *tackys* (tachies) when we arrived at home. That was the name that we called our shoes, sometimes they were called *plimsoles*. They were like tennis shoes but were hand-me-downs from the generations of children in the orphanage.

The clothes that we wore were also hand-me-downs, and they were very coarse blue—denim-like dresses. We would rummage through the piles of dresses to fine one that would fit us. Everyday we had on the same color during all our years in the Orphanage. We had navy blue dresses that we had to wear when some important figure was expected to arrive. We always had to wear big white bows in our short cropped hair. They were part of our uniforms, and we wore them all day long until we went to bed at night in the dormitories.

All the children had different tasks to do before and after school: Cleaning the hallways, classrooms, dormitories, and bathrooms, and helping in different places like the kitchens. There was more than one kitchen, and for a while I was sent way far down to the lower kitchen. We called this kitchen "Annie Ippy's Kitchen to distinguish it from the others. This lady would be down there all the time. She had a room set aside off the kitchen which we figured was Annie's bedroom. No doubt, the reason that Annie lived there was that she probably couldn't make it up the stairway. To this day, I have not seen such a large woman as Annie Ippy. Her name was used many times throughout the day to scare us children. We ourselves would scare each other saying, "Annie Ippy is coming round the corner," and we would take off running so fast. It became kind of a game with us. Annie had some very serious illness and weighed, I figure, about four-hundred to five-hundred pounds. When I went to work down in her basement kitchen, I got used to her and she was kindness itself underneath all her gruffness. During our time of fun we would sing the song refrain from the song: She'll be coming round the mountain when she comes, "Singing Ay, Ay Ippy Ippy ay, ay," and so on. We had so much fun with her and got up to lots of pranks.

Every morning, after getting out of bed, we would head for the bathroom and after we had washed we would be checked over by the nun in charge.

Once the lavabo inspection passed, we would get in single file and walk upstairs to the chapel. We often had quite a show in the chapel. The elderly people were on the same level as the chapel. They would stroll in one by one with walkers, wheelchairs, and walking sticks. Many of them had hearing problems d would talk out loud to the others, especially if someone was in their wrong pew. To us children the conversation would be really funny. Some of them would be so upset that they would bash on the pews with their sticks. We children knew that we would be severely punished when the nuns caught us laughing or giggling in the chapel. Trying to smother our laughing and giggling just made it worse, and how many times did I kneel aside the pews out in the aisle for punishment because of the giggling. When things were really funny, there was no way of controlling ourselves. Trying to keep the silence in the chapel also made it worse for us to control ourselves. Sometimes the older folks would talk out loud at the most solemn part of the Mass. Many of them would bring in their snuff-boxes. They would have a little sniff during the mass. They would roll the snuff between their thumb and forefinger and sniff it up their nostrils. This often caused a loud sneeze reaction, which of course triggered off the giggles again which we had tried so hard to control. We visited the chapel throughout the day on a regular basis for formal prayers, but there was nothing to beat that early morning show in the chapel!

After the services were over in the chapel, we got in lines to walk down to the refectory. There were girls who helped to line us up and they were in charge of us, like assistants to the nuns. We walked in single file to the refectory and sat on the long benches. When the bell rang, each table had to pick up the tin plates in front of us and walk over to where the porridge was being dished up. We had the same ritual for each meal. We also had the same big pots with mush, kind of soft but thick mush, for lunch and dinner. When the meal was over, we would get in line again, and go to the next duty that we were assigned to. I would stay on in the kitchen with some other girls and wash then tin plates and the big cast iron pots, leaving everything ready for the next meal.

The rest of the children would go after breakfast to their respective duties. There was plenty of work to get finished before school began. The aides to the nuns would supervise everything and finally line us up in the play hall for school. I think that there were nine or ten long lines in the hall. An assistant girl would be in charge of each line. We would be inspected as we passed the nun on the way out of the hall to go to the school.

School was the best part of the day. I loved school. Arithmetic was my favorite. There were problems in the books that puzzled me however, not the math problem itself but just reading the puzzles. An example would be "The mother would send little Susie to the shop to buy sweets, and she would give her six pennies to go shopping." I wondered about the word 'mother' and it puzzled me at what was a shop. I did not know what pennies were, or why Susie had to have pennies to go to the shop. The problem was not math, but the meaning of ordinary things that we did not understand. There was no one that we could ask, we dared not speak in the classroom, unless we were spoken to by the teacher. I guess we had a lot to be grateful for. We were fed, clothed, disciplined well, and we were taught how to work. There were the basic things that were missing in our lives. We, as children, did not know anything was missing; we were too busy everyday with all kinds of chores, as well as going to school.

Now looking back what was missing there was no affection or recognition of any good we did. On the material level, there were many things missing. We had to wash our hands with carbolic soap back then. We cleaned our teeth with our forefinger. I never saw a toothbrush or even knew of the word toothbrush. I remember combing my hair with the first comb that I found in the bathroom. I did not know about a hairbrush. When we washed our hair, it was with red carbolic soap. Generally, we had a tub bath once a week on Thursdays and I think we washed our hair in the tub bath at the same time. The girls who assisted the nuns cut our hair short. It was easier that way to keep the hair clean and it was more manageable. I guess that with the large number of children as we were, that was the only option the nuns had.

I mentioned that once a week on Thursday we had a tub bath. It was like a race to see how fast we could be in and out of the tub. There were two children to a bathtub and the same water was used 'til it really needed to be changed, only then did they change it. The girls were told to conserve water and not to change 'til they had seen about ten children go through. The two girls in charge of the bathrooms had to hold up a sheet between he two children in the tub, so that we didn't see the naked bodies of the children being exposed. We also wore a chemise in the bathtub for modesty, it was the same wet chemise handed on to the next child in the tub, and the next, and so on, down the line. The line of children kept moving along like a relay race.

We had good moral development and a very structured upbringing. All beds had to be made as soon as we got up in the morning. They also had to be in a straight row and the floors cleaned. Clothes were neatly stacked and nothing was to be out of place. In the classroom, we learned to knit, sew, and darn socks. I remembered that there was a group of girls who sat in a room, and darn as many socks as they could get through. This was on a Saturday morning, and I wished that I could join that group because they didn't have to scrub and polish floors like the rest of us children. Saturday was always the big cleaning day in the orphanage.

Every day in the orphanage was the same routine. We lined up for everything. We lined up from the time we arose in the morning 'til we went to bed at night. It became a routine for us. One day we all had to line up and there was such hustle and bustle, and suddenly there were men in the orphanage who were helping us to get into line, and they rushed us outside into the courtyard behind the orphanage. This was a large quadrangle where we often saw the horse and buggy carts which drove the nuns to different places. When we arrived outside, the men took over and organized all of us. We were each given a mask to put on over our head and get into the jeeps as quickly as possible. There seemed to be so much excitement. Prior to these goings on, black drapes were put up on all the windows. The assistants to the nuns were kept busy. I remember standing still and looking at all the army jeeps (I don't know what they were called). We heard that the men were "Air Raid Wardens". I saw the horrible picture of all the children in the jeeps with their gas masks on. The looked like scary animals with their gasmasks on their faces. I saw this picture, and my little legs took off as far away as I could. I remember one of the Air Raid Wardens catching up with me; he slapped me on the backside with his hand, and hoisted me into the jeep with the other children. I only remember how scary it was in the pitch-black jeep inside. I have no recollection of whether we drove off or stayed on the grounds.

Every day after that incident of the jeeps, we all, each individual child, had to carry a gasmask with us. It sat on the floor next to our desks, and we put them on the floor next to our beds. We carried them to the chapel in the mornings, and they were our constant companions. There were times when we didn't have to carry them around; then again, we had to take them everywhere we went. They were bothersome!

We did not know that there was a war on, but we soon learned what a war actually was. I recall the worst times of all for me, and indeed for all of us, including the nuns and people in charge of us children. The "Siren" would ring out, which meant that we had to go to the lowest basement, generally we had to get out of bed, grab a blanket, and walk or run down to the basement single file. Everyone was huddled in the basement. We had our gas masks with us and we were told when to put them on, they had straps that we would put over our faces and large snouts in the front of our faces. The snouts filtered the contaminated air from the outside so that we would be breathing in cleaner air.

All the windows in the convent and orphanage had black drapes. They were opened in the mornings and after a certain time in the evening they had to be closed. If any light escaped from the windows, heavy fines were imposed from watchmen who guarded the streets. If the sirens would go off during the day, we could see our way, but at night, we couldn't have any light showing anywhere, so we would cling to one another and grope our way down to the basement. We children were probably safer in the orphanage basement than the people outside who had to leave their homes to go outside in the streets to the "Air Raid Shelters".

I recall having to climb out of bed and make my way to the basement. I would be throwing up and really sick from just listening to the siren. Psychologically, I think the sound of the siren itself made me feel sick. Many of us were sick, and the nuns took no notice of us because they weren't able to do anything anyway. The nuns would pray out loud all the time, and sometimes I'd wish they would stop praying for a while. Whatever prayer or. enunciation they would say, we children had to repeat it after them. Sometimes they would break out into song, and we had to sing along with them. I was too ill to join in the prayer or enunciation they would say, we children had to repeat it after them. Sometimes they would break out into song, and we had to sing along with them. I was too ill to join in the prayers or hymns _____. Now, when I hear the song "Bless this house O Lord we pray. Keep it safe by night and day," I still recall the awful sickly feeling and foul smell all around us from those long ago days.

Sometimes trying to peep through the black drapes to see what was going on outside scared me too. Many times one couldn't see anything. The thick heavy smoke outside the windows was dark and frightening. We children thought it was the end of the world. I guess one child heard some remark about dying and it spread around the orphanage so fast, we all thought that we would die soon. I had seen a number of children laid out in what we called the "Dead House" in the orphanage.

I imagined that the thick fog outside was going to get worse and worse and spread all over us, and then we would die. I was concerned, in my own little mind, about how they would be able to fit us all in the "dead house" and who would be still alive to do all this work of putting us all together in the room we called the "dead house".

Many times the air outside was so thick. Today I would compare it to the "London Fog" but much thicker than that and it had kind of splinters in it. This was what we called "The Black Out".

Most of the nuns were very, very kind and all we children noticed that, and we just loved those nuns, especially the teachers. I remember the one nun in the classroom, when she saw that I had finished sewing a pair of mittens that she had cut out for me to do, was jubilant and showed the mittens to all around her. It was some kindness and appreciation that we didn't experience too often. She patted me on the back and it felt so good. One of the Sisters who was in charge of the babies used to pass by on her way to the nursery and we would put our hand out for her to put a spoon of sugar into it. She always carried a bowl of sugar the same time each day and we would try to be there when she passed. We would open the nursery door for her and hope for a spoonful of sugar in return.

Other nuns we just didn't like and shuddered when we saw them. Fortunately, there were only a few of those. The principal of the school was so very, very strict, her name was Sister Colman. She taught the very last class, eleven and twelve years old. There was no class beyond that class, which was as far as it went in the orphanage. I often wondered where some of the girls had disappeared to. One day they were sitting in school, and the next day they were not there. This just occurred in Sister Coleman's classroom. It puzzled me, and I did wonder. I'd be doing my chores with the same girls everyday, and suddenly they had vanished, never to be seen again. I knew that maybe some of the children had gone to work in the laundry and kitchens in the orphanage instead of coming to school. I often wondered sat at my school desk, in Sister Colman's classroom, and looked around, just wondered what happened to everyone. Sister Colman was an excellent teacher and at the same time so very strict. She was tireless and kept us back after school to drill certain subjects into us. I remember how she attempted to teach us Shakespeare and we were just hopeless. We did not understand any of its meaning. We learned by rote, not understanding any of it. Sister Colman was strict, she punished us on the spot in the classroom with the ruler or the cane, but she was not really cruel.

We actually did have a nun who was cruel. I will call her Sister Cruel. Every nun in charge of us gave us a whack with their cane or ruler when we needed it (sometimes when we didn't deserve it). It was all part of the discipline and order which they had to maintain. I recall sliding down the banisters outside the dormitories, starting from the top floor. We must have had about eight flights of stairs to descend. When we would get to the bottom of each flight of stairs, we had to turn, and check down below that no nun was around. I enjoyed this ride for some time before I was caught one day sliding down the banister by none other than Sister Cruelty herself! She was standing like a statue at the bottom of the stairs. When I arrived, she grabbed me by my hair and ears, and swung me around and threw me into the door of the play hall. The play hall was used for all occasions. We gathered in the hall for every function, like a multipurpose hall. Every Friday, all the children gathered in this hall, after dinner. We all just dreaded when Friday came around. The nun, Sister Cruelty was in charge of us on those Friday evenings.

After dinner, on Friday evenings, we knelt in a semi-circle in the hall. There were about three circles, the outer, the inner, and the center circle. Sister Cruelty, accompanied by her girl assistants would start in the center, go around each child's place, and examine her clothes before they were sent to the laundry. We were prepared beforehand by the girls before Sister came on her inspection rounds.

Each child knelt with arms outstretched. We only had one piece of underwear_ It was a one-piece, from shoulders to bottom, and fastened at the back with buttons. We undid the button on each side to let the flap down in order to go to the bathroom. We called the pants 'drawers'. We turned our drawers inside out and held them over our left arms, so that the nun would inspect them to see if they were soiled. If they were soiled, we were in for a fierce caning! This Sister Cruelty would produce the cane, which hung from her belt, and we would be whacked unmercifully. Some of the girl assistants were just as bad as she was. They seemed to think that because they were helping this Sister, they had to be cruel also. If we said a word, the girls would not hesitate to lift us up by the ears and the hair of our heads and swing us around, and then throw us, so that we would slide along the floor 'til we either bashed into something or came to a halt. This punishment was given out any time that the nuns thought we needed it, and, for some reason, I automatically expected the nuns to hit us anytime and anywhere, but I just hated when the assistants would do the same thing to us. I have figured it out now, that if the nuns did it, the assistants could get away with doing it too!

To avoid being punished on Friday if our drawers were soiled, we would try to wash them on Thursday nights, lay them out wet under our bottom sheet, and sleep on them so that they would be dry by the morning. If they were still wet in the morning, it didn't matter because we had all day Friday to put the drawers on us to let them dry all day. The drawers were made of thick denim material, the same material as our dresses, so it took a while to get them dry before Friday evenings. Buttons were not to be missing on the inspection, so we sewed them on beforehand. The nuns, I don't think, were ever aware of the entire goings on before Friday. We would do anything to avoid the punishments. We lived every day in fear of the cane. There was very little chance of us getting into trouble. We did, of course, get up to pranks but we were not always caught.

There was a high wall surrounding the orphanage grounds and behind the wall the very end of the orphanage was what we called 'The Dean's Garden'. It was actually the presbytery, which was next to the Church. They had apple trees growing in the garden at the back of their house. Some children, who were daredevils, would try to climb over to pluck the apples from the trees. I was afraid to try because I had seen some girls climb back over the wall in a worse condition than when they left. There was barbed wire with glass on top of the wall and these girls would be bleeding and so severely punished, if they were found and caught. I did help to hoist the girls up, so that they could reach the top of the wall, and climb over. I recall once that we all had to be in the play hall for recess and the dean came to talk to the whole school. It was about stealing the apples. It seemed to me that the fact that children had not only stolen apples but were on holy ground, which was a worse sin. I did not dare help any girl over the wall after that episode.

The parochial church on the Ormeau Road was situated parallel to the back wall of the orphanage. You could get to it by climbing the wall or walk down the Ormeau Road. It was the Holy Rosary Church. This particular day, I was to go to the Holy Rosary Church to be baptized. I thought to myself, why me? Why was I going to actually go out of the orphanage, to be baptized and christened? Naturally, I didn't ask any questions. Why did the other girls not come with me? Why was I going by myself? I do remember thinking that I must be special. I had on a white dress, white shoes, and white stockings and black patent (shiny) shoes. I had a veil on my head. Annie Lamont accompanied me to the church. Annie was one of the sewing nun's assistants in the sewing room. Maybe she had a part in making my dress for Baptism.

I clearly recall walking out the big front gate and walking down the road with Annie alongside me. I don't know what happened, but I suddenly gave a hop, skip, and jump, while walking along, I guess I was happy at the way

I looked, and also being outside the four high walls for the first time. I fell and scraped myself. Annie Lamont let some loud voice out of her and told me to walk properly. I was going to church she said, and I ought to know how I was to behave. She would tell the nuns about me when I got back to the orphanage! I recall, walking into church, it was pitch dark, I tripped going in to the pew, walking after Annie. She scolded me again. I didn't know then the significance of Baptism, or how old I was. Years later, I found out that I was eight years old.

As I sat in the dark church and I heard a loud bang, it was the priest at the top, closing the doors of the sacristy behind him, and walking down the aisle towards us. We were both sitting in the last bench. "Who made you?" he shouted. I immediately answered, "God made me," Maybe he didn't shout, but the loud masculine voice was what I was not used to hearing in the orphanage. "Why did God make you?" I replied, 'To know love and serve him in this world and be happy with Him in the next." I was told to stand up, and follow Father to the Baptismal Font which was right behind where we knelt. I was so terribly nervous that I wet the floor and was afraid to come out of the stall in case Annie Lamont would notice what happened. I had to stand on a stool that was there, and as if they poured the waters of Baptism over my head, I bent over the font and the flow of water trickled down my legs over the stool. I was so very frightened. I walked back up the Ormeau Road to the orphanage and felt ashamed of myself. It was the month of February back then, and I'm sure it was a bitter chill day in Belfast.

We witnessed some of the children who had died in the orphanage. Each child that died was taken to what we called 'The Dead House'. We took turns going to the 'Dead House; and we would walk around and around the slab, saying the Rosary or praying with the Sister or girl who was in charge. I recall seeing 'purple grapes' at the bedside of this particular child who was very sick and we were very curious to know what they were. None of us had ever seen anything like a bunch of grapes before. I was truly intrigued and I just couldn't take my eyes off them. Not only because I was longing for some of the grapes, but I thought they were beautiful colors.

There were many things that I could write about. I'll limit myself to a few. I recall, as I was about nine or ten years old that as we sat in our desks in the classroom, walked three black men! We had not seen a black man before this. We children instinctively hid under the desks. We were petrified. It took some coaxing from the teacher to get us up from under the desks. But, when the men started singing we gradually appeared from below, we children enjoyed the singing so much, and the men were very funny. I guess they were some kind of comedians. They sang songs for us and had us join in with them. "Way down upon the Swanee River," "There's a Yellow Rose of Texas," "The Red River Valley," etc. It was the first time I heard these songs. We could probably say that it was such fun, a first time that I recall having such a good time. The three of them gave out candy, toothpaste, toothbrushes, and Lux soap. This was the first time that we had ever seen another color of soap. Oh, but what joy they gave us! We did not want them to leave us. I just loved these black men. They did leave, and the girls were told by the nun to collect up everything that the soldiers had brought. The soldiers went to each classroom and also performed for them too, and gave out the goodies, which we all collected and we were never to set eyes on any of the gifts they brought us. How I wished that I could meet those same men who gave us so much joy during those war years, when they were assigned to Belfast, Northern Ireland, in the 1930's

Another time that I recall in the orphanage was on a certain Sunday of every month. We had to be looking our best. A group of people would come to see the children. We had to sit on tables in the center of the hall, while the people walked around and looked us up and down. They wanted to adopt a child. We children didn't know what that meant but we knew they would take some children away with them. When I began to understand a little better, then, I wished that someone would have taken me too. The people never spoke to us, just walked around and stared at us!

Another significant happening was the arrival of a new Chaplain, Father Geoffrey Lynch. This priest totally changed the face of things in the orphanage. He took a great interest in all of us and organized more play for us. He brought in hoops, stilts, tennis balls and rackets and set up netball. He would come to the classrooms in the evening and read to as. He tried to put a stop to all the work that we did all day long. "All work and no play," he didn't believe in it. This was the first time that anyone had ever read a story to us. I was, like the rest of the children, so happy to have Father Lynch. He would be out in the play yard when we were out there and we just liked him so much.

For some reason, there was friction among the nuns and Father Lynch was the cause of it. The nuns did not like him. Father Lynch tried to stop the nuns from giving us the cane so often. So I think, back then, he was interfering with the way the nuns were treating us. I just loved the sports he introduced. I was delighted with all the changes that were taking place and I just loved this priest.

Chapter 2

"The Situation Girl"

One morning; as I was I was sitting at my desk in school, our class teacher, Sister Colman, returned from her morning break. She was standing at the doorway looking directly down at me and at the same time beckoning with her finger for me to come forward. When I reached the door, Annie Lamont was there standing outside waiting for me. Annie Lamont was a former orphanage girl who worked in the sewing room and who was mentioned as my sponsor at baptism. In silence, I walked with her to the sewing room in the basement. Clothes were handed to me to put on and to dress quickly. The, pants were not the same as what I was used to wearing, they were a beautiful peach-pink with elastic at the waist and the legs. Orphanage drawers or knickers were one piece from the shoulders down to the knees. I spent too long looking at the beautiful color of the knickers and also trying to figure how to put the pants on me. When Annie Lamont returned to the sewing room, she said, For God's sake child are you not dressed?" She proceeded to put the clothes on me and marched me out to the front gate of the orphanage. On the way, the knickers kept slipping down. Annie produced a string from one of the side rooms and secured them from falling down again. The long navy burberry coat that I was wearing covered a lot, but if the pants slipped down again, I would feel so ashamed of myself. I had tried so hard to keep the top elastic of the pants held up tight under my armpits and the elastic in the legs high up on my thighs. I was happy to have string holding up the pants and I felt free to walk, but the legs were so loose and though the pants were tied up, the legs kept slipping down below my knees. I didn't mind pulling on the legs to keep the elastic above the knees, so long as the pants, themselves, didn't fall down again. Being so preoccupied with the clothes I clothes I hadn't thought of what was happening to me or where I was going. I began to feel excited within myself though dare not show it. It appeared that I was singled out from all the other children to go somewhere. I tried to walk along with my head held high and shoulders back, as taught, and began to feel some excitement. So, unknowingly, I did a skip and jump while holding up the knickers. So, Annie's look of disapproval accompanied me through places in the orphanage that I had never seen before 'til I arrived at the front gate. The nun responsible for opening and locking the front gate was right on time to let us through and with keys rattling she silently bowed to us but no words were spoken and it was all done so ceremoniously, the gates closed behind us. There were two gates to go through. For a split second or maybe longer, the thought occurred to me that perhaps I was going to see my mother. No words were spoken. I was outside the convent walls and it was also frightening. Across the street, was a double-decker bus, which I often saw, everyday from my classroom window up on the second floor.

From over the orphanage wall a bus stood outside at the terminal, it was a little daily glimpse that I had in the orphanage of the outside world from my classroom window. This was my first ride in a bus. The bus started to move and as it passed the orphanage, I saw the building from a different perspective for the first time. An overwhelming fear or dread and a terrible sense of loss (as I saw the girls in the classroom) came over me. I was unable to control my feelings, so I sobbed and sobbed, and all the years of pent up feelings of not ever being allowed to cry erupted! I do remember this incident well. It was so frightening for me to be out of control in this way. My companion, Annie Lamont eventually shook me to try to get me to come to my senses. She told me that I was a disgrace to the orphanage and just wait 'til she goes back to tell the nuns how badly I had behaved. If I didn't stop the balling she would bring me right back to the orphanage. She said that the lady that I was going to work for would not like that behavior or put up with that nonsense. The harder I tried to take control of myself, the worse the floodgates opened and I was sobbing, shaking, and shivering, out of control and so afraid! Of what was I afraid? I don't know. So I was not going to see my mother, but going to work for a lady.

I have no recollection of arriving at my first job, neither do I remember any days that followed. I was to be the maid and nanny to this wealthy Comerton Family. Mr. Comerton was the brother of one of the nuns at the orphanage. There were four children in this family and I gradually learned the daily routine. The first thing I was to do was to light a fire in the morning. Mrs. Comerton taught me how to do this. I was to collect papers and sticks in readiness beforehand and store them in a shed at the back of the house. First, to make a fire I was to light the paper, then the sticks would catch on, large coals in front, and slate packed in at the back. The coal and slate would be delivered every week also and I was to keep the shed door where the coals were stored closed and not allow the children in there at any time. I became an expert at keeping the fire going all day, I was very frightened of the fire in the beginning because the flames would leap up and I was frightened of something catching fire. I had never witnessed seeing a fire. When I was busy the children would try all kinds of tricks and they needed constant watching. The four children were all about one year apart from 10 months to age 4 ½ or 5 years, three boys and one girl. With the dampness in Ireland, lighting the fire was a big chore at times nothing seemed to be dry, especially firewood in the winter. Peter, the baby, was at the crawling stage and I had to watch him constantly; he loved to crawl over to the fireplace and pull the fireguard down. So in the midst of chores I had to attentively keep a watch on him. I gradually learned the ABC's of daily living in the Comerton house. While in the orphanage we only used spoons and one enamel plate, we had the same for every meal. The food was always dished out of a large pot and you got a scoop on your plate dished out with a ladle. This was the same for each meal. So I had to learn everything in the Comerton kitchen, including all about the utensils and what a knife, fork, and spoon were for and how to use them. I set the table for breakfast, lunch and dinner and with the routine I became familiar with everything in the kitchen. I do recall standing and watching a pot boiling with eggs in it and I was fascinated! As I stood watching, I wondered how that happened. How did she get that water to bubble like that?

Of course, I was frightened to ask any questions, for fear of looking and being stupid and of doing the wrong thing by asking questions. I would never have asked questions in the orphanage. That was the way we were trained, just brought up that way. The work in the Comerton's was not as heavy as the work in the orphanage, but I was kept busy all day. I was good at cleaning and knew what I had to do, the cooking was the problem, and the kitchen stuff, but I was ready to work at that, it was nevertheless fascinating for me to learn all the new things.

My day was filled. I lit the fire in the mornings. I set the table for breakfast. Sometimes the children would be up and about. Sometimes the Master and Mistress would be up, but if not, I had to call them by a certain time. Mrs. Comerton would cook the breakfast and I would carry it in to the dining room. I had to see that nothing was missing. I then ate out in the kitchen while the family was eating in the dining room, but I had to be ready to answer the bell which the parents rang if they needed something. Many times when I answered the bell it was to take Peter, the baby, who was crawling and screaming out to the kitchen with me so that they could eat their breakfast or meal in peace. There were times when Peter would (as he got older) stand on his toes, bang on the door of the dining room to get out and scream and scream. I had to come and rescue him. The mother or father would often pick him up, bring him out, and put him on the kitchen floor for me to take care of. So this is how it went for all the meals. I loved Peter, he and I had so much fun together, he followed me around the house everywhere I went, so it was sometimes difficult to get my chores done. When he began to make sounds the only sound that he made was to call me by name. My name was, Maud. Peter would call, "Maw, Maw" all day long. I took the children to school in the morning after breakfast. I brought them back home in the afternoon. I really enjoyed these outings as I could see everything outside the houses, which I passed, the gardens, trees, and parks. The Cavehill Mountains in the distance and I really looked forward every day to getting outside. I always took Peter with me in the pram when I was taking the children back and forth from school. Once I was used to these outings, I was told to take the dog, with me, his name was Rowdy. I was told to take the children and the dog to the Park after school every day. The park was on the way home on the Cavehill Rd. where we lived. Every afternoon, on the way home, I would see children out playing in the streets outside their homes. One particular girl, whose name was Ann Maguire, would always want to speak to me, but I was afraid of talking to her in fear of getting in trouble with the mistress. How I envied Ann that she could play outside in the streets, I longed to do just that. My thoughts often flew back to the orphanage as I walked along with my brood and wondered what the children were doing now and if Fr. Lynch, (Fr. Geoff) as we called him, knew where I was, or, if anyone knew.

Rowdy the dog was probably old because he was slow in his movements, and when he went for a walk, I had to wait for him to catch up with us when we were in the park, I was longing to get on the swing myself, but out of fear that the oldest children would report me to their mother when I returned that, "Maud was on the swing." I did not get on. I was to watch the children, and stick to my job, which I did very conscientiously. So one day, a moment of weakness came over me and I quickly jumped on the swing while the children were all playing together and the pram was next to me. Suddenly Rowdy became true to his name and began to frisk around as I had never seen him before. The corner of my metal swing bashed with force right into his nose. I had nothing at hand to help the dog, who was bleeding from his nose. I had to call the children to start walking home so that I could get the dog home quickly. Eventually the dog was not walking properly so I hastily picked him up and put him in Peter's pram. And I walked home as fast as I could. Arriving home I placed him in the shed. There was no one at home to report to about the dog; I kept going in and out to watch him. As soon as Mrs. Comerton arrived home the children reported that the dog was sick. I told her what happened while in the park, but did not tell her that I was on the swing for fear of punishment from her. I cannot recall what happened afterwards. The next morning when I went in to the shed to fetch wood for the fire and check on the dog, he was dead. I shed silent tears and blamed myself for getting on the swing in the first place. It was a lesson for me to behave myself in the future. I missed the dog very much, especially at feeding times and when taking him for a walk, he was a good companion.

In the afternoons, I cleaned house and every day I was assigned different chores. E.g. cleaning the brasses one day, the silver ornaments from cabinets another day. There were no vacuums in those days and once a week I cleaned the bedrooms, it was difficult cleaning the carpets with a small brush while on my knees, and dust around the skirting boards in the rooms. The stairways had to be swept every day and the dining and family rooms also. I did my duties well, but sometimes when Mrs. Comerton was home, she saw that I hadn't cleaned the stairway properly and would pass me on the stairs just to point out what I hadn't cleaned. This followed with a slap across the face when she was in a bad mood. The first time that she hit me I was in a kind of shock and it left me wondering "why" and it put a damper on my spirits. I did not feel like working at all after that, no matter how good or hard I worked, it did not satisfy Mrs. Comerton. She did not hit me in the beginning when I began to work for her but after a while the hitting began. I then tried to keep out of her way as much as I could, but that was not possible. I set the table every evening for dinner and tried to be sure that nothing was missing, as I hated to be called in to the dining room and be reprimanded in front of the children. The family was all assembled for dinner in the evenings, like a major ceremony, no one sat down 'til everyone was present and grace was said. I carried in the dishes and cleared them away. In between, I would try to eat something outside in the kitchen and wash dishes at the same time. Depending on the weather the children would go outside to play after dinner. When it was time for bed

I had to get the children in the bathtubs and to bed. When all was clear I began the washing of the clothes which was by hand in those days using a washing board for heavy stains.

Generally, Mondays were washing days and Thursdays were the days for ironing. But, every day was washing for me it was only the bigger washings that I spent time doing on Thursdays e.g. sheets, tablecloths, towels, etc. The most difficult thing that I had to do was to wash the master's collars, scrub them so hard on the scrubbing board to get the ring of dirt out. My fingers would be so sore and burning especially in the winter months. I was to starch the collars immediately after the shirts were washed and iron them, then hang them up in the kitchen near the stove to help them dry fast. I had to make sure that there was a clean, starched shirt for the master every morning. That was my biggest worry in the winter, to get the clothes dry. I would iron the shirt over and over in the evening to help the drying process quicker and first thing next morning, I would bring the shirt up and hang it on the banister outside the master's bedroom. So I had my days cut out for me. I actually lived in fear that I would do something wrong.

One Saturday morning, I answered the doorbell. Two nuns all in black with their faces almost covered were standing there like statues. I thought I was seeing a vision and I was unable to speak. I must have been in a state of shock. Without saying a word I went inside to tell Mrs. Comerton that there were two nuns outside. She invited them in, and I was so frightened of being told to go back to the orphanage. I went about my work in fear and trembling 'til I saw them leave again. Once a month or sometimes every two weeks, I saw nuns coming and going. They were out on their begging mission for the orphanage. Most of them I did not recognize.

In those days in the 1940's the bread van would arrive and deliver bread to each house, the smell was so good like just having a bakery right at your front door. The milkman would deliver the bottles of milk on the doorstep and when the bottle stood for a while the cream would be at the top of the bottles and I would carry the bottle steadily one at a time, so as not to disturb the cream at the top of the bottles. I had to pour the cream at the top of milk bottle out into a jug to be used for different meals or for cooking. The children always had to have the cream in the mornings on their porridge. The coalman would arrive and drop off the coal down the shoot into the shed. In the summertime the ice cream man would deliver ice cream and also ice to those who went outside to buy from him. I enjoyed all this kind of activity that was in the area.

The war was still on and most of this activity ceased when the air-raids were on.-I dreaded these times when the siren would go off loud and clear and everyone had to grab a blanket and head for the air-raid shelters close by. It was literally a nightmare to be wakened out of sleep by the sound of the siren, get ourselves together, bundle the children up and get out quickly. I recall being packed in the shelter like sardines. We all had to put on our gas masks which we carried with us wherever we went. They were frightening times for sure. We were not so tightly packed together in the orphanage as we were in the air-raid shelters.

During this time of war we all had to line "queue" up for our ration of food. One family of our size was allowed two eggs, maybe a duck egg, a little butter and a certain amount of sugar. We also had the ration book to help as to buy clothes. I would queue up for the family and then ask food for myself as I was a single girl on my own without a family. So what I got with my ration book I brought home to the Comertons and we ate sparingly. Even people who had the money to buy food could not do it without the ration book. Only a limited amount was allocated to each family. The same rules held for buying clothes. I heard later that many people got into the black market and bought coupons so as to be able to buy clothes.

Those years of Blitz in Belfast with the air looking like a London fog except, that the air itself was so thick, we had to grope our way through it; it was really difficult outside to find our way home during the time of blitz. This scared me very much along with the feeling of being lost and trying to grope my way out of it. So, I was a little servant girl during those years of blitz; coupons, ration cards, queues miles long, shortages and deprivations. It all entailed a lot of uncertainty not knowing where the next meal was coming from, or whether we would live to see the next meal. The one piece of information about the war came through the radio. I remember clearly the day the war was over, excitement everywhere but the rations continued even after the war. More information on the radio just brought more sorrow and grief on hearing the news of sons and daughters, families and friends killed, maimed or missing in action.

One morning, as usual, I came down to the kitchen to get things prepared. I found a strange lady there, she was dressed in white with a white cap on her head and she was bustling around, had a tray in her hand and she asked me if I was the maid. I replied that I was, and I asked if I could help her. She wanted to prepare a breakfast tray and take it up to Mrs. Comerton in her bedroom. I helped her to prepare the tray and get the breakfast ready. Away went the white lady in her starched uniform, up the stairs leaving me wondering what was going on up there. I thought that maybe the Mrs. was sick in bed. Some fleeting thoughts went through my mind that if she was ill then I was free to get my work done without interference from her. I happily started to move fast to get things done, enjoying the freedom of being by myself to do everything I had to do. I was determined to show that I could be relied on to get the work done. The children were dressed, had their breakfast, and were off to school without a word. The father, Mr. Comerton, told the children and me that we were not to go into the bedroom as mother was sick and she had to be kept very quiet. No one was to disturb her. The master was a very strict man and we dared not to disobey him. After taking the children to school I returned still very happy that I felt as free as a bird in the house.

I had the house all to myself, so I thought but I could hear talking coming from the room upstairs. I was very curious as to what was really going on. It was all so hush, hush. It was an eerie kind of uncertainty, and I could not ask any questions of anybody in the house because there was no one to ask. In spite of the silence in the house, I was delighted to be by myself. The front door opened and the master arrived. I pretended not to see him. I continued to do what I was doing, without looking upwards. I had never seen the master come home during the day. I wondered what he was doing at home. As a rule he came home in time for dinner. I could always rely on the toddler, Peter, to tell me who was home because as soon as Peter saw his dad, he would come screaming to me and calling, Maw, Maw! All the children were afraid of him and of doing anything wrong, especially when dad was at home, ain't misbehaving then! I can still hear Peter screaming while he clung to my legs, I would pick him up and sing and talk to him 'til he calmed down. The master seldom spoke to me, not even to greet me the time of day, ever and back then I was very much afraid of him.

In the orphanage I was used to children being sick and often children lay out on the cold slabs in the "Dead House". We children took our assignments at different times to walk around the slab or table and pray for the dead child and all the children who had died at the orphanage. Most of the praying was saying the rosary aloud or singing the well-known "Deprofundis Clamavi ad te Domine". In English it is "Out of the depths I have cried to thee 0 Lord", taken from one of the psalms which we children knew by rote in Latin. So my busy curious mind told me that as a consequence of being sick or following sickness you just died! So I wondered, if Mrs. Comerton had died and would I get another lady or Mistress in her place. My mind was spinning with all kinds of things that might happen. Maybe this new mistress would be nicer to me. My mind was thus preoccupied when I heard Mr. Comerton calling me. I was to go upstairs and wait outside the mistress's room. I was to wait for the nurse to come out. So that was who the lady-in-white was, she was a nurse. I recall in the orphanage seeing a doctor for the first time and was our one and only time in our lives to see a doctor. We had to undress and stand on a scale; according the other orphanage girls there was a nurse there too but I do not ever remember seeing her. Though I was scared of the doctor I couldn't take my eyes off him, I had not seen a man before in the orphanage except the priests who said Mass. He fascinated me. I heard many years later as I talked to the orphanage alumni that the doctor told the nuns to see that we were fed properly, and be wanted to see some weight gain on all these girls on his return, I have no recollection of this. I only remember the doctor and my standing on the scale. So here this was a real live nurse in Comertons! The bedroom door opened. I heard swish-swish of her starched uniform. A bundle of white sheets was thrown into my arms, with a clear command to soak them in cold water only. We never had warm or hot water anyway, unless we put the kettle on to boil. I carried the sheets down to the outside sink next to the kitchen and as I shook them out before putting them in the water-Lo and behold, blood everywhere! I rinsed them under running water and then soaked them. Again, I had no one to ask questions of, I just did as I was told.

Now I knew that Mrs. Comerton was very ill and going to die or was already dead and of course, they would not tell me. Later I hung the sheets out on the line to dry. As I continued with my work, I kept pondering about so many things and I wondered what had happened to the mistress to cause her to bleed so much. I went as usual to pick up the children from school and was told to stay longer at the park after school. The master, Mr. Comerton, wanted me to stay out longer. In those days, I did not possess a watch and there were no phones either. During summer in Ireland, there is the twilight which means that it is bright outside 'til about 10 or 11 p.m. So, I returned to the house quite late to find some relatives in the house who were having a meal. The nurse was out, but came back to spend the night after the relatives left. I was still in the dark about all that happened. No one had spoken to me and I had no right to ask and I dare not speak unless I was spoken to. I went to my attic bedroom away from all sights and sounds. The next morning, the nurse was carrying a shoebox or some kind of box. And she called me to come over quietly and have a look. Amidst the many folded clothes was a baby. I was looking at a tiny little face. I was so astonished and wondered how it got into the house. Of course the baby belonged to the nurse as it came into the house with her. The baby's name was Mary. The nurse stayed about a fortnight. I did not get to know her or talk to her; I had to keep my place as the servant, out of sight, but appear if they needed me. I missed the nurse when she left, part of the excitement went with her, but she left the baby behind. Mrs. Comerton was up a little every day and came out of her room eventually. So she did not die and she took care of the baby christened Mary. So the children ranged from the oldest, John, Paul, Elizabeth, Peter, and Mary, the latest arrival. Life continued moving as usual again and Peter remained my favorite. As I recall the baby weighed approximately 4 lbs.

One day, I received a small parcel in the mail. The postman came to the door and Mrs. Comerton answered the doorbell. I of course, had never received anything in the mail before, we never, ever received mail in the orphanage. This little parcel puzzled me quite a bit but it was very exciting. Then I thought, Oh, maybe it's Fr. Geoffrey Lynch. I had often wondered if he knew where I was and now, he is sending me a parcel? I was elated over this. I did not get to see the parcel, never mind opening it. That evening before going to bed the master, Mr. Comerton, came in with Mrs. Comerton to the kitchen and told me that I was to open the parcel which Mrs. Comerton had held until the boss came home. I don't remember who opened the parcel, but I was excited to see there was a brooch inside the wrappings of paper. Mr. Comerton then appeared really angry. He said, "You are to tell me who sent you this brooch, you must know who, if you don't tell us then I will have you sent back to the orphanage or that place across the street from the orphanage. You will own up to this." A few minutes later, Mrs. Comerton asked me if I had a boyfriend that I was not telling them about. I would never see this brooch 'til I owned up to the truth. It would be dangerous for me to wear that brooch if I didn't know where it came from. I was shaken to say the least and the next morning I was afraid of meeting either one of them. I was indeed perplexed and scared.

Inside the gift box was a typed folded paper, folded up with the brooch inside which read:

> From someone whom you do not know
> And whom you have never met
> Is sending you this little brooch
> To wish you, "Many Happy Returns"

I was as scared as I could ever be and didn't know where to turn to ask for help about the brooch. It took me a few days to get over the shock of the

"Brooch". Then I began to turn over in my mind some of the things the Comertons said to me and questioned me about. The one thing that got me started was BOYFRIENDS! Now that's an idea. Where on God's green earth would I come up with boyfriends?

I was ignorant regarding males, but Peter the baby had unknowingly taught me my first anatomy lesson of the male species when I changed his diaper. We had a charwoman who carne twice a week to do the laundry. She washed the heavy things on Mondays and ironed them on Thursdays. I was comfortable with Rose around and was always happy to see her. I asked her about the brooch, but she did not know anything at all. I was not afraid of Rose and I gradually was able to talk to her about anything. I asked her what "Many happy returns" meant on the paper and she answered, "Lots and lots of birthdays to follow after this one." Then she said, when is your birthday? I honestly didn't know for sure, only just when the new girl in the orphanage told me she peeped in the School Register and told me that it was November. I did not know that people had a celebration on their birthdays. So must have had a birthday and someone must have known about it occurring in November. I tried to recall if I had told anyone about it but there were not too many people that knew me. I certainly would not have mentioned anything in that line about myself. Sometime, many months later, I was walking home from church, a girl caught up alongside me, it was the maid from the large house behind me. I only met her when she or I were hanging out clothes on the clothesline as our yards were back to back. We seldom talked, maybe exchanged a few words here and there. When we were walking towards home, we were able to talk freely. I grew to like this girl and it was good for me to have someone on my level to talk to without being on guard as to what we said. We always walked together after we got to know each other. Her name was Betty. When we first got acquainted on our way to and from church, she had asked me when my birthday was and I hesitated to tell her as I was afraid! "Come on; tell me, it's good to know when it is." I answered, "November, but don't know the date" I wanted to make up a day myself as I was afraid of Betty thinking that I was stupid. She did not know that I was from an orphanage and did not know or keep birthdays. The lady that Betty worked for owned a jewelry shop and it was she who sent me the brooch. Betty did not know that Mrs. White, her employer, had sent it to me. It was while working in the back yard many months later, that Betty mentioned the brooch and wondered if I had received it. I was still afraid of getting into trouble, so I told her that Mrs. Comerton was keeping it safe for me. So I was happy to know where the brooch came from and so I could clear myself of any wrong doing.

I still recall some incident that happened while I was at Comerton's. As I mentioned the bedrooms had to be cleaned weekly. I couldn't help but notice some pretty clothes in the closet; in fact, I cleaned in there occasionally, and had to move the clothes out of the closet in order to clean properly. Mrs. Comerton was usually present when I helped her with this project. I loved to look at the pretty dresses, there were so many of them. I looked forward to seeing her go out some evenings all dressed up, she looked so lovely! How I wished that I possessed at least one dress of hers. As it was, since the time I arrived at Mrs. Comerton's I had. the same clothes, except for the maid's uniform. I was blessed to have a uniform to wear while working. My possessions from the orphanage consisted of one dress and the one pair of shoes which I wore each day, not to forget the peach-pink bloomers I wore daily. The length of the knickers was from under my armpits to below my knees; these were the same knickers that I left the orphanage in and had difficulty holding on to them, keeping them from falling down. A safety pin is a useful thing, and two safety pins were better than one, so by this means, I kept my pants on! You may wonder how I managed so long with one pair of pants. In the summer months, they dried quickly, but in the winter it took the knickers a long time to dry. I used the method I learned in the orphanage, of washing them, and wringing them in a towel and laying them under the bottom sheet spread out flat. I would sleep on the sheet, and in the morning they were dry when I got out of bed and so I'd put them back on again. So, back to the dresses: I was longing to try one of the dresses on. I had to be very careful that no one was around when I attempted this, especially not Mrs. Comerton! Generally, she was not around during the day, so I waited for the opportune moment. The chance came, and I was admiring myself in the mirror. I was about to take the dress off when I definitely heard footsteps on the stairway. The dress was half off, and I immediately ducked alongside the bed on the floor but could not slide under the bed. I lay very still holding my breath for the longest time. The person came into the room for one minute and then out again. Oh, God! Help me! I was relieved and very happy that I was not caught in the act. I slowly moved out and speedily changed back into my uniform. Never, never again would I try something like that. Looking at me in the mirror was just great, in itself! There were no mirrors in the orphanage anywhere, we children use to look at ourselves in the spoon we used at meals we would shine it with spittle and rub it on the hem of our dresses. The mirror in Mrs.

Comerton's wardrobe was not visible; it was attached to the inside of their closet door. I would be cleaning and taking a good look at what I looked like! What a revelation! Really seeing myself in a mirror was wonderful, I mean the mirror itself was wonderful, what a thing to possess, something that showed one's own reflection.

Another incident happened while I was at Comerton's. Window cleaners would go from house to house on the block. It was the same window cleaner who always came to Mrs. Comerton's. He carried a stepladder, a bucket, and cloths for cleaning windows. I had never spoken to him, only the mistress would talk to him. He was cleaning our windows for as long as I could remember, since I first started to work for the Comerton's. This particular day while I was at the kitchen sink, someone from behind suddenly grabbed me, and it was the window cleaner. In no time, I was on the floor, and he wrestling me. I knew this was not what should be happening, and fought back with my fists as hard as I could. I didn't know I was capable of such strength. The peach-pink knickers I was able to salvage and I escaped over to the neighbor's house all the while yelling and screaming. Everything happened so fast that when I did come up for air, at the neighbor's house, I was in shock and disbelief. I did not do anything to annoy him, so why did he do this to me? Mrs. Magee was the neighbor whom I ran over to and she, Mrs. Magee, reported the incident to Mr. Comerton when he came home. Of course, the window cleaner lost his job and at that time, I felt bad that I was the cause of him losing his job. I was afraid that Mr. Comerton would put the blame on me somehow. I was really scared of the master's approach and his comments to me. He seldom spoke to me, but when he did, I kind of shriveled up. If Mrs. Comerton reported me at any time to her husband, he would lash out at me. He would say things to me such as: "Didn't they teach you anything in there," or "You can go back to the orphanage where you came from", or "We have never had anyone so stupid," and so on. I lived in fear of this man!

As time moved on, I was getting older, but I often wondered how old I was. Looking back at another incident that happened to me while I was at Comerton's, suddenly I was bleeding! Thank God it happened to me on one of those days when the charwoman, Rose, was at the home. I tried to do the best I could to protect myself, I felt really sick but tried to go on with my work 'til Rose, the charwoman, arrived. The toilet paper in those days was a whole lot of paper squares on a hook, mostly newspaper cuttings. I had this as one of my duties to see that there was enough paper in the bathroom. So I went to my supply source of paper, I could not use what was in the bathroom because it would be noticeable if the paper was being used faster than usual. In the meantime, I used the newspaper or any kind of paper in sight. Paper cost money, and money was scarce and there was no easy access to either of them during this time of war. I had a problem, how was I going to walk the children to school? So I found the next best thing to do. I grabbed a towel and walked with it packed between my legs and the peach-pink bloomers holding everything together. Wonderful, I was on my way! Once I dropped the children at school, I went to look for a bathroom! I continued my walk home and all the while wondering what was going on with me. I really thought that I was ill and maybe going to die. I made so many Acts of Contrition to God, orphanage upbringing taught us those prayers in the time of need, and it helped me to be prepared to go to God. I was not going to tell any of this to Mrs. Comerton.

Rose duly arrived. She saw that I was looking a bit peevish. I immediately told her that I was bleeding and didn't know what to do. Am I going to die from this? "Oh God, no child, you are going to give life from this." She then explained to me that this would happen every month. I was horrified even to think of this as a monthly occurrence. She produced a pain tablet for me from her bag. The tablet worked magic for me and the terrible cramps were gone. Come to think of it, I never saw any kind of pills in the orphanage. This was, no doubt, the first pill that I had ever swallowed. Rose, a rose even more in my estimation. No pain, I was able to do my work. My mind was always working, trying to figure out so many things on my own as I went about my duties. I had at least one private area where no one had access to, and that was my mind! Later on, every time Rose was working at the house, I was happy to have someone to talk to. Rose always warned me not to talk when the mistress was around. So I really did not want to think of this monthly thing which was going to happen but I had to be prepared. Rose suggested that I tear up some old rags, from old sheets that were up in the attic, and I would have them in readiness for the next time. Trust me, I was going to be prepared! Any time I was in trouble, no matter how insignificant, the mistress would talk down to me or reprimand me. Occasionally, if it was of a more serious misdemeanor, then the master would deal with me. So the master appeared in the kitchen one evening and I knew I was in big trouble when he appeared. I didn't have time to think of what I had done. Looking back now, as I write, I think that Mr. Comerton's voice could have been louder than what Ian Paisley's voice was known for in Belfast a loud booming voice! In the confines of the kitchen, when Mr. Comerton was reprimanding me on this occasion, he was, it seemed to me, full of fury.

His anger was visible. "So, what did you steal? I want the truth!" and on the next breath, "Do you know that I could put you in jail this very day for stealing?" I owned up to cutting the material, stating that it was an old sheet with frayed edges. "Does that make it right to steal? This will be your last time to steal, because if this ever happens again, you will not have another chance. You'll go to jail." Of course, I had never heard of "jail," and I asked Rose what "jail" meant. I had had some idea that it was a terrible place. I was so frightened. In fact, I was so frightened of so many thin s now. My little world, but a big world to me, seemed such a terrible place and I felt like such a bad, bad person. My one relief was walking the children to school and walking back in the fresh air. I could be alone and have the time as I walked to mull over in my mind so many things that had happened.

So I talked to Rose about this jail that I would be sent to, and talked to her of so many things that were happening that really worried me. I was frightened to death of everything now. Thank God for Rose at that time in my life. She was my lifesaver. I wish I would meet her today 60 years later to really *talk* and to say a *big thank you!*

Rose had explained to me that the new baby belonged to Mrs. Comerton. It was not the nurse's baby, she only helped to deliver it. In my understanding at that time, it was a delivery like all other deliveries that came to the house of bread, milk, coal, etc. When deliveries arrived, Mrs. Comerton would sometimes give me cash in my hand to pay straight away for the delivery of goods. I handled the money, but I did not yet understand what money was all about. You bought something and you paid for it. So I figured that Mary, the baby, was bought from the nurse. So I thought and thought about it. I still often wondered how the baby was delivered by the nurse. Where did she get the baby? I had so many questions, and only myself to answer them. I was always thinking and trying to figure things out for myself, sometimes it just left me more puzzled than ever. I had so much to think about as I went about my daily chores. During the course of my time with the Comerton's, Rose explained the facts of life very simply when the occasion arose. When I washed the blood on the sheets for the nurse, I then thought that Mrs. Comerton had her period that was what Rose had said. I asked Rose, how was it that Mrs. Comerton had her period at the same time she had the baby? Would I have a baby some time when I had my period? How is it that there isn't always a baby when a girl has her period? I thought that I was going to be in trouble for asking too many questions. Rose was not always able to answer because of the heavy load of work but she tried to answer if the mistress was not within hearsay. Rose said that you have to be a mother to have a baby, and she left it at that. I was okay with that statement, but later on I had more questions for her.

Rose had a secret plan which I did not know about. She was trying to talk to Mrs. Comerton about it. One day, when Rose arrived for work, as usual I had tea ready for her in the kitchen: Mrs. Comerton came in to the kitchen and told me to get on with my work as she wished to talk to Rose. The kitchen door was closed behind me. I was really frightened that Rose would tell Mrs. Comerton things about me, maybe that I had been asking her too many questions and keeping her from her work. I was so afraid of the outcome of the private meeting. The meeting was over. Mrs. Comerton went out. I was afraid to show myself in the kitchen. Rose eventually called me downstairs to the kitchen. She unfolded the plan that she had told Mrs. Comerton about. She had been trying for some time to "adopt" me but Mrs. Comerton would not hear of it. She said that I was her responsibility while I was working in this house and that the orphanage would not give her permission either. Apparently, they argued back and forth. Rose argued that I was only a child and should be in school. Rose herself was married and had one child, a girl named Margaret. Rose thought Margaret and I could be sisters and good pals. What's more, I was very much like her daughter, Margaret, in appearance. So Rose goes up to the orphanage to speak to the Mother Superior about the matter. It all fell on deaf ears. Rose tried everything possible to achieve her goal of adoption for me, but it was to no avail. Though I tried not to show how I really felt about all this, I was jumping for joy inside; I could hardly contain myself at the thought of being adopted. Rose explained the meaning of the word, "adoption" to me and I was literally walking on air at such a prospect. I knew that Rose did not get permission for adopting me but just the very idea that someone would want me! I felt on top of the world! There was a spring in my step and a hop skip in my jump as I went happily about my work. So I was waiting for big things to happen. I had hopes.

One day, I awoke early for some reason, and I was hardly able to get out of bed, I just felt weak all over, with muscle aches and pains. I tried to go about my work as if nothing was wrong but the Mrs. saw me struggling to walk. She told me to sit down in the kitchen and offered me a cup of tea. Though I was feeling so weak and wanted to lie down, I felt so bad because Mrs. Comerton had to do some of my work and take the children to school herself. When she left to walk to school with the children, I had no option but to lie down on the floor in the kitchen, I was unable to stand upright. I was afraid that if I was unable to do my work that I would be sent away. I don't remember if it was the day for Rose to come to work. The only thing that I recall was up in my bed in the attic and Rose taking care of me bringing me black tea and crackers, and generally being there for me, just watching and observing. When I had a few days in bed and fell a little better and was able to walk, Rose then took me with her on the bus to her doctor. I recall being in the doctor's office. He told me to take off all my clothes, which Rose helped me with, and I felt so naked and exposed. He then asked me to walk around the room. I felt so cold, scared and shivering. I thought the whole place was shaking but it was only me. I was hardly able to touch anything as I was trembling so much. My teeth were shattering and I was unable to answer any question that the doctor asked me. Rose was very helpful in putting the clothes back on me and I felt so good that she had taken over for me and spoke to the doctor. I returned to Comerton's and spent some days in bed while Rose took care of me. It was so good to have someone to care for me and I would have liked this care all the time, it was so comforting for me. Rose would bring me hot soups, tea, and scones. I loved every minute of it! Rose was a large size, buxom lady and so motherly, I grew to love her dearly. Oh how I longed to have her as a mother and to go and live with her. So I gradually continued to get better and was happy to be able and useful again. My hopes were high when Rose told me that she was going to try to get me adopted, no matter if they turned her down, she would continue her pursuit. I was all for it, and this is what kept my spirits up while working at Comerton's. I would wait for that day. In the meantime, life went on as usual.

Rose showed me photos of her daughter, Margaret. She was probably a few years older than I, and was in high school. I would have liked to have seen her; I liked the photos of her. I would have really liked to have Rose as my mother. Would it ever happen? Wouldn't it just be wonderful? According to Rose everyone had a mother and I needed a mother. Rose, did I have a mother? If everyone had a mother, what happened to mine? I would like you to be my mother if I don't have a mother. I had so many questions that puzzled me. When doing math problems in school, there would sometimes be mention of the father and mother and children in the books. I understood it all in theory. For example, if a mother sent a child to the shop to buy eggs and bread, the child would be given money to buy the eggs and bread. I understood the money part of shopping, but had never seen any money. I understood the theory of having a mother and father but never knew what it really means as I did not have the experience of ever having seen a family. We only saw nuns and the same crowd of children everyday, over

two-hundred and forty children or more on the roll. When I was in school
years later, I heard that many of the children were sent out early to work
during the war years, as it was very hard to feed so many children. I guess
that was the reason that I was sent out at such a young age. Domestic work
with those rich families ensured a place of safety where we had a bed and
food. We were situated hence the name "The Situation Girls". As I did not
know my birthday or my age when I left the orphanage, I of course then
did not know how long I had worked at Comerton's. I figured it was about
three years.

Chapter 3

"To Catch a Bus"

I'm guessing that I was approximately three years in my first job at Comerton's. It was a Sunday afternoon. The doorbell rang and one of the children jumped up to answer it. I heard, "Mommy, there is a lady at the door, she wants to see Maud." I could scarcely believe that someone asked to see me. Mrs. Comerton told me to see if I was dressed respectively before she checked out who was at the front door. I straightened myself up and all the while wondering who would know me and who would know my name. Mrs. Comerton led me into the front parlor. What an unbelievable surprise to see one of the girls from the orphanage. Her name was May Kennedy. She stated that she had just come to visit me. I asked Mrs. Comerton if I could walk with May to the bus stop. Once outside on the way to the bus stop we got into a conversation. May found out that I was not too happy. She gave me some money for the bus fare and said, "Maud, be ready on Thursday to catch the bus right here. I will be here for you. The bus will take you to the city hall. Just in case I'm not here at twelve noon, you can take the bus yourself and wait at the bus terminus in town. I was afraid hat May would not turn up because I had never been on a bus by myself since I left the orphanage. She gave me a brown paper bag and folded it up so that I could hide it inside my dress. The bag was for me to put my meager belongings in it on Thursday. May waited for her bus to arrive and she called out before stepping on the bus, "Don't forget to catch the bus on Thursday at twelve noon!"

As May left on the bus, I kept my eyes on the bus 'til it was out of sight, then walked back to the house. I counted the days 'til Thursday. I worked hard on the few days that I had left at Comertons. I guess that I was energized and relieved that such luck had befallen me. To my surprise, May arrived early at the house on Thursday. She said that she had to do some business with Mrs. Comerton. May had to inform her that she was taking me back with her and that she would have to get another servant girl. I was so afraid but excited at the same time. I would not have been able to have the courage to talk to Mrs. Comerton the way May Kennedy did. Some argument followed about money. May asked about the money that was due to me but Mrs. Comerton said that I didn't receive any money for my work, that I had my food and lodging. I walked out of the house accompanied by May Kennedy. I would just have had one wish on leaving Comertons and that was to take Peter Comerton, the three year old with me. After all the confrontation in the house, I was glad to leave it all behind me. Together May and I walked out of the house, turned the corner up and arrived at the bus stop. What joy and delight to be waiting to get on a bus again, and to be with someone I knew. This was my second bus ride, both rides so different and truly unforgettable. May did not come directly from the orphanage as I thought but was already out working for some years. She loved the job that she was doing, working for a Miss Morrow. May spoke very highly of her and hoped that I would be as lucky and happy as she was in her job. Miss Morrow had helped May Kennedy in so many ways and helped her to buy a little house.

I duly arrived at May's house, #1 Inkerman Street, off the Falls Road. I felt that I was in a doll's house comparing it to Comertons. I felt at home in this small house and especially with May who came from the same place, the orphanage as I did.

Here, I belonged. When I got to know the neighbors, I was one of them. There was always something exciting happening. Part of the excitement was the fact that there at the corner of the street was a pub. As the war was still on and things were scarce, some of the pubs sold cigarettes etc. At this pub, one could almost buy anything. The neighbors loved to send me over for cigarettes. Oftentimes, I would be given the change to keep and others would give me a few pence. When May saw that I was excited about having my very own money, she gave me a cigarette box to keep my money and save it. May helped me to identify the different moneys. Belfast was under the British rule, so we had British money and it took some getting used to and learning. Starting from the smallest there was the halfpenny, the penny, two penny, three penny bit, as we called it the sixpence, the shilling, the two shilling piece, the florin, and the half-crown the pound and the twenty-one shillings which was called a guinea, equivalent to twenty one shillings. Now,

I remember learning all this in the orphanage, but now it was hands on see what the money looked like. I grew to love the neighbors there was so much happening. I could pop into anyone's house and was always welcome. There was a great sense of community and we all seemed to belong together. We, of course, had to still keep the curfew, and keep the blackouts. No lights were to be seen after curfew.

Chapter 4

"Jobs, Jobs and More Jobs"

From this time on after staying with May, I had many, many other jobs. I knew that I could only do domestic work for the simple reason that I would have a bed to sleep in at night, a place to stay, while I was working. Whatever happened I would always have May Kennedy! She was someone to fall back on in time of need.

One job I got was working in a house for a teacher, a quiet lady who seldom spoke. She outlined the duties that I had to do throughout the day. She had a house full of books, shelves and shelves of books. She allowed me to read if my work was finished. She was a single lady who lived by herself, never married. It was so quiet there compared to the Comerton's house. I was there for two weeks. One evening, the lady came in to the kitchen to have a word with me. She said, "I don't have any complaints about you, Maud, you seem to be a good girl, but I detect an expression of sadness on your face. I don't want to keep you if you are not happy." She gave me my wages and told me that I could leave the next morning.

I was out on the road again, looking for another job. First back to May on Falls Road, but I knew I could not be relying on May every time. I can't recall how I got some of the jobs afterwards. One time I landed in another job, with what I thought was a very strict and very strange family. They had two daughters and one son. I hardly ever saw any of the children except in the evening. The only time I can recall was that the son, when he was ready for bed, he would kneel upright on a chair, and not move. At first, I thought he was a statue. I had the hardest time when passing him not to touch or push him off the chair. I don't know how he knelt in that position and not speak or move and eyelids closed. In the orphanage, I had heard stories of saints who were motionless like that when they prayed. I was afraid, if that's what he was doing, then he must be a saint! I was truly afraid of him and we never spoke. One of the daughters in the house was often sick and I spent a lot of time meeting with not only her needs, but her demands. The second girl was probably away in college. One incident that I recall was going away to the country for a week with the family. I was to take care of all of them as usual as if I was not on holiday. I. was to do the work as usual. I brought a book along with me. The master of the house saw that I had a book in my hand. He grabbed it and asked me where I got it. It belonged to the family and was to be put with the rest of the books on a shelf. He told me not to touch any of the books, he said I had no permission to read while I was in his house. That night I slept in a little make shift outhouse and was reading with the aid of a small flashlight under the covers. I then placed his book under the mattress just in case the master would come in and find the book. The next morning, the master came in, threw back the mattress, picked up the book, threw the book at me, and told me that I was fired. How did he know that I had a book and what's more, that I had hid it under the mattress! They were truly weird people.

I returned to Belfast with the family at the end of the holiday, and back to May Kennedy's house. May told me that Father Geoffrey Lynch was enquiring about my whereabouts and the job situation. He was in the process opening a club for the "Orphanage Alumni." May and I were asked to look up as many of our girls as possible, and round them up to help with cleaning and putting things in order before the official opening of the club. This period was spent doing just that, polishing floors and general cleaning. I enjoyed every minute of this time because it was spent with all of my friends. We had so much fun and lived on bread and jam. We had makeshift beds which we set up in the evenings. The club was like a large apartment flat on the second floor in a building on a corner of Castle Street near the technical college in Belfast. I often saw students coming and going at the technical college. Some of the young girls would come over to join us at the club in those early days, and I had been curious to know what they were learning at college. I found out that anyone could go and learn what they were interested in. The government ran it free of charge to any students who were willing and motivated to learn. The government also helped people after World War II. I couldn't wait to get back to school as it were and I loved reading anything I could get my hands on. I gave it all some thought and decided to put first things first and learn cooking because I could get a cooking job in a kind of institution or orphanage. I guess that was the sum total and all I knew of my world at that time. The real reason was that if I got married one day that I would know how to cook. That was important to me. I needed to be prepared and know how to cook.

There was a girl working in a fish shop on the Shankil Road in Belfast. She was due to have her baby soon. The owner of the shop was trying to find someone to take her place. I can't recall how I got to know of this place. I worked about a week, being introduced to everything in the shop before the girl went on leave. The girl's name was also Maud. It was fun for me learning how to handle the 'til and learning all the different kinds of fish. Plaice fish was sold more than any other kind of fish, probably because it was inexpensive. I did enjoy working in this shop. Plenty of people were coming and going and at jokes were being told. I was delighted to be in a real job where I could go home in the evening and be free. I, of course, came home to May Kennedy every evening. I would guess that I was there at the fish shop for maybe two or three weeks when father Geoffrey Lynch came to visit May. Father was horrified when he heard about the place where I was working and told May to get me out of there fast. I would have gone to the moon for either of these two people, May and Father Geoff May would not let me go to work there any more because of Fr. Geoff s wishes. It left me feeling very, very angry. I began gently arguing with May, telling her that I loved that job. Also, this was the first real job that I had! (Meaning that I was not in domestic work.) I was devastated. I had just gotten into the swing of things, was doing well, earning a good salary, I was able to take money home with me. The owner liked me and had told me that he would keep me on the job even after Maud returned. He jokingly would say, "I'd have two Mauds working for me . . ."

So I never returned, and it left me with a terrible feeling of frustration and anger. For once, I was trying to stand on my own feet but the mat was pulled out from under me. I felt that I was being very disloyal to the owner of the shop. Why, oh why, could I not work there? The answer was, according to Father Geoffrey, "I was a Catholic and they were Protestants."

Many times, I was in and out of other jobs, either they didn't last long or I didn't stay long in any job. One of the orphanage girls who was working for a family of eleven or thirteen children, only one girl in that family, the rest were boys. As I was free at the time, she asked me to come and help her sometimes, this I did. A few houses away was a family who was looking for a domestic worker. I was happy to get the situation, but it was the same old domestic live-in. I was not keen on it, but beggars can't be choosers! I took it, partly because my friend, Kathleen, an orphan, was close by. Kathleen and I kept in touch. I had some free time during the day so I would go over to help Kathleen with the children. I had more free time in this job than in any of the other domestic jobs. Kathleen and I would go to early mass on Sunday and walk to church and back together. We would be back in time to get the children out of bed and start the day's work. One thing I recall was that after the war was over, the black curtains came down. Kathleen was an expert at the sewing machine, so she got busy and started making clothes out of the blackout war material hanging on the windows! She made a black skirt and blouse for me that I could go and play tennis with Father Geoffrey Lynch. Father had a sister who was a nun in the Dominican College on the Falls Road. We had access to the tennis courts because of her influence. I just loved sports.

Father Geoff taught me how to play tennis and I would be picked up every Saturday afternoon by him to go to the Dominican College to play on the tennis courts. Kathleen would be going with a too as we both lived close to each other. This was great for Kathleen and I. We went to the Irish ceili (dance) every Saturday night. The family I worked for at that time in Belfast was moving out to the country, so I was on the road again looking for another job. I found a temporary job in another domestic situation where one of the orphanage girls worked, her name was Mary. Mary worked for a very wealthy family and the second maid was leaving to go take care of her mother who was ill. I was chosen to replace her, I was again so happy to be working with one of my own. We had the best time together. We would round up any of our girls and walk miles to get to each other, have fun together, and then walk back to our situations. We couldn't get buses at that time of night, and even if we could we did not want to spend our hard earned pennies on buses when we were able to walk. We would walk home at all hours of the night. The twilight in Ireland made it easy for us to see our way, and life was safe then. Free as birds were we on Ireland's roads, and not a care in the world!

While in this temporary situation, I had time to look for another job. Mary was a few years older than I, at least she was out of the orphanage longer than I was, and she seemed so smart in regards to the ways of the world. Mary had clothes, especially beautiful dresses, and I would try them on. They were given to Mary over the years when she worked for different people, especially the family that she worked for at the present time. So I thought that I was coming up in the world by wearing these fancy dresses! I changed my black tennis skirt to a white one. One Sunday evening, I arrived at our club for a party gathering wearing one of Mary's taffeta dresses. This party was for May Kennedy's engagement. The party, at that time, was not on such an elaborate scale as they are today. It was bread and jam, and a cake made by one of the girls. The girls were admiring our dresses, but not so by Father Geoff, who thought wearing these dresses was out of place. He called me aside to tell me that what I was wearing was unbecoming for me, this did not fit in with my character. (The dress was a V-neck dress.) "Please, this is not you Maud," he said, and shook his head and showed his disapproval of the dress. I really liked this priest so much, he was the only father figure that we all had, and it made me sad to hurt him like this. On the other hand, Mary was not affected the same way as I was affected. He was not going to tell her what she could wear. Father Geoffrey Lynch was appointed Chaplain to the orphanage after Mary went to her first situation, job so she did not really know him the way I knew him. He meant so much to me at that time. Anything Father Lynch said was like God talking to me, that's how high he was in my estimation!

Another job I got was just opposite the King's Hall Ice Skating Rink. Fr. Geoff knew the family and they were looking for someone to help with the domestic work. This, of course, was my next job. I was, as usual, glad to get any job that came my way. If I didn't have a job it meant that I was on the streets as it were. There was always May Kennedy to fall back on, but May was going to be married soon, and move to her own little house. I came to know her fiancé, David Ferris. We called him Dave for short. I wasn't sure how far away they were going to live. I wondered if I would ever live with May again. Would things change now that she would be getting married? I did not fully understand what getting married was all about, but I did know that things, as I knew them, were changing. Was I going to lose May forever? This thought made me so very sad, and the more I thought about it, the worse it became. Now, looking back, fifty years later, I guess I was moving away from the only mother figure or security I ever knew!

I was working well at this new job, opposite the skating rink. I was shocked to find how large a house it was. I thought there were far too many rooms to clean, but it all worked out. The family did not seem to bother too much about me. I was not connected with them on any level. They more or less left me to get on with everything and use my own judgment. Father Lynch was away in Newcastle. Most of his free time was with his parents as neither of his parents were well. The Lynch family lived in Newcastle, N Ireland and this took an hour or maybe longer for him to get there from

Belfast. Consequently, I did not see as much of him as I used to in the past.

I recall one interesting time at this new place where I worked. There was a famous ice skater by the last name of Fleming, who was coming to skate at the King's Hall Skating Rink. I don't remember what year it was, I am guessing maybe it was 1946 or 1947. This girl, Fleming, stayed in the big house opposite the ice rink where I was working at the time. I can't recall if the girl was coming from America to do the solo exhibition, but I remember her well. One day she had some time and she came to talk to me. I was very fascinated by her. She wanted to thank me for taking care of her dresses that she wore for skating (I washed and ironed them for her) while she stayed with us. She was full of questions about me. She was just interested in how I got the job and if I was happy there. I found her a very down to earth girl, and I think she may have been about my age then. I remember her playing a tape back so that I could hear my own voice! I had not ever heard of tapes and this all surprised me to no end. It was spooky, back then, to hear my own voice! She had recorded for me just for the fun of it, and I was totally unaware of what was going on. Fleming stayed about one week and I don't recall where she was headed for after Belfast. What a display the dresses were, some of the most beautiful I had ever seen! The sequins that caused the glitter were so fascinating for me, not to mention how she looked while on the ice. She actually got a ticket for me to go one night and see the show. Wow! I was in heaven at the sight of her ice skating and all the lights. What splendor, and the music was wonderful!

One day before the ice skating show, May Kennedy had come with me to buy my first pair of shoes! I had told May that I had a ticket for the ice show, and May decided that I needed to dress up appropriately. We went to visit Mary to borrow a dress from her supply, and Mary came with May and to buy a pair of shoes. I didn't have sufficient money but the girls helped and I was to pay them back later on. I was really in dreamland; it was the first time I had ever gone shopping. It felt so good to have my very own dress and my very own shoes! They were mine! I put them away after that occasion, but I would take a peep at them now and again. They were brown and white with a Cuban heel. I was so very proud of those shoes. Mary gave me some kind of dye that I could put on my legs so that it would give the impression of wearing stockings. Not very people could afford to buy stockings in these post war rationed years, so I thought that I was growing in the ways of the world at that time, and loved every bit of excitement and fun.

Chapter 5

"Unforbidden Territory"

Father Geoffrey Lynch hired a bus one day and we orphans all went for a two week holiday (vacation) which was planned well ahead so that as many as possible would be able to go. It was a place called Portstewart, right by the sea. We stayed right close to the strand, or the Promenade, as it was called. There were about fifteen or twenty of the orphanage girls. It was the best time we all had at Portstewart, just to be together, have fun, and talk as only we could about our common experiences, in and out of the orphanage. Some of us had not seen each other since we were in school together. On the last Saturday that we were in Portstewart we went to the pictures (movies). Coming out of the cinema, we all decided to go down to visit the fishermen at the wharf. It was all within close range of where we stayed. As our vacation was coming to an end, we were out to have our last minute fling! No one knew where we were and that's what made it special. There were twelve girls altogether and the fishermen told us that if we got on the boats it was our own responsibility to find our way back. The fishermen were going to a place called Portrush. We, all twelve of us, went on three small boats and sailed away all the while shouting and screaming over to the other boats. We were enjoying this forbidden trip! We arrived in Portrush at one in the morning. We looked at the high wall where we docked and wondered how we would get over this wall. The fishermen were letting down ropes, and one by one we would grab tightly on to the rope and walk our feet up the wall at the same time. Some of us, the more daring ones, were not afraid as we had climbed over the apple orchard many times while at the orphanage. The high walls at the orphanage had barbed wire and glass on top, to deter us from stealing the apples in the Dean's garden on the other side of the orphanage wall. So we helped the more timid ones to clinb the wall to make it to safety to the other side.

Now there was a big question as to how we would make our way back to the vacation house in Portstewart. It was more than a two hour walk back. We had not gone too far when we saw an army jeep. I went over to ask the soldiers if they were heading our way back to Portstewart. They certainly were, Portstewart was on their way to where they were going. We all hopped onto the jeep. We had so much fun with these soldiers. An ideal set up as there were twelve men and twelve girls. One of the fellows shouted, "Hi, there's one each for you all." There was not much space, but the soldiers sat on the floor of the jeep and each soldier had a girl on his knee. We were so happy to get a ride and we sang all the old Irish songs along the way. What natural innocent fun we had! Some of the soldiers were trying at the end of the trip to make dates. It all went so fast that I don't think they got a chance. We stupidly told the fellows to drop us off at the actual place where we were staying in Portstewart. The back of the jeep opened and out came the crowd of girls to face Father Lynch, May Kennedy, and the owner of the house where we stayed, Mrs. McLoughlin! There were some other people there that had been helping in the search to find us. What a letdown! No dates and we were is big trouble! When we were on the jeep it was four a.m., so no one got any sleep on account of us runaways. Who was blamed? Me! I should have more sense as I was one of the oldest in the group. Father Lynch expected more from me and so did May. Oh, was I in hot water! They were told that I was the ring leader. I had the idea of going down to the fishermen, I told them to get on the boats, and I managed to get the ride back. My response to Father Lynch and May was that we had fun, and it was the best time ever. However, it was just a real nightmare to them. Naturally, they just could not understand how so many us could be missing.

One day we were meeting in the club for former orphanage girls. May Kennedy was the president and she had asked this question: If anyone of us was not happy in the jobs we were in, to let her know or if we knew of anybody who was looking for a job. The person for the job would need to be reliable and trustworthy, a good upright character! Oh boy, that would be hard for me to apply after the big incident that had just happened on the previous Saturday night in Portstewart. By and by I heard rumors that it was Fr. Geoff who was looking for someone to help with his parents at their home with the domestic work. It would be a live in situation. How I hated to even mention this "live in" situation. I acted like I did not know what was going on. What's more, I would not tell on the girl who told me, just in case that girl would get in trouble. I continued to work in the big house opposite the King's Hall Skating Rink on the Lisburn Road. The club was downtown but it had moved to a large room also on the Lisburn Road, so it was easy for me to walk straight down the road to the club. In this new place, I was helping again with the cleaning, and spent a lot of free time cleaning at the club, just like when we started at the first place. While I was cleaning the stairway, a friend of Fr. Geoff's came by to bless the place and we were not finished cleaning yet. It was Bishop Conway, a good friend of Fr. Geoff. They were in the seminary in Rome together. The club was a large room on the second floor of a house downtown in Belfast. It was close to the Belfast Technical College. Fr. Geoff had acquired the room so that the girls would be able to get together when we had half days off work.

In the orphanage, we cleaned for any priest who was visiting, so since it was a bishop, we super cleaned! It didn't really matter if the cleaning was not finished in time though, because the two priests were friends and so the cleaning could wait. May Kennedy's big day also arrived, and we celebrated the wedding reception in the club. This time we celebrated a little more than with the tea, bread and jam! It was a beautiful day. It was the first wedding that I had ever heard of or ever seen. We all had a wonderful time.

This wedding made me do some thinking, about things such as why people get married. Mary Murray enlightened me in some things, she was wise in the ways of the world, and so through her mostly, I was given information. I would pound her with questions all the time, because one piece of information would lead me to another question. She was older than I was, and knew so much; at least I thought she did. I was happy to ask questions of somebody I knew. I had been working for so long and dare not ask questions of anyone. My head contained so many questions unanswered. I couldn't go anywhere with the things that puzzled me. I was stuck, as it were, until I received more information on what I needed to know. Life was a puzzle in so many ways. I tried to solve them all by myself, at least 'til now, when Mary came along. When I had time off, I would sometimes go to where Mary was working and we would talk and talk. I did me a world of good. I was basically a happy go lucky person. I showed an outward face of happiness. It was when I was busy that I was at my best. For some reason, if I was busy and active, I could cope with life and all its ups and down. When I was by myself, and alone at night, I had the kind of thoughts that would drag me down to the depths. I was then that crying took over, and sometimes I felt so out of control. With my stoic training in the orphanage

I would never let myself cry or let anyone see me crying. In the orphanage, I had learned that crying was a sure sign that we were guilty. It was a sign of weakness as well. I was in shock that this crying thing was happening to me. Again, I would not tell anyone about this, I kept it to myself. Not even my friends would know about how I felt. Now I know this was part of adolescence that I was going through, and of course I had no knowledge, nor had I ever heard of the words puberty, adolescence, teenagers, or crisis. I would try to figure out myself, just why I cried at night and not when I was busy during the day. I wished it would not happen and just go away altogether because it drained me and I was so tired the morning after I had been crying.

Chapter 6

"Mom, Where Are You?"

The always dominant questions in my mind from the time I left the orphanage was: "Where is my mother? Did I have a mother? If everyone had a mother, and that's a known fact, so where is mine?" These questions were always on my mind, the moment I was alone, I would think about it and wonder and wonder! Of course, I dared not speak of this to anyone:

Where did I come from?
Who is my mother?
I wonder does she know about me?
Did she (my mother) drop me here?
In this place we call Belfast City?
Who dropped me here? I'd like to know.
Someone did!
Who am I?
Does God know about me?
I didn't put myself here. Who did? And why? Was it a lady in white?
Someone dropped me and said, "You're on your own!" To fend for yourself.
Does not everyone have a mother!
Where is mine?
Who is she?—
So out of nowhere I came!

The words "orphan" and "abandonment"
Call up feelings in me that never heal.
In the presence of others, I feel insignificant,
Undeveloped, and very awkward at times.
I don't know where I've come from.
No background to fall back on.
Always a piece of me missing.
I keep looking at people and the faces of strangers that pass me by.
Hoping for some recognition.
Will anyone ever recognize me?
I longed to belong
But I won't ever be part of anyone's life.
Not part of any family.
I will never be missed by anyone.
Who am I?
Where am I going?
Why do I look the way I do?
Do I look like anyone?
Does anyone look like me?

I'm all alone.

So life went on and I carried on as best as I could in spite of the depressing thoughts that dragged me on a downward spiral. Feelings of loss and hopelessness were with me for the longest time. I was afraid for myself and frightened for the future. I was not trained or used to showing any emotion so it was frightening. After I left my first job at Comerton's and found my way around Belfast, I had a one track mind: to find my mother! I told May Kennedy that I must have had a mother and that I would really like to find her. I thought the very first step was to go back to the orphanage and ask the nuns. May answered, "Good Luck, hope your luck is better than mine." I arrived at the front gates of the orphanage and the little nun answered the door and let me in. I forgot that at the orphanage school was in progress, and so the nuns that I knew were not around to help me. I did speak to some nuns that I stopped, who were passing by, and said, "Please, Sister, I was brought up here and I have a question for you, could you help me to find who my mother was?" She replied that she had no permission to do that and she had doubts if anyone would know anything about my mother. I begged her to just take me to the place where the books were kept which contained all the information on all of us that were brought up here. "Child, I never heard of such a thing. I will call the Superior to deal with this." I was ready to take on the whole convent of nuns to attain my goal. Unfortunately, the Superior was out, at least they could not find her at that particular time. I persisted and insisted on seeing the information book. I was guessing about there being a book. No one had told me about a book, I just figured that there was bound to be a book with our names written in it! I knew there was a School Register, and there may be some more information as well. So I was frustrated about it all. I had the free time, but it was a fruitless visit. I left, but I was coming back again to pester them!

All the jobs I had since I worked at Comerton's were of short duration. I was continually trying to find some information on my mother, but how? I discovered the kiosks, or telephone booths, out on the streets of downtown Belfast. I asked someone passing by to show me how this telephone worked. She asked me if I knew the number I wanted to call. I told her that I was going to look up the number (all the while, my knees were shaking). I immediately looked for my last name. It was nowhere to be found in the telephone book. At that time, there were not that many people with the luxury of a telephone. From then on, every telephone booth that I came across, I would be in there looking for my last name. I never passed by a telephone booth (kiosk, as they were called) without going in and looking for my last name. I certainly would not ask or tell any of my girl friends from the Orphanage what I was trying to do, and for some reason, they never talked about trying to find their families. We just never brought up the subject. So I was entirely on my own in my limited search. Occasionally, something would come up in conversations about family. The most common response was, "They didn't care about me, why should I care about them?"

We, the orphanage girls, usually had a club gathering every week which began with a meeting. The most important person, Father Geoff, was not present for the meeting. A number of us would discuss what we did the last week for the hospital visits, and what our plans would be for the following week. For example, we visited the sick people, we talked with them and tried to bring them some comfort. We would see if they were in need of anything and bring any kind of magazines to them. We had some of the girls involved in collecting magazines for the hospital. The reason we became involved in this kind of work was that Father Geoff, at that time, was the Chaplain of the hospital. He certainly got people involved; at least he had mostly orphanage girls at his disposal. I asked May Kennedy-Ferris (Ferris was her married name) where Father Geoff was, she said that he would be arriving later. She took the opportunity to ask again (while he wasn't there) if anyone would like to work for him. This priest had done so much for me and this reason, together with my love for him, made me make the decision.

Chapter 7

"A Nurse Overnight"

I had to tell the family that I was working for presently that I was going to work for someone else. I had not ever been in this position of resigning. It was awkward for me, to say the least! Who was I to have such power in my life, to actually tell them that I was resigning? It was a frightening experience. I expected some terrible reaction but nothing happened that caused me to be worried. I collected my few belongings together over the course of the week. Where were my shoes, the only one pair of decent shoes that I had possessed? I had bought them myself. Wow! I was afraid to ask if anyone had seen them just in case they would think that I was accusing them. Who was I, asking them, my employers, if they knew where my shoes were? I was sure I knew where I had put them, but they weren't there now. I did finally pluck up the courage to ask if anyone had seen them. They were not found by the time I was ready to leave.

Father Lynch picked me up in his car and we drove all the way to Newcastle, situated at the foot of the Mourne Mountains. "Where the mountains of Mourne sweep down to the sea." What a beautiful picturesque sight to behold! I was right by the sea. Could anyone want for more? I was introduced to the Lynch family. The father of Father Lynch was standing beside his wife. Father Lynch told me to call her "Mama," that was the name that everyone called her. I could not call her "Mama," it didn't ring true for me to call her by that name I had not called anyone "Mama" in my life and it was difficult for me to say the word. I did get used to calling her "Mama" eventually. Mama had a stroke and was paralyzed on the right side and her speech was affected. Besides the domestic work in the house, I had total charge of Mrs. Lynch (Mama). I fed her at mealtimes, I bathed her or washed her everyday, I walked her at certain times each day. I took her out in the wheelchair when the weather was warm enough. I would read to her and put her to bed, and see that she was comfortable before I myself went to bed. I was really happy in this situation and taking care of Mrs. Lynch was a joy. I was not rushed in any way and I myself enjoyed the stories that were chosen for me to read to her. I loved every minute of this. Taking care of her made me feel that I was useful and I was needed.

Father Lynch's father was a very tall man. (Up to that time I had never seen a person that was that tall.) He generally had to stoop to go through the doors. Just his very presence exuded gentleness and kindness. I don't remember that I ever saw him sitting down. He always stood, leaning against a wall, or was helping me with the care of his wife (Mama). For some reason, I suspected that he was not well. No one had said that he was ill. He was so very attentive to his wife and helped with feeding and walking, and would help me to turn and position her in the bed. Such attention and devotion to his wife, and also to me was a new experience. I grew to love and revere this man and felt the loss of his presence very much. He was admitted to the hospital and died soon afterwards. Mama then became my sole attention and I grieved for her loss as well as my own. I always expected to see him turn up just at the right time but he was gone forever, and it took me a long time to realize that he would not be coming back anymore.

With the death of the father, all the family arrived at different times, so many children with their children, and I got to know everyone. Father Lynch was the oldest of thirteen children, two of whom died in infancy. He also said that I ought to get out more often now that there were enough people to take care of Mama. So, while his family was visiting, I would take the bicycle and go off to the bottom of the Mourne Mountains and watch the waves come in (to quote the Irish song) where the "Mountains of Mourne swept down to the sea_" I just loved this place and its beautiful scenery. I couldn't get enough of it and I would go back to the same spot as often as I got the chance.

Once I was able to learn to ride the bicycle, I thought that I could try a few daring tricks. I had some pretty bad fall but I did not say anything in case I wouldn't be allowed to ride the bicycle again. There was a gate at the entrance of the driveway to the Lynch's house. Coming home one evening, I opened the gate wide and attempted to ride my bicycle over the bump or hump in the center, and I was thrown some distance. The bicycle was badly damaged and I hurt my left hand. One of Father Lynch's brothers was a doctor and he happened to just get home that evening, so he bandaged my hand, and put a splint on it. Apparently, I had broken the last three fingers of my left hand. I was at a loss for a while but was able to accomplish quite a lot with my right hand. Because of the fear of ever riding the bicycle again, Father Lynch insisted that I keep riding once my hand and fingers healed properly. Not a word of reprimand about the broken bicycle. The brother who was a doctor said, "You know, Maud, there's only one of you and you could never be replaced, Mama loves you dearly. A bicycle can always be replaced." Those words were music to my ears and I kept going over and over the words that he said: "Mama loves you dearly!" These were the first words of "love" ever spoken to me.

After the death of his father, Father Lynch moved back to Belfast. We all moved into a house right near where the orphanage was were I grew up, and I continued to work and live in Father Lynch's home in Belfast.

Chapter 8

"What is a Vocation?
Did I have the Call to Religious Life?"

In many European countries after World War II, but I think especially in Ireland, nuns from religious orders were sent to different high schools to give talks to the girls on religious vocations, or the call to religious life. It so happened that one of these nuns was sent from Africa to Ireland. Her name was Sister Gerard. Father Lynch was the chaplain of a convent where she stayed while in Belfast, so that is where he met her.

Father Lynch, in the course of the conversation with Sister Gerard, mentioned my name to her and suggested that he thought that I was a good candidate. Father Lynch arranged for me to have an interview with her. So, one Saturday afternoon, he drove me to the convent to meet her. Never before did I have an interview or one to one talk with anyone, so I was naturally nervous. It was a frightening though. It was when I stepped out of the car that I got the shivers, and walked towards the front door of the convent that reality hit me. Before the door opened, I whispered to Father Lynch, "Don't leave me."

I was escorted to a large parlor room where Sister Gerard was waiting for us. She was a large robust woman with the kindliest smile I had ever seen. Sister welcomed me warmly. She saw that I was trembling, and scared. Father Lynch was heading for the door to leave, and glancing at him, I said, "Don't leave." I sat down in the chair directly in front of her. She placed her hands on mine and assured me that she was not going to take a bite out of me. I had never been shown any tenderness like this in my life before, no one had ever touched me that way before and it frightened me, though it felt good.

Father left me alone with Sister Gerard. There was a tray of tea and scones on the table next to us and she offered to pour the tea for me. I was afraid to lift the cup of tea because I was still trembling so much and was afraid that I would not be able to hold the cup in my hand. I couldn't help but think that I'm the servant; I should be pouring the tea, not the sister.

The fact that Sister Gerard was very friendly and motherly did help somewhat to calm me down. "So Maud, I heard that you want to be a nun. Is that right?" I was like paralyzed. "Isn't that why you came to visit me?" "No, not really," I answered. Sister said, "That's not what I heard from Father Lynch. Then why did you come?" I childishly answered, "Father Lynch brought me." "Have you ever thought of being a nun at any time before up to now?" she asked. I replied "No!" "Well, Maud I think that you must have told Father Lynch or he wouldn't have driven you here to see me. Is that not so?" "Yes, I responded to Father Lynch when he asked me if I wanted to be a nun and I told him that I wanted to do well and help people but, I didn't want to wear that long dress and cover my head. If I did that, then people would think that I'm a good person, and I'm not a good person. Father said that there was no way today that I would do that kind of good except to enter a convent. I'm not good enough for the convent really." Sister said, "I can see that you are not afraid of me anymore and that you actually found your voice." She joked a little with me, and then she said, "Have you told anyone in your family about this?" I replied "No!" She didn't ask any more questions and soon after that Father Lynch knocked and came back into the room again. I started to drink the cup of tea while they were both in conversation. My throat felt parched. Sister came back over to me and said, "You know Maud, we don't enter the convent because we are good people, but because we want to do good for other people, and there are many out there who need help." She proceeded to inform me that there was a group of girls who would be traveling back to England with her, and would I like to go back with them? I turned to Father Lynch for an answer-and before he could respond I replied, "I'm too young to go now." "How old are you now Maud? Does that mean that you want to come later?" I was afraid to say an outright 'no' so I replied, "Maybe, but I am only fifteen." It was the summer of 1946.

The interview over, I followed Father Lynch to his car. When we were driving along the road, Father said, "Sister Gerard said that you were extremely bashful." "Yes," I answered, "she told me that and asked me why

I was that shy." Was I always that way? I didn't know what bashful meant until Father Lynch explained the meaning of the word to me. Up to that time, I wasn't aware that I was shy. I told father that "I am just that way when I meet strange people for the first time. I can't help it that is why I feel awkward when I go to a new job. I'm meeting new people again."

Later that evening, when I was finished with my work at Lynch's and had put Mama to bed. Father said that I could go out for the evening. I went immediately to visit with my friend Kathleen. I related all the happenings of the day to her, especially the interview with Sister Gerard. Kathleen exploded, "My God, Maudie, are you out of your mind? Don't go; don't do such a stupid thing. Do you want to be like the nuns in the orphanage?" "I sure don't, but if I set foot in there, I'd fix them all," I said. Kathleen responded, "I'd kill them Al, that's what I'd do." "How could I ever come up with such a grandiose idea that I would ever change the nuns. I had a long way to get myself settled in life. Later on, I found out that the nuns in the orphanage did not accept orphan girls from their own schools. There was a rule that they did not allow it within their order.

That Saturday was quite a unique experience for me. I could not fall asleep that night because my thoughts were going at a mile a minute, my emotions were running high, and I felt real bad that I had let Father Lynch down by not going along with Sister Gerard. I hoped that Father would understand my reasoning.

The next day was Sunday. I went to Mass wearing my red dress that I wore for the interview the day before. It had been given to me and I loved it. I thought that it went well with my black hair; it was a warm dress, and I had a black coat of Mama's. I felt awkward wearing it for the interview, but I was delighted to wear it again when going down the road for Mass. I thought it was just wonderful to wear such beautiful clothes. The boys that usually hung out at the corner of the Ormeau Road by the church noticed that I was all dressed up, and began calling out to me, "Hey Gypsy! Hey Fenian! Where's the gypsy going?" They were whistling until I was out of sight. I was afraid to go back the same route so I took a back route from then on to the Lynch's house.

Sunday at Lynch's was generally easier for me in regards to the work. I had no laundry or house cleaning except washing dishes. I still have to cook and care for Mama. So this Sunday I was spending more time with my thoughts and all that happened the day before. In regards to the question "Have you told anyone in tour family about this?" it sent my mind thinking of a family. Why don't I have a family, where are they all? There were so many questions that I needed to knew and no one to ask. If I could find my mother then I would know who my family is, that would stand to reason. Where is she?

When I worked at Comerton's, and all the domestic jobs afterwards, I was instructed to call the two adults in the house "Madam" and "Sir". The children in Comerton's would call them "Mum" and "Dad". I had no concept then of a "Mum" and "Dad". When I began to figure out what family meant, and was educating myself in my limited way, then I awoke to the fact that everyone had a mother. So began my search, in my mind anyway, of where she was and who she was. She is the reason that I exist so she has to be somewhere. I've got to find her. Sunday, being a more relaxed day at Lynch's, I would go for a walk or take the bicycle and stop at every kiosk to look in the book for my last name. No one ever knew that I was looking for my mother. I was ashamed to even mention the idea to the orphanage girls. At the club, all the girls were so happy to be together and have fun. They never talked about family because that didn't exist for them. If questioned, their usual response was always the same. "They didn't t care about me, why should I care about them?"

Chapter 9

"Simple Adoption"

One day I got a big surprise, I saw the chairwoman Rose from Comerton's standing in the club and talking to Father Lynch. I was taken by surprise to see "Rose" at the club. Her 16 or 17 year old daughter Margaret was with her. Rose looked so different all dressed up for the occasion. I was curious to know how she found our club. She had tracked me down through Father Lynch, and found out that I was frequently at the club.

I was extremely happy and excited to see Rose again, we had such a good time together at Comerton's and I could talk to her and learned so much from her. I never knew where she lived, and telephones were a luxury for only a few. I dearly loved Rose and thought about her often after I left Comerton's. Here she was visiting the club, and being persistent in her desire to adopt me and come to get permission from Father Lynch. Father told me that adoption was out of the question. The reason: "Rose was Protestant and I was Catholic." I never saw Rose again!

Working in the Lynch's house was the best job that I ever had and I was happy. I had more free time and a certain amount of independence. I was earning a little money, which I had not ever received before. I was able to go to the Irish Ceili's and set dances on a Saturday night with some of my friends, and Kathleen Palmer always came with me. I so looked forward to getting away for a while.

The Trainor family was very helpful to Father Lynch and the club when it first opened. There were seven children in the family, two girls, Rita and Kathleen Trainor, and five brothers. They had been friends of the Lynch family. They were so knowledgeable about everything and we orphans felt stupid in their presence, but then we knew that the people outside of the orphanage were smarter than us, orphans. Father Lunch used to say that the girls in the orphanage were a few years behind the outside world. We did not develop physically or mentally as fast as they did. We all just felt like a square peg in a round hole after we left the orphanage to start working outside.

Rita Trainor was going on an outing to Bangor and the Hollywood seaside resorts traveling east from Belfast. She and four of her brothers were going and they asked Father Lynch if I could go with them. It was a Saturday and Father got his sister's bicycle out for me and checked if it was in working order. So we set off at eight o'clock in the morning and it was just great, the freedom of being outside, riding a bicycle! About halfway there, my bicycle started to give me trouble. Rita told one of the brothers to stay behind and help me while she and the remaining brothers went on ahead. They were to stop at an arranged place to catch up with us. I was scared to be left alone by myself with another boy; just the two of us together scared me. It was not that I thought something bad might happen, but (at that time) I did not know anything about boys. It was frightening out alone in the street. I was so awkward and felt shy and tongue-tied in this boy's presence. Rita told me later that her brother said that I was a beautiful girl, but I was so quiet and she doesn't talk!

Chapter 10

"Big Decisions"

One Sunday morning, I came home from Mass and was feeding Mama her breakfast. Father Lynch also came home and came straight over to me. He said, "When you are finished I want you to come up to my room." It seemed like a summons and so solemn! I was afraid to go up and began to wonder what I had done wrong. My conscience was clear. Mama knew and saw that I was worried and that I was so afraid. I had never seen Father Lynch in such a serious mood like this.

I entered the room, and Father immediately said, "Sit down, Maud, I want to talk to you and I'm asking you to be serious." I think that I was acting in a frivolous manner trying to cope with the unknown situation. He repeated, "Maud, I'm serious, and I want you to give me a serious answer." Oh dear me, what had I done wrong? Father said, "Do you still want to be a nun?" "Oh no! I don't know," I stuttered and stammered and was so taken by surprise and had no chance to discuss it with anyone. Father said that I had had two years to think about it. I replied, "Yes, I know, but I didn't think about it up 'til now." This was the month of July. I loved to get out of doors and all I could think of was being locked up in a nunnery and never seeing the outside world again. "So if you still want to be a nun, Sister Gerard is back again, and is leaving for England in two weeks time," he said. "Oh Father, it's too soon, I'll go later." He replied that I had given the same answer the last time. "You know Maud, if you fight this call from God you may regret it for the rest of your life," he said. So, just to get this over with, I said, "I'll go next time." Father reminded me that I also give the same answer the last time to Sister Gerard. He continued, "There may not be the same chance next time around." I said, "I can't go now, but I'll be ready the next time for sure." I was feeling so bad that I had let Father Lynch down again; it was the last thing that I wanted to do to him.

A private nurse began coming from the hospital to assess Mrs. Lynch about twice a week. I still continued to care for her basic needs of feeding, washing and taking care of her. I read to her any time that I was free and Mama loved it. She seemed to understand even though she couldn't speak or express it. This job gave me the only chance I had to read a book.

The private nurse became interested in me, and asked me if I would be looking for a job if Mrs. Lynch would pass away. She would take me to Guernsey Island where her home was. "You would love it there, you are young, and it is good to travel and see the world." It seemed wonderful, but this nurse did not know that I had no family and no money to travel. I thought about it but it was also very scary going to a foreign place. I would have to leave my friends behind! No, I couldn't do that. It was an unknown future, besides it was already settled I would be entering the convent in January.

The only time I had to myself was at night, when I went up to bed. Alone in my room I was free. I always brought the book that I read to Mama up with me at night so that I could prepare the reading for the next day. This was to check ahead of time and be prepared for any big words that I could not pronounce or understand.

That particular Sunday night, my mind was in a whirlwind, I couldn't fall asleep thinking of all the happenings, especially the interview with Father Lynch. Everything was flashing through my mind. Life was great at this time and I was enjoying myself much better than I had ever had the opportunity to do before. I could go out for a ride on my bicycle, I could visit my friends, I would play tennis every Saturday morning, I enjoyed the Ceili's, I was meeting more people, and I visited the hospital. I loved working at Lynch's and had grown to love Mrs. Lynch. This was the best period of my life since I left the orphanage. I would have to leave it all behind if I entered the convent.

Chapter 11

"One More Try"

The foremost thought in my mind was to find my mother before I ever thought of entering a convent. But where could I find her? Anytime I went to Church or to the hospital or in any public places where I happed to find myself, I would look at every woman who had black hair and brown eyes, looking and hoping for some kind of recognition. I knew that there were very few children in the orphanage with black hair, I being one of the so I innocently thought that anyone with black hair and brown eyes that I met in Belfast could be a relation of mine, maybe even my mother.

As I mentioned before, I was within walking distance from the orphanage. I knew that if I entered the convent, it would please the nuns in the orphanage. That in itself was a great reason for them to give me information before I entered.

When I would visit the orphanage, I would try to get in without being seen. Hence, I would go in through the large back gate from the Ravenhill Road. If I went in the front gate at the Ormeau Road there would be too much red tape, and a nun would have to let me in the front gate from the Ormeau Road. Pretty soon everyone would know that I was there and I tried to avoid that. The front entrance was where the nun's convent was situated. The nuns would see me arriving and the sister answering the front gate would have to report any person who arrived.

While strolling through the orphanage one day from the back entrance, I found myself eventually in the laundry room. There were so many girls working there. One of the nuns in there asked me it I was looking for someone. I said, "No, I'm just taking a look around." "You know that this is not allowed, you need to have a sister or one of the senior girls to accompany you." "Does the sister at the front gate know that you are here?" I replied that I was just taking a walk and would leave soon. One of the girls recognized me, "Hello Maud!" She said to the nun, "That's one of the situation girls! I know her!"

Soon the girls in there were all gathering around me to ask me if I liked it out there. The nun let me alone when she found out that I was one of their own girls, brought up in the orphanage. We were called the "Situation Girls". It meant that we had left school and were situated in wealthy homes as maids. The girls in the laundry were all brought up in the orphanage and so were all the others working in the different departments. I enjoyed talking to the girls and after that I wandered around on my own, waiting for an opportunity to find a nun that I could talk to about my ongoing persistent question

I came upon a nun whom I didn't recognize. She greeted me so politely and while bowing head as if to move on, I stopped her. I thought, this nun doesn't know me so I can pretend that I was requesting on behalf of someone else. "Sister, would you be able to help me? I'm trying to help a girl who was brought up here, she is getting married, and has to find out some information before she gets married," I said. "Who can I ask or do you have a book that you could look up for me?" Sister said, "Follow me." So down the long corridors I went 'til I was put in a little parlor to wait 'til the sister returned. I thought that I had pulled that good excuse off very well. My hopes were up, but I was afraid of another nun returning who would recognize me. My brain was working fast. The nun returned with the superior, Mother Elphege, I wasn't sure of her name. She recognized me as having been there before. I told her why I had come. She knew what I wanted but told me the same response. "I would have to speak to the girl herself, we are not allowed to give out any information except to the girl herself!" she said. I told her that I could understand that, then I said, "Now, I have some news myself, I'm going to enter a convent and I also have to find out about my family before I leave. I will be going to England in January."

The nun had no permission to look up anything, and there is no book here, she said. I was just beginning to get desperate and really frustrated about ever finding out anything. I said, "Mother, this is the last and only opportunity that I have. There must be a way to get this information. If there is someone else in higher position than you to talk to, I'll ask them, please tell me where I can go to find out." The Mother Superior left, and returned with a small piece of paper, Written on the paper were four things:

Baptized March 1939
Confirmed March 1941
Entered 1936
Left Orphanage 1942

I took a quick glance at the 2x2 inch piece of paper and there was nothing written there that was of interest to me. "Mother, could you please tell me the year that I was born?" I knew when I was born, from a girl who peeped at the class register during a lunch break when I was still in school. However, I had never been told officially, so now I would know my birthday for sure, if the sister would look it up for me.

"Sister, I have so. many questions that I want information about, but I have only one question that I really want an answer to. Is it not too much trouble, and why is it such a secret?" I asked. I was trying so hard to hold in my anger! Why does no one on this earth know where my mother is, or how I got here to this orphanage? The nun replied, "I said already, Maud, we do not have permission to disclose any information." (I thought I must look up the word "disclose" when I get home.) "Did God personally drop me down right here in this place in the orphanage? Is that how all the hundreds of other girls got here? Mother, I can't believe that we are not told anything," I said. So I left the orphanage accompanied by the sister and the little nun who had the keys to let me out the front door. There were two locked front doors after going through one door, then you went through the other door. Outside on the Ormeau Road, I tore up the small piece of paper. I was so mad at all of them back there. I walked home to the Lynch's house and tried to show a smiling face to Mama. She was alone waiting for me. I had always thought that I was put in the orphanage as a baby and if I looked on that wee piece of paper more carefully, I would have noticed that I was put there at six years of age. In 1997, I found out that I was placed there when I was five almost six years old. Why do I not remember any of that? May Ferris, who was older than I, remembers when I arrived in the orphanage. I had a yellow dress on and the nun's assistant was trying to get the dress off me to put me in the orphanage uniform. May said that I was impossible! I kicked and screamed and was so afraid of the nuns. I would scream and yell every time that I saw a nun, but pretty soon they had me subdued.

As I already mentioned, there were hundreds of children in the orphanage. It was not noticeable when any child was missing but when I reached the senior classes in school, then I began to notice that some girls who were always sitting at certain desks were not there anymore. Periodically, the numbers would dwindle and the girls were gone. Of course, no one would dare question this.

It was while I was out working that I realized the children were put out to domestic situations like I had been. Years later, I often wondered where they were and what happened to all of them. Some children, more than others, remained in my memory. After I left Comerton's, I saw some of them when they would come to Father Lynch's club but many of them I never saw or heard of again.

Chapter 12

"A Trunk in Passageway"

One day, while working at Lynch's, I saw a big trunk on the floor in the passageway outside. There was a key with a tag attached to it on top of the lid of the box. I wondered how the trunk had got there and was naturally curious to know what was inside the case. Pretty soon, I found out when Father Lynch came home. It was for me! I was told by Father Lynch to get my personal belongings together, I had to be in England to enter convent with the group that were entering on the 20th of January. I thought that I had plenty of time to get my few belongings together. I didn't have much. I could carry my personal belonging in my hand. A brown paper bag was all I ever needed. Why the big trunk?

Father told me that I was booked on the train to Dublin the 17th of January. I needed to spend a few days in Dublin in order to buy all the requisites needed for the convent. Then I would leave Ireland from Dublin, and sail for England. None of this information really sunk in but gradually I was beginning to realize that this was it! It was actually only about four hours by train from Belfast to Dublin, but it was a long way for me, my first time traveling on a train. When I realized what was going on, I asked Father Lynch why I had to have this big trunk box, because I didn't have enough possessions to fill the trunk. Father showed me the long list of requirements that Sister Gerard had sent him. In the north of Ireland, we still had our ration books; I would not have had enough coupons for all the convent requirements, so that was the reason for buying everything in Dublin. Black market would have to be the way of getting coupons, but who had the money to do that? Many of course did still.

Apart from buying the one pair of shoes, fish and chips, and the occasional candy, this was going to be my first shopping spree. I did not know what was going on or how I would shop, but someone was going to be with me in Dublin would meet me at the train station in Dublin. It was a friend of Father Lynch's.

On the 17th of January, I was all set to leave. I checked if I had everything, I had already put my gas mask in the trunk and this helped to fill some space. Father had put some things in for his relatives and friends and the lady who was to meet me in Dublin would take care everything.

On the 17th of January, there was a cold bitter wind that was blowing and Father had told me to wear a hat. I couldn't arrive at the convent without a hat on my head. I was leaving, so I had plucked up the courage to say something about the hat. Father knew that I didn't like to wear a hat at any time, and he always insisted that I had to wear one, and that was the time when you weren't dressed unless you had your hat on, especially for church. I told Father that I was going to put the hat in the trunk. I argued that I didn't want to wear it now, but I'd put it on before I arrived at the convent in England. He won the case, and I walked out of Lynch's with the hat on my head. Father was driving me to the Belfast train station and as I was getting in to his car, the hat blew off my head. There was such a gale force that I never retrieved it. I had run after it, but it was gone with the wind. In the car, Father said, "Well from now on, I won't have to worry you about a hat again. You will always have one on." I always remembered those words, but still I didn't catch on to the fact that I was really off and on my way to a convent where my head would be covered. Somehow, I think that all the newness and excitement took over my real fears of the unknown future.

I arrived at the train station in Belfast. Father gave me his final blessing while he laid his hand on my head for a few seconds. This gesture sent shivers up my spine; I was trembling and unable to steady myself. I don't remember who lifted the trunk out of the car or how I ever got on the train, but I remember being on the train and sobbing and sobbing and unable to stop. I was suddenly alone and lost. I had left everyone behind and Father Lynch was gone forever. I was going too far away! There were many people traveling on the train but I felt all alone. I wanted the train to go back to Belfast again. (As I write these memoirs, I find that I'm still reliving and crying and I will have to give myself some time before I come back to the story.) The continual puffing of the train and watching the green fields out the window just added to my melancholy. I tried to behave and straighten myself up in front of all these people traveling in the coach with me.

I cannot recall being fetched at the train station in Dublin. I did remember shopping in Dublin. Father Lynch's friend drove me around in her car to the different shops. Some of the stuff on the list I had never seen or even possessed before. I questioned the fact that I had to buy so much toweling material. In addition to the towels and washcloths, I had to buy yards and yards of white toweling materials. "What am I going to do with it all?" Father's friend replied, "Cleanliness is next to godliness. You'll be washing a lot." We laughed so much, and it broke the tension that I was under. I was to sail for England on the 19th of January from Dunleary. I do not recall arriving or getting on the boat. I do remember sitting out on the deck, and unable to move from the bench that I was sitting on. I was very sick, and so was everyone around me. My name came over the loudspeaker, more than once, but I couldn't respond. I knew it was probably the girl, Maureen Keane, trying to find me. I was to meet Maureen on the boat and together we were to travel to Euston Station in England and then on to the convent. As it happened, we met up with all the girls at Euston. I cannot recall how I got from the deck of the boat in Ireland to Euston Station in England, it's a total wipeout. I do recall, while I was sitting on the boat bench, some young lads were having a great time and they sang mostly Irish songs out on the deck, but the first song that they sang with such gusto was Gracie Fields,

"Now is the hour when we must say goodbye.
Soon we'll be sailing far across the sea.
While I'm away, oh please remember me."

That's all I needed to hear at that lonely hour on the deck leaving Ireland. I do not recall how long it took for the boat to sail from Dunleary/Dublin to England. I remember it was drizzling. (Soft rain, as we call it in Ireland.) I was shivering from the cold while sitting out in the open deck. I guess the boat took three or more hours because Father Lynch had booked a bunk bed for me. As I said, I was not able to move from where I had plunked myself down. I was so very sick. It was difficult for me to reach the deck rail to even throw up, even though it was only a few steps away from where I was sitting. I remember a lady sitting nearby. She was covered with a Galway shawl. I only saw glimpses of her when she would lean over the deck rail, like I tried to do but I felt so very bad that I myself was not able to help her. I wished that I had a shawl to cover me. The wind would be so strong and sharp, and it was freezing. The cold, wet wind, along with the rain, kept blowing and I was not dressed for an awful ordeal like this. The young lads were still enjoying themselves and singing up their own storm. I wished they would stop and realize that all of us on the deck were sick and they should have had some consideration and pity on us, and stop singing.

Chapter 13

"On the English train as it pulled along my thoughts were of Belfast and Ireland"

While on the train in England from Euston to London, my thoughts flew back to those years in the 1940's, between my job at Comerton's and before I worked for the Lynch's. Some of us orphan girls would plan to get out of the domestic situations. We'd plan all kinds of things. The one thing that we all wished for was to get out of domestic situations and find day jobs for ourselves. This was more of a problem than we thought. We seldom got the same time off together, if we got any time off at all. Generally, we had a few hours a week, so planning was not easy. I recall a bunch of us going up to the Catholic area on the Falls Road. We'd split up, and go separate ways, and meet up again to relate our stories. We had so much fun telling our stories and just being together.

We were obviously not thinking at all of the times that we were living in, we were just out to find a day job. The war was on, and we were restricted in so many ways. Food was scarce, and rationed out to each family. Many times, I waited in line queues for the family that I'd be working for to get two hen eggs and one duck egg, along with bread and two ounces of butter. If you were under eighteen you got extra milk and an occasional fruit. We were only to go once a week for our rations. We couldn't cheat because a check off was done on our ration books, and a date saying when we were last at the pickup place.

Some of us found a day job working in Fish and Chip shops. They were popular during the war. So, the big question now was, where will we live if we have a day job? So, the next time that we head off to roam the streets, we went in search of digs. A group of us could rent a single room, if we found one. Most of us working in homes, doing domestic work, got no pay except maybe two shillings and sixpence, a half crown, a month. Most places that I worked at, my board and lodging was my pay, so we had no spending money. We thought that a day job would bring in more money. We looked for hideaway places to sleep in, outside buildings and under bridges where we could use our coats to cover us. We would go wherever we found shelter, no matter where, so long as we were together and out of the domestic situations. We had to stay in our old jobs 'til we were sure of a place to go at night. The air-raid shelters were great places to hide in because we were protected from the cold winds and rain but the air-raid wardens kept a watch to see if anyone was in there, and we'd be in big if the police found us.

Father Lynch got wind of what we were up to, and he kept trying to keep us in our domestic jobs where we were safe, but we still pursued our goal looking for day jobs.

Those memories remained in the forefront of my mind as I traveled to the convent in England on the train from Euston Station to Liverpool Station. It was all like a dream. Yes, here I was, on my way, to a convent "live-in" situation. In my wildest dreams, I had not conjured up this situation.

I traveled with the group of girls about to enter the convent with me at Euston Station in England. Sister Gerard, the nun who interviewed me in Ireland, was there at the station to chaperone us in the right direction. Some of us were from different parts of England, some from Scotland, but the majority of us were from Ireland. I was the only person from the north of Ireland. We boarded the train from Euston Station to a place called Chingford. The name Chingford sounded to us like a Chinese name. We duly arrived at the convent where a big welcome awaited us. We had been traveling all night, so breakfast awaited us and we were sent to rest and get some sleep. Later on that day, I recalled the hustle and bustle of unpacking our belongings. There were about ten or more postulants in the group ahead of us, and they knew the ropes, having been in the convent six months or more already. It was all so different and so strange and we were all dressed in black. We had to look for black dresses that fitted us and we were given a short black veil to wear on our heads. The period of being a postulant in a convent was a testing period. Depending on how we conducted ourselves all round during that period determined if we were found suitable to be received officially into the Congregation one year later. We had to meet certain standard requirements, and studies pertaining to the Religious Life began immediately.

Chapter 14

"A Postulant in Training"

Therefore, I became a postulant on the 20th of January, 1949. Everything was so very new. A postulant is a candidate for admission to the novitiate. She becomes a novice, generally a year later after she has completed the postulancy. We were in a new country in England, but it was the newness and strangeness of the convent that was so foreign to all of us, a totally different way of life. We might as well have arrived in China (the place was called Chingford). In spite of this, I at least had an advantage over the other postulants with regard to having been accustomed to the rules and regulations of the orphanage, and having a much disciplined childhood. I grew up with hundreds of children and so, I loved to get lost in the numbers, where I wouldn't be noticed. Besides all the postulants, there were about thirty or more novices, all at different stages in Religious Life. Somehow, I was enjoying the whole set up, at least at this stage of being a new girl, so to speak. All of us were in the same boat, heading in the same direction, all dressed in the same uniforms, black shoes and stockings, black dresses and short black veils. We also wore a black cape over our shoulders which hung down to our waists. We were often nicknamed "The Crows." The more mature postulants, in the group above us, were to assist us in the ways of daily living and conformity to life in the convent.

Basically, a person with a true vocation enters the Order or Congregation to give her life to God. He or she may have sincerely felt this longing to serve God for some time, or may have had the calling to serve God and was internally fighting against it. This is the big day when this step is finally taken and full of enthusiasm, the postulant is ready to take on great things for God. The postulant not only brings herself, but also her God-given talents. The superiors are happy to use these gifts and talent for the good of the community. Anyone who enters, because she has these talents for the sole purpose of writing, painting, art or music, is not entering for the right reasons.

The period of postulancy is a time of discerning on the part of the postulant and the Superiors. I thought that I was young, only to find out that some of the girls in the group above me were fifteen years of age. The ages ranged from fourteen to girls in their twenties. One girl in my group was thirty-three and we joked about her being so old! So, whether it was because we were really young and immature, or we felt awkward in our new surroundings in the convent and as if the whole focus of attention was on us newcomers, I think that we all felt so clumsy at would have normally been familiar to us seemed strange.

As postulants, we were to eat well, sleep well, and laugh well. We were to be happy, healthy, and hearty. I became so familiar with these phrases and really tried to live up to them to be a good postulant. I thought to myself, if that is all that is required of us, then I am capable of living up to these standards, and what's more, I liked this kind of life, it was going to be just great! To me it seemed carefree and happy. No more worries for me to find a place for myself. I would never have to worry about a job again. I was delighted with myself and the whole world! How could I have been so fortunate? This life was just great! What really appealed to me was the fact that I would always have people around me and never be alone again.

Looking back now, this was probably the honeymoon phase and life continued on cloud nine for a while. It felt good to be secure with no worries! Oh, it was more than I ever asked for, or ever deserved, or ever dreamed of, for myself. I was always grateful to have landed in such a place. We had a reception ceremony for the admission of the new postulants, beginning with a church service, and the celebration continued throughout the day. I was deliriously happy and, of course, ready for anything.

Living the life in the Novitiate House as postulants was different from the novices and the Professed Religious Nuns. They were separated from us though we saw them every day in the chapel and in the refectory, and when they were going about their duties. We were not allowed to speak to them, just bow our heads in acknowledgement as they passed us in the corridors or elsewhere. Gradually, all the newness wore off and we became part of the whole set up.

The typical day as a postulant was all planned out for as. We arose at five a.m. with the rest of the community, awakened by the sound of a bell.

We washed in a basin next to our beds, which we had filled with water the previous night. We dressed quickly and went straight to the chapel. We had about fifteen minutes from the sound of the bell 'til we arrived in the chapel. We were not to come in to the chapel late because that was a distraction to the choir of nuns who were absorbed in prayer.

In the chapel, we joined with the nuns in reciting the Divine Office (the official prayer of the Church). It was all in Latin (the official language of the church). We postulants just listened and tried to follow along in the book. We then sat in our stalls or knelt for a half hour of meditation. Mass would follow at 7 a.m.

After mass, we had breakfast, and then we all headed for our assigned duties. By ten a.m., we had to assemble in the Novitiate. Instructions were given by the Novice Mistress. She chose a spiritual book to read a chapter or more to us each day. We had to learn the Catholic Catechism and learn about Religious Life. The Rule of St. Augustine, and the Constitutions of our Congregation, was to be read, and we would study these books in detail at a later date. I enjoyed the instructions and coming together in the mornings.

Afterwards, we went back to our assignments, and waited for the lunch bell. After lunch, we gathered again in the Novitiate for the "recreation." Recreation meant sitting around the table while we talked in a subdued voice. We had to do embroidery for the convent or darn socks during Recreation time. We had to keep busy with our hands, and the Novice Mistress kept repeating that "the devil finds work for idle hands." As we were new, we didn't have socks to mend, so we were happy to mend for the novices and junior Professed Sisters. After recreation, we passed the chapel for a visit to pray and then continued on to doing our jobs. To continue our routine, we responded to the call of the Bell for dinner in the refectory. This was our routine every day. We were segmented throughout the day by bells, prodding us from one activity to another.

The Divine Office mentioned earlier was divided into canonical hours throughout the day. Matins was in the early morning, Prime, Terce, Sext and None during the day, and Vesper was in the evening. Added to all of the Divine Office was the meditation, the Rosary, and the Litany, in the evenings. The duties and assignments I wrote about were tasks in general, such as cooking, cleaning the convent, washing up the dishes after each meal, and setting the table for the next meal right away.

Sisters also had their own specific charges or assignments. The bursar treasure, choir mistress, novice mistress, Superiors, cooks, laundry mistress, sacristan, sewing mistress, musicians and teachers were all various other positions. So the nuns and postulants would frequently be seen filing in single lines to go to the next call of the bell. We were to walk sedately by never to hurry or run, that would be considered a breach of discipline or decorum. This was a busy life.

Silence was maintained throughout the day. The Profound or Great Silence was from 9 p.m. 'til after Mass the following morning. No noise was to be heard of any kind. Silence was kept throughout the day and we spoke only when it was absolutely necessary and even then it had to pertain only to the work on hand. Silence meant not only did we refrain from talking, but also there was to be silence with everything around us, walking silently and quietly, no banging of doors or closing them noisily, or dropping something that might make a noise. We had to grow accustomed to all this, but in the meantime, the postulants were readily excused if we broke the silence, or did something which would have been out of place in the convent. We were still new girls on the block! The postulants were shown more leniency in everything as we were not yet novices.

When springtime arrived, and we were able to get outside, I realized that there was a lot more work to be done. Besides the large Tudor house that we called the convent, there were two more houses to be taken care of, right next to one another. One of the houses was a school, and this is where I saw some of the sisters going off to school each day. It was a boarding school. The house in between the convent at school was used as an extension, with three or four classrooms and a section for an old age home. The gardens behind these three Tudor homes were enormous, where one could get lost. At the end of the garden behind the convent was a fowl run. At the end of the garden behind the middle house was an open air stage. A Montessori school was at the other end of the school. These were just huge grounds, and all three were connected to make one big playground for the children.

Our charges began to expand from the convent to these other houses. Every Saturday, we postulants would troop over to clean both houses. In the basement of the school was the laundry, where some of the postulants were to spend so many hours every day washing clothes by hand on scrubbing boards. Laundry was done every day, but Monday was the big laundry day. Thursday was the ironing day; though there was ironing every day as well as washing. So I would think, "The devil finds work for idle hands". This was an expression used often in the convent. It was certainly not a saying for the nuns, novices, or postulants! We had our assignments, which changed every week, like taking turns at serving in the refectory at mealtimes or reading from the podium in the refectory during mealtimes while silence was otherwise kept.

One of my first assignments was the fowl run. Besides my full time duties, I was to feed the chickens, keep the area in good order, do whatever I had to do there and collect the eggs. Wow! I didn't know how I was going to do this. One of the older sisters was to initiate me in how to be responsible for running the chicken business. So, not being from a fram in Ireland, or even from the town, I had been cooped up in an orphanage. I had never ever seen a chicken in my life. I thought that I was actually afraid of nothing, that I could manage most almost anything, being so well domesticated in the orphanage. So with confidence, I walked up with the sister in charge to the fowl run. I began to feel frightened. I was scared of all those chickens, so many of them seemed to be scratching at each other and coming towards me and running away from me, and jumping on the sister, and generally they were all over the place. I did not know how I was to control this situation; I soon learned to control my emotions of fear and learned obedience in a very practical setup. The older Sister, I think, knew that I was scared, and told me that this is how I was to learn how to obey. I would be taking a vow of obedience and that meant that I had to do what my Superior assigned me, even if I didn't like it. I did learn a lot in the fowl run, basic things that I ought to have known in the first place.

Things were going well—I was getting used to the chickens, and really liked the outdoor part of it. One day, one of the postulants in my group, Maureen, who was from Galway, on the west coast of Ireland and lived on a farm, was walking towards the fowl run. She spoke in a low voice telling me that I had to go with her to the chicken house, which was a classroom-sized room at the end of the garden. We both walked together and suddenly she stooped down and grabbed one of the chickens by the scruff of the neck. I was frightened to death. I backed off, and refused to venture another move. Maureen said, "I didn't know that you were such a chicken!" I didn't think it was funny and told her that this was all so new and strange to me. "Well," she said, "You're in the convent now, and you have to learn obedience. I'm from the country and grew up with the chickens, so I'm sure it is all new to you, but you'll learn fast." I went in to the fowl house after her and watched her kneel down and slit the chicken's neck with a knife while kneeling on its wings. I took to flight, and I was running as fast as I could to get away from the gruesome scene. One of the sisters stopped me and said, "I had the same experience, it is good for you to go back in and be brave, that is what the saints are made of." I returned back and saw that the chicken was still running in a circle with no head on it. "I can't, I can't do it," I thought, and I was outside the house again. I stood trembling, and at the same time afraid of what the Superior was going to do or say to me. I felt a total failure for not being in control of myself or the situation. This experience ended after one month, when another postulant took over the chickens.

After about three weeks of feeding and cleaning up after the chickens, one of the chickens died. I thought I was responsible for killing the chicken. I was beside myself. It was lying there, and I was afraid to touch it, or go near it. I went to find another postulant who was brought up on a farm in Ireland. She was a very lively girl and I really liked her. I told her that one of the chickens was dead, and asked if I should tell the Superior; or should I do something else about it. She said, "Oh, don't worry, leave it to me dear, I'll take care of it." Later on, she told me to be up in the fowl run and she would meet me there at 3 p.m. I was delighted to know that she was taking care of it all and she was helpful without scolding me or not speaking to me because of the silence.

I met the postulant at the other end of the garden where the stable used to be, and was now used as the fowl house. I noticed that she was preparing for some big occasion, which puzzled me, but I didn't question. The chicken was picked up and put on a large platter and covered with a black cloth, like a pall. As I was curiously watching this strange situation, the postulant picked up the covered chicken on the platter and walked out of the fowl house. Immediately, when she came out, there was a crowd of about 20 sisters who appeared and began to intone the "Deprofundis" in Latin. The procession started around the fowl run and all the novices and postulants had long black cloaks adorned for the occasion. I did think that this behavior was weird, but I didn't say a word, just watched in amazement. The novices followed the sister who was carrying the dead carcass, on the platter. The sisters singing in intoned voices made it all sound and appear very solemn. I was so intrigued by this solemnity and wondered what in the world was happening! The novice carrying the carcass then announced as she turned to face all of her followers: "Let's celebrate the life of the chicken, and roast it and toast it!" I was absolutely flabbergasted. Of course, the chanting of the psalms by the junior sister and postulants had been carried by the wind to the opposite end of the fowl run where the convent was situated, and no doubt caused some alarm. What the senior nuns saw from their second and third floor convent windows was a scene that totally disquieted them. I remember that we as postulants were not expected to know any better. We were not punished but the novices were punished because they took part knowingly in a sacrilegious act, and should have shown a better example to all postulants: Later on in the day, when we postulants got together, and there were no novices or senior sisters within sight, we exploded with laughter. I laughed so much and I felt so out of control. I couldn't stop laughing even if the Mother Superior or the Pope had come on the scene. What made the laughter for me even worse was the fact that everyone thought that I was the leader and cause of it all. After all, I had been the person in charge of the chickens. Also, I was known for giggling at anything and everything. Up to this time in the Novitiate, the only thing that I was reprimanded for was giggling in the wrong places, that of the chapel and refectory in particular. These were places where there was not to be any talking whatsoever. We postulants, not being used to keeping the silence, would try to get our message out whatever we had to say, to the other person by making signs and hoping they would get the message. This in itself stirred up more laughing and giggling. After all, we were teenagers, really! Not called teenagers in those days.

I had a cutting from a convent paper which said, "Postulants are young religious creatures who laughed at everything and often at nothing. They giggle in moments of silent solemnity. They have a rare talent for making such noise in cloister, but they themselves hearing none of it." I guess postulants are the same the world over. The solemnity and not speaking to each other just added to the nervous condition of all of us. We seemed to become worse at giggling, the more solemn and silent that certain places became in the convent precincts. My first impressions of the convent were a real surprise to me. Every minute of every day was filled, with so much work. I felt that when I was wading through one duty, I would hear the bell calling me to something else. It was like having unfinished business all the time. We were to live by the rule which taught that whatever we were doing, at the sound of the bell, we had to drop instantly and go to the next duty because it was "God Calling."

Some of the spiritual books that we read when we were postulants stressed the Superior may be wrong or in error on certain commanding issues but the subject is still right in obeying her commands and orders. We did not question, we obeyed orders. We all had to learn the lesson of obedience.

The Mass and Liturgical prayers were all in Latin. Liturgy was the important part in our life in the convent. We learned how to pronounce the Latin words in the Liturgy, so that we were able to join in the prayers and chatting of the Daily Office with the rest of the community. Many years later, the Mass was changed into the vernacular, as well as the Liturgical prayers. A lot of discussion took place over this change and according to some authorities, "Changing to English took away the mystery and reverence from the Mass and the prayers." I was, at least now able to pray to God in my own language which I understood. Part of the mystery was not grasping or understanding what the prayers meant in Latin. The length of time we spent learning the Latin pronunciation, instead of learning the language itself, was just for the sole purpose of being able to join in unison with the rest of the community in the Liturgy of the Word. Some of the Latin words were easily understood, but for the most part it was just a case of saying the Latin words correctly. The Liturgy of the Word was sung in plain chant and this added to the solemnity of the chapel. At Easter and Christmas time, the services were beautifully done. Of course, a lot of choir practice took place before the actual Feast days.

Silence was strictly observed in the refectory building during all the mealtimes except breakfast. The tables in the refectory were in the shape of a horseshoe, a long table at the top and long tables put together to reach full length of the refectory. At the center of the top table sat the Superior, flanked on both sides by her councilors, the senior sisters, and finally those professed sat according to their rank and in the order that they entered the convent. We postulants were at the tail end of the rank. We filed into the chapel in the same order of seniority. In the center of the refectory was a podium or rostrum used for public reading in the chapel or refectory.

Chapter 15

"Doubts and Temptation to Leave"

We recited the Divine Office daily in the chapel. Different sections of the Divine Office were recited or said throughout the day. It was divided up in Prime, Terce, Sext and None. Early morning we arrived in the chapel to begin the first part of the Divine Office which was Matins. At night, we sang Compline. The Office itself was interrupted at Matins for the Reading of the day. It was generally the same book, which had readings for every day of the year. It was called "The Roman Martyrology." It sort of gave as a pause to think after reciting everything in Latin. At least this book was in English. So we relaxed, and listened to the sacred readings. The Sister chosen for reading that week had to step out from her stall and go to the center podium. The Roman Martyrology had some very difficult words to pronounce and I dreaded that when my turn came for reading in the chapel, that I would be unable to get those big words out properly. I did not look forward to duties like public reading in the refectory or in the chapel. These special duties of reading and chanting solo in the chapel scared me. They were performed by the Sister appointed for that week. Even the act of leaving my stall, and walking out to the center, frightened me so much. I was doing fine in a crowd where I was unnoticed but if I had to do that assignment when my turn came, I knew ahead of time that I would disgrace myself. I also thought that all of these Sisters had schooling and I had not been in school since I was eleven years old what was I going to do? I couldn't possibly get out there and read! I had worked myself up into a frenzy and no matter what I thought, I couldn't convince myself of ever doing this public reading. I knew that I didn't have the education but how could I tell the Superior that I had not been to school since I was eleven years old!

Nor would I dare even mention to the postulants with me that I had not
had any education, and I certainly could not tell anyone that I was from an
orphanage. So, my mind was very busy, while I carried on with my daily
duties. After much thought I decided to take to flight, leaving the convent,
which was one way to escape it all.

So one morning, I made a beeline for the attic, I got the stool to stand
on to help me jump up into the attic. I found my trunk that I had entered
with and for some reason, I was happy to see it again. I sat up there all by
myself, and just to be by myself was wonderful! I thought of Father Lynch
packing it for me, and I thought of all my friends . . . Oh, how I missed
them, and wished that I could see them again. I began to cry and was so
homesick. I had not known what homesickness was but I think that's what
it was. I wanted to get back to them all, to go home to them all! I missed
Belfast, so the next step for me was to find the clothes that I had on me the
day that I entered, so that I could get dressed and be ready to leave. A few
days later, I had it all planned to go to the Superior and tell her that I was
going to leave, that I didn't think that I had a vocation to the Religious Life.
The Superior got the news that I was planning to leave before I could tell
her myself. I was up in the attic and suddenly I heard the superior's voice
calling, "Who's in there?" I climbed down from the attic and faced the
superior. How did she know that I was there? I had not thought that the
stool would be a giveaway! It was a nun who had seen it and reported me to
the Superior. The Superior who was the novice mistress was also in charge
of the postulants, and had to report any misbehaving to the top Superior.
This particular novice mistress was just temporary until the newly-elected
novice mistress arrived from overseas. In those days traveling was by boat,
so it would take a couple of weeks until the real appointed novice mistress
arrived from Africa.

So, I followed this presiding novice mistress to the head office as it
were, the Head Superior's Office. I was instructed beforehand that I was
to prostrate myself on the floor at the feet of the Superior. This was one of
the many customs in the convent. We knocked, and I walked in after the
Superior called, "Come in." I duly fell on the floor, but I was so scared, I felt
that I had offended God and expected punishment. The Superior knocked
with a little hammer on the table; this signaled that I was to get up. I faced
the same nun, Sister Gerard, who was the top Superior and the same person
who interviewed me in Belfast. I felt more at ease when I saw her smiling at
me. She said, "Maud, what is this I heard? Are you going to leave us? Why
do you want to leave us?" I was taken aback by questions which made me

feel that I was being so very disloyal, and I couldn't answer her because I felt tongue-tied. My tongue dried up in my throat, as it were. I somehow was able to get the words out that I thought that I did not have a vocation. Sister Gerard replied, "Well child, you have not given yourself much of a chance, have only been here a couple of months." She continued to talk to me on the spiritual plane and what religious life was all about. From the second floor window where we were, the Superior looked out and said, "Look at that man down there on the horse and buggy. He is happy." The man was going around with his donkey and cart and calling out loud, "Any old rags, any old rags, any old rags?" He looked up at the window with a big smile, and showing one white tooth, and waved. We waved back to him. Sister said, this beggar man was happy, why was I complaining? I tried to get a few more words in before I left the office, but eventually blurted out, "I'm homesick." Mother Gerard retorted, "Now, if I heard that coming from the other postulants I would understand, but what are you saying? You never had a home." As she said it, she smiled at me and dismissed me. I do not think that she meant to hurt me, it was like saying, "I know about you."

Chapter 16

"I'll Try Again"

I came out of the Superior's Office, made a bee-line for the bathroom to wipe my face and straighten up before anyone would see me. I made a promise that I would try again and conform to the life that I had chosen. I would never in my wildest dreams, have chosen this life for myself without the assistance given me. I was here now and maybe it is God's will that I'm here. So, I would give it my best. There were a lot of rituals, rules and regulations that I had to learn, and conform toeven if it goes against the grain! What was bugging me was having to take my turn, like everyone else in doing the public reading in the refectory and chapel. I felt so very incompetent. Scrubbing and cleaning was my life! Each week, a different Sister was assigned to read publicly in the refectory and in the chapel. The theory was that while we sat in silence eating our food for the nourishing of our physical bodies our minds would be nourished and fed with the word of God.

As postulants, we did not read in the chapel, only in the refectory. Just knowing that my turn to read would eventually come around scared me. Just the thought of reading alone in front of all those nuns made my stomach churn, just the thought of it! My turn came and I got one of the postulants to prepare the reading with me beforehand. Nevertheless, I ascended the podium, intoned the Latin phrase "Jube Domine Benedicere" which means "Pray Lord A Blessing". I began to shake and tremble so much. I don't know how the Sisters heard a word of my reading through my shattering teeth! Standing up on a podium, in front of a crowd of silent nuns, totally unnerved me. My throat felt paralyzed, but once I began the reading, I kept on going 'til I finished. I knew I couldn't stop anywhere, or I'd never be able to start up again. Immediately after I stepped off the podium, I wanted to become invisible but. just taking two steps down from the podium, I tripped and lay sprawled out on the floor. One of the postulant servers came over to help me to my feet, and she said, "Who did you fall for that time?" Then as I stood up, she whispered, "Don't forget to make the venia!" So down on the floor again in a more dignified position, I lay 'til I heard the knock with the hammer to get up off the floor. The criticism that followed was that I read like a speed train, so fast that no one understood.

The word "venia" was from the Latin meaning pardon. The venia involved prostrating oneself on the floor and lying there until the superior knocked on the table with the gavel for you to get up. This knock meant giving you permission to get up off the floor. The venia was made for many reasons. For example, coming late for the chapel, or being late for meals or any duty. It was made to another Sister if we had offended her in any way. One had to walk to the center of the Chapel in order to make the "Venia" or to the center of the refectory. There was a special way of making the venia and we had to practice it in the beginning of our training. If the Superior was not present to knock with the hammer, we remained on the floor 'til the next Sister in rank after the Superior knocked to give us permission to rise. Getting down on one's knees and stretched out flat was a gesture of apology to the community.

Anything that happened to cause a stir in the midst of the silence would send us beginners off into giggling and laughter. The silence and solemnity of the occasion often made things worse. for us and caused more laughter and giggles. I remember early one morning in the chapel, while we were meditating. A Sister came in late, made the venia and lay there because she was not given the signal to get up. The Superior who should have knocked with the gavel had fallen asleep, so the next Sister in rank gave the knock, and the Superior woke up and called out, "Come in." I was unable to contain myself; I had to walk out of the chapel to contain my laughing. I really thought that at any time, I would be told to go home because I was so very out of control.

So many things appeared to be really funny. I couldn't understand how some of the Sisters would not move a muscle during these times but kept their decorum religiously. Some of the readings in Chapel in the morning hours were written with a sense of humor. For example, the Roman Martyrology had the story which we read one morning, of the saint who was placed in a cauldron of boiling oil, and who asked be turned over because he thought that he was cooked enough on one side! I sat in my stall shaking with laughter and the more I tried to stop laughing the worse I became. I was sure that this giggling would be the cause of my being sent away. This was certainly not "nunlike" behavior. I was going to make a big effort to act in the appropriate manner as a prospective Sister.

Silence was to be kept in all places. I loved to talk and have fun, so this was a sacrifice for me and for all of us as well. However, I was in trouble so often, for giggling and talking out of place. If we broke the silence we had to prostrate ourselves on the floor in the venia. This was a humiliation which was supposed to keep us humble. I ought to have been the most humble person around when I think of how many times I lay on the floor!

A well used phrase which I got used to hearing in Religious Life was "Striving for Perfection." It was a phrase which I just didn't like to hear. It could be read in any of the spiritual reading books. I just bristled every time that I heard the phrase. Why it had the effect on me to make me feel anger and want to lash out against it, I don't know. Connected with "Striving for Perfection" was that we did all things, in every detail, as perfectly as possible. To aid us in this striving for perfection, besides the keeping of the silence, and doing things quietly and doing all our chores perfectly, was a session every week called the "Chapter of Faults." This was held in the refectory, generally on Friday nights.

"Keep the rule and the rule will keep you." This was how we really learned to study the Rule and the Constitutions in their every detail. Outward demeanor was very important. The novices had to walk with their heads down without looking to right or left. Eyes were to be cast down, and hands kept under the scapular, which was part of the nun's habit. In addition, there were to be no long strides, when walking. We had to take short steps, with no running or swinging of arms. Our hands had to be folded under our cape or under the Scapular if we were not using them. After we were finished eating at mealtimes we immediately placed our hands under the Scapular. There were many exterior religious rules. All this was to help us keep strict guard over our five senses (but my sixth sense was very strong), so that we would be better able to cut off all distracting thoughts and have our minds more attuned to the God dwelling in the center of our souls.

So the "Chapter of Faults," or the weekly public confession of faults held in the refectory, was a public accusation in view of the whole community of nuns. Each Sister walked to the middle of the refectory and publicly made her confession of faults, whereupon the Superior forgave her in public and the sister would prostrate herself in the Venia and only get on her feet when the Superior knocked on the table with the little gavel or hammer for her to get up and go back to her place. This was what I dreaded, "The Chapter of Faults." Generally, we accused ourselves if we did not adhere to these rules and regulations. Any breach of the Rule had to be publicly confessed. I used to feel so very tied in and tied down at these sessions. Many of the faults that we accused ourselves of were downright silly to me, and so stupid. For example, the accusations went something like this:

> I accuse myself of having talked during the Profound Silence.
> (Which was from 9 p.m. to the next morning after Church Service.)
> I caused another Sister to break her silence.
> I broke a saucer, etc.
> I ran instead of walked.
> I did not keep custody of the eyes.
> I came late for chapel or refectory.
> I made a noise which disturbed another Sister.
> I banged a door.
> I dropped a utensil.

We also had to give the number of times we did things wrong. The Superior also had her say. When each Sister was finished with the accusations of her faults, the Superior would reprimand each one of us as she deemed necessary. Oh, how I hated Fridays. It reminded me of Friday in the orphanage.

In the first years of probation in the convent, we had to cut off all connections with the outside world. We had to free ourselves from everything that this world would offer. We were in the world but not of it. All connections by letters were severed except family. Even family were restricted to every three months of writing. I could not write to my friends in Ireland, as they were not family. We never saw newspapers, periodicals, or magazines. Only books were read that were of spiritual value and they were from the convent bookshelves. In addition to reading at mealtimes, we had a spiritual reading book read to us for 15 minutes at the beginning of the recreation hour.

Our letters, coming in and going out, were censored by the Superior. This naturally prevented us from being open in our writing, as we knew that the letters would be read. I was called up for writing to Father Lynch and told that this had to stop now. I didn't know how to explain that Father Lynch meant so much to me. How could I say to anyone, "This priest is like my father?" I was so angry about not being able to write any more to him. I went to bed at night and as this was the only time that I had had to be alone, I would be in tears before I even climbed into the bed. I just felt so alone in my thoughts and could not share them with anyone. I was really angry with everything that was happening, but because of the silence, I wasn't able to talk, so I showed a brave front. In some ways I was glad I couldn't talk, but I so desperately felt the need to talk to someone. All these deprivations were eating away at me all day long but at night, I could cry as long as I wanted to cry. I was trying so very much to be a good religious person, and a perfect one at that. I needed to work hard so that my Superiors would accept me. I didn't know then that none of us are perfect, but because it was indoctrinated into us, I worked really hard to achieve it. I was thinking that only then would I be accepted among the nuns, when I became a good religious person and a perfect being. I was constantly adapting and changing, and had an internal fear of doing anything wrong.

During the season of Lent, we did not receive any mail. The mail that arrived was stored in the Superior's office. At Easter, the letters were placed in the refectory on our places at the refectory table. I remember walking in to the room and seeing a blue airmail form lying on the table all by itself, I wanted to cry. All the other places had many letters, and even some parcels. My one airmail letter was slit open, and when I noticed it my immediate thoughts were, "Oh God, the Superior has read my letter. I hope Father Lynch didn't write anything that would let the Superior know anything about me." I was afraid of the Superior's reaction towards me after reading Father's letter. Easter was a time of celebration and we could talk to each other that day. I really spent my time trying to help with carrying the snacks and coffee in and out of the room. The reason behind this little service was that I didn't have to talk about my family. We were allowed to write home for special times, like Easter, Christmas, and specific events that occurred in the families, anniversaries etc. However, we had to ask permission individually of the Superior beforehand. I had written to Father Lynch for Easter. I guess I wasn't very spontaneous in my letter to him, because he wrote back and asked if I was all right. He wrote, "Come, come now Maud, this is not like you to write like this. What is the matter?" I do not recall the content of what I wrote to him, but I guess I was trying to write the perfect letter that would please the Superior and just write general information, nothing personal. I found it hard to write to anyone as the convent news would not have been of any interest to the outside world.

During the meals in the refectory, we were served by two servers. Different servers were assigned every week. If something was missing at the table we did not ask for ourselves but only for the neighbor, sitting beside us. As we did not speak, we signaled for the server to come, and then whispered to her what we needed, i.e., if something was missing like a knife, fork, etc. I remember a talk that was given during a retreat at the convent. The priest was talking about the silence, and told us the joke about the monk at the table who had a small mouse in his soup. He signaled for the server to come, and as he was not allowed to ask for himself, he said to the server, "My neighbor has no mouse!" This was not for himself, it was his neighborly concern! We were to think of others and self was to fade or die a slow death, to use the expression of the Novice Mistress.

I recall part of Father Lynch's letter to me. He wrote that "Mama" really missed me. She kept saying by way of signs that she hoped that I was happy. Father Lynch continued writing. He wrote, "I feel as if I was on crutches and someone had pulled them away from me. I've lost a great support and feel that something is missing. But please God you will be a great success. Your high calling, means giving up the nearest and dearest to you. God will be your light and your life. He is to be first in your mind and thoughts. It was a sacrifice for me to let you go . . ." Of course, every time I read the letter I would sob and sob myself to sleep. Somehow, the Superior got word that I was crying at night. She waylaid me in one of the corridors and questioned me, "Why are you crying so much, you seem to be a happy person, is there something going on that makes you cry like this at night? The postulant in the next cell can hear you." I gave the same response that I was homesick, and missed all my friends. "That is to be expected, it's a big change, but remember that you are giving your life to God and we don't want unhappy people in the convent.

Chapter 17

"Free Again"

As a postulant in England, the convent situated about half an hour by train from London. So, in the summer of 1949 we were taken on outings to London. I so enjoyed every minute of these trips, a great getaway from the convent enclosure, and an opportunity to see the world again. It felt so good to be free for a day. Most of the places that we visited were historical places like Buckingham Palace, St. James' Palace, Kew Gardens and so on. I remember on one of those outings when we all entered Westminister Abbey there was singing in the distance, and as we approached the Church, opened the door, inside there was a young boy up on the balcony. He was singing with a powerful, pure voice, it was hard to believe that voice was only one voice of a young eleven-year-old boy. This incident held me spellbound, and this is all I can recall about that Abbey. I'm not even sure if it was the Abbey or the Cathedral in London. The boy's voice was so "beautiful a gift," that it stayed with me.

On one of the outings, we "Black Crows" as postulants were called went with a Sister Margaret Mary from the professed community. Sister enjoyed the outing, and explained everything about London to us, and we were so terribly interested in the whole surroundings. There was so much to see, and it was all steeped in history. Sister Margaret Mary, originally from Cork, in Ireland, really knew the places that we visited. She had lived in the convent in Chingford for ten years. That seemed a very long time to me! We visited St. Paul's Cathedral, Westminster Abbey, and the Houses of Parliament, in addition to walking along the "Thames Embankment" to Tower Bridge.

The next day was a great surprise for us. We went again to the riverside near Big Bend along the Thames and stepped on a boat, which was to take us down the Thames River. The highlight for all of us was the Tower Bridge that opened up to let our boat pass through. Wow! We thought we were royalty itself just for the day. It was exciting indeed, and a never to be forgotten trip. We passed so many bridges on the way, until we saw Windsor Castle in the distance, a tiny spot which became more visible and larger the closer we got to it. It was like a fairyland to me. Just before we reached Windsor Castle, we passed Runnymede on the banks of the Thames going towards Windsor Castle. Sister Margaret Mary gave us some history lessons. This is the place, at least on the opposite bank, where King John first signed. The Magna Carta, or Great Charter on June 15 in the year 1215. One of the postulants, the same fun person who had the funeral for the dead chicken, said to me, "You know what, King John was trying to conquer Ireland, and it was here at Runnymede that he lost his bag and baggage and he never made it to Ireland. The story goes that if you or anyone tries to reach over into the water, the spirit of King John will grab you and pull you into the water. So don't lean over too much *because the English will get you.* I was so gullible and tried to keep in my seat in the boat after that story_

Chapter 18

"The Novice"

So my time as a postulant would soon come to an end. We had to prepare for our religious exams within the convent. We began a ten-day retreat which included a whole day preparation for our official entrance into the Order. So life was getting serious. I enjoyed the retreat master very much. He would tell us jokes and sometimes it would only ring a bell with me later on, at a most solemn time. I had to listen carefully to his English accent so that I wouldn't miss anything. One day during the retreat as I was working in the front garden, the retreat master passed by and tapped me on the shoulder. He said, "You're a great girl, please keep up that "sense of humor" of yours, it will carry you a long way." I had not heard the expression "sense of humor" before, so I looked it up in a dictionary.

Our new novice-mistress had arrived from Africa, and immediately took over her position after some small ceremony for her accepting the responsibility as Novice Mistress. She was stall and stately and had a kind of tan. She had worked out on the African missions for many years.

We postulants had a special ceremony after the retreat was over. We had to go individually to the Novice Mistress and to the top Superior to ask to be received into the Congregation. We had to use special words and formulas for the request, and it was almost like begging to be accepted. I didn't like the "begging" for the Religious Habit. We had to use words to that effect, and get down and prostrate in the Venia before both Superiors.

Reception day arrived. We would be wearing a nun's habit from now on. It was a very serious ceremony. The Habit was presented to us and each postulant was given a nun to assist her in getting dressed in the habit. I was given the new Novice Mistress, her name was Sr. Malachy. We walked in single file into the Chapel. The bishop and priests were sitting at the top of the chapel behind the altar. We had on our long white dresses, like brides. The dresses made such a swish as we walked because the dresses were made of sheet material. The first part of the Ceremony was the "Cutting of the Hair." The bishop went to each of us, said some prayers about dying to self, and whacked a piece of hair off with the scissors. My hair was almost to my waist and it was long, black and wavy. One of the senior sisters greeted me after the ceremony and said, "I'm generally surprised that you didn't go overboard long ago with those beautiful waves of yours." The Novice Mistress who helped me put on the habit said, "I'm going to tie this belt on you so tight that it will never come off again." I didn't understand the symbolic meaning of what she said at the time. I kept fiddling with the belt during the rest of the ceremony, as it wasn't fitting properly, it was twisted somehow!

I thought she had strapped it on tightly, but I unfastened it, straightened it, and all the while I was doing this the Novice Mistress' eyes were watching me. It was awkward trying to fix the belt as I had the scapula and long black cloak or mantle on top of the habit, which got in the way.

One of the most significant parts of the reception ceremony was the change of names. The bishop announced the change of names to each Sister individually, with the words, "In the world you were known as 'Maud Friars' now in Religion, you will be known as 'Sister Mary Peter'."

Generally, the names were given to the postulants without any discussion or choice about them. It seemed that our group of postulants was given a choice, and this was the first time that a choice of names was given. Mother Gerard had asked me what name I would like to have in Religion. I responded immediately with "Peter". She said, "I have three names and you will be given one of them'.' I must have looked at her longingly because smiled back at me and patted me on the back. I wanted Peter because that was Father Geoffrey Peter Lynch's name. Peter was also the name of the two-year-old boy at Comerton's. (The name chosen had to be a saint's name.) So I was delighted to be given the name Peter and I wanted to jump for joy on the altar steps when I heard the name "Peter." I would still have a connection with Father Lynch! I couldn't wait to write and give him the news. I liked my new name better than "Maud".

So at eighteen years of age, I began a new life as Sister Mary Peter on October 7, 1949. I had completed nine months as a postulant. I was beginning a new life with a new name, dressed in a habit, and I was now a "novice". I was to be a novice for a period of one year to the day. This year was called "The Canonical Year".

I entered the "noviceship" with great zeal and fervor. I would eventually be at the end of my one year novitiate and be taking my three vows, which meant that I would belong to Christ forever. I reasoned in my mind that this was the ideal life for me. After all, I didn't have a soul in the world that I belonged to, and my search for my family would be at an end due to the restrictions in the convent. I would put that quest well behind me. I would learn all that I had to learn in this year, and leave the material world behind. Nobody out there knew about me or the new life that I was adopting. And so, with single purpose of mind, I set my mind on the highest spiritual attainment. The Canonical Year meant also that we were confined to the convent: Plenty of domestic work for our physical bodies, and our minds were to be on the spiritual life that we would continue to nourish and pursue in order to become the "Spouses of Christ".

Now that our Canonical Year bad begun, we knew that this year was to be a very secluded year with our whole mind, he, soul and focus on the spiritual life.

It took some getting used to the new Habit that we had to wear. It was quite an art to put the headpiece together. The forehead-band was a rectangular-shape-that we shaped ourselves each week, so that it sat on our foreheads and the rest of the veil pieces fitted on top. The forehead-band was starched so that it was a stiff piece that held all of the rest of the pieces together. Straight pins were used to attach the veil to the center starch piece. The guimpe was the soft part worn over our heads and was starched around the neck and bib. We really looked stiff-like and starched. Only our eyes, nose and mouth were visible. "Maud" did not exist any more; she was buried and the new Sister Mary Peter emerged. The habit was down to our ankles. We wore a broad belt around our waists, and a scapular hung over the habit, which was one long rectangular shape going down the front and back. When we were not using our hands, they had to be folded under the scapular. This was a fault if we did not adhere to this rule. We kissed the scapular before kneeling down to make the venia for a fault. We also kissed the scapular toward the Sister we disturbed or to the Superior when we received a reprimand. There were new rules and regulations regarding the habit, and particularly the scapula. We had to fold the scapula in its creases at night and not allowed to let the habit touch the floor at any time. It was really quite awkward to walk around in the habit in the beginning. We had to remember to hold the habit up in the front when going up the convent steps, and hold it up at the back when. coming down the steps. To me, this was a natural thing to do, but some of the Sisters had to practice walking up and down the steps as they couldn't get it right. I thought this was hilarious and tried so hard not to laugh. I was told to help a Sister Anthony who was a sister in my group. I was bent in two laughing so much at how ridiculous it all was. For my penance for laughing, I had to spend a week showing and helping Sister Anthony. Of course, I wasn't laughing at the Sister but at how funny it all looked to me. It seemed so simple to me. I couldn't understand how anyone had to be taught doing steps with a long dress.

My years, as a novice, went by fast. Every minute of every day was occupied with prayer, meditation, and works of all kind—the Novice mistress gave our daily assignments, duties, spiritual reading, and instructions. We did go out for a walk occasionally in Epping Forest right opposite the convent. The convent in Chingford was situated in a beautiful location. One Sunday, as a group of as were walking along a track road in the forest, we came upon a group of people sitting around having a picnic. The people seemed to be all looking in our direction. Suddenly this girl in the group jumped from a sitting position in the grass and called out "Maud, what on earth are you doing here?" It was one of our orphanage girls. I was so surprised to see her. The Novice Mistress came over immediately to check out the person who spoke to me. I said, "It's a school friend of mine." She replied. You know' as a novice you are not allowed to talk to the outside world."

On another occasion, which was a special feast day in the convent, we were allowed to go to Epping Forest for a picnic. I was excited to be going out and I grabbed a spiritual reading book to take with me. I put the book under my arm and walked along with the other Sisters, two by two. Suddenly from behind, I felt someone had pulled the book from under my arm. It was the Novice Mistress. She said, "Take the book, walk right back to the convent and wait in the Chapel for us to come back." I missed out on the picnic. I read some pages of the book while I sat alone in the chapel. The title of the book was, "The Man Who Got Even With God." How I wished I could get even with that Novice Mistress!

Another incident that happened to me at the beginning of our Novitiate year really frightened me. I thought maybe I was losing my mind to have done such a thing without thinking of the consequences. In the convent, it was a very serious matter. On a Sunday morning, the profound silence was kept later in the morning, usually until after breakfast. Our basins of water in our cubicles or cells had to be emptied before breakfast. We all made a beeline and stood in line outside the bathroom to empty our basins. We were still new to the wearing of the Habit and feeling awkward. I stood next to one of the Sisters who was holding a basin that had a chain attached to it with the stopper or plug in place. I was so intrigued and fascinated by this and instinctively pulled the stopper. Water, water everywhere! The novices scattered in all directions while trying to hold on to their own basins. Smothered laughs could be heard and the Novice Mistress appeared from nowhere. I wiped up the water from the floor and made the venia on the spot where I found a dry patch. The profound silence was broken, and we novices were told by the Superior that we had to make restitution. As I was the cause of the disturbance I had to hold up the basin with the chain attached to the rim in the refectory during the meal and like every good thing, punishment, it can be overdone. This is what happened with regard to holding up things in the refectory. It was meant to be penance for a serious offence of some kind. Our new Novice Mistress, Sister Malachy, reveled in the idea. So every day, I saw one or more novices kneeling in the refectory holding up some object.

I remember when all the novices and postulants were sent to clean up the garden and cut the hedges, etc. When the bell rang to cal us to the next duty, most of us dropped everything immediately and answered the call bell. The next evening, all the novices and postulants, including myself, knelt in front of the podium in the refectory, each holding up a garden tool: forks, shovels, clippers, spades, buckets, etc. There was audible laughing and chuckling among the rest of the Sisters. After the reading of the Gospel, we all placed our tools on the floor beside us. We then proceeded to prostrate ourselves in the venia on the floor among the tools we had put down. The correct thing we should have done was to put the garden tools back in the garden shed where they belonged. We looked like forces in array, ready for battle.

While on the topic of holding things up in the refectory, I actually had to hold my own Habit up one day. The sleeves of all the Habits were very wide, and each sleeve had to be folded back about six inches. I had returned home from hospital to the convent after having my tonsils out. Sister Valentine, the same person who had the ceremony for the chicken, sewed up my sleeves supposedly, so that I would have a clean habit to wear when being discharged from the hospital. Instead of sewing the sleeves back, she put safety pins in to hold them back. A safety pin was a useful thing but certainly not to be seen on a religious garb like a habit. The next day after being discharged from the hospital, I was told by the Novice Mistress to hold up the habit in the refectory. I very carefully folded the habit and held it up folded that way. I could not make any excuse that I did not put the pins in the habit. I was not the culprit. One did not excuse oneself in any way. The Novice Mistress met me outside the refectory and explained when something is held up in the refectory, it should be held in such a way that the community knows the reason for my holding it up. The next day, the Novice Mistress was waiting for my arrival, and before I walked in the refectory, she demonstrated how I was to hold up the habit. I knelt in front of the podium and held the habit up. The body of the habit was folded with the wide sleeves hanging down, and turned inside out, so the safety pins were visible for all to see. Coming out of the refectory I was stopped by one of the elderly Sisters who said-to me, in a whisper, "Who told you to hold them trousers up?" I guess that's what they looked like from a distance. More giggles and laughter.

It was my understanding later on that at the Community of professed Sisters did not approve of all these kinds of penances, that is, holding things up everyday. It had been carried too far. Everyday there were some Sisters kneeling in the middle, holding up something. Sister Valentine had to hold up her nightgown, then sit down in the center of the refectory, and sew on a button that was missing. It had become a source of fun, a disturbance and so ridiculous.

Chapter 19

"A Practical Nurse Again"

Now that I was a novice, I was assigned to work in the infirmary for a period of three months. Anyone who was ill, or recovering from surgery, would be taken care of by me. Was this ever scary!!! I had no idea about anything, let alone being a nurse, so to speak. There was a Sister Michael who was bedridden. She was the only chronic patient in the infirm. In those days her disease was called "Creeping Paralysis". Taking care of Sister Michael was something I was happy to do. It so happened, I became quite attached to Sister Michael. She was a beautiful person. It was just like taking care of Mrs. Lynch again. Sister Gerard said, "I think you are just cut out for nursing. Would you like to be a nurse?" I wasn't able to answer her because that would have been too far a goal to reach, and knowing my background, it would not be possible. Having not had the basic schooling, I knew that I did not have a chance.

Sister Gerard, or Mother Superior, as she was called, would visit the infirmary just about every day to see how Sister Michael was doing. On one of those visits, she noticed that the chamber from the commode that Sister Michael used was very badly dented and rusty. So one Saturday morning, Mother Superior went shopping and was thrilled with her purchase. She had bought a new delph chamber pot for the commode. She was delighted to have found a "delph" one at that! One would have thought she had found a pearl of great price. I showed her that I too was delighted to have a brand new pot. Believe it or not, it had a short lifespan. The following Sunday morning, I lifted the pot from the commode, and as I went outside the infirmary to empty it in the nearest bathroom, I accidentally knocked it against the door. The contents were all over the place and I had on my

Sunday habit. I cannot describe how I felt—just terrible and sick at the thought of everyone hearing the news at was the Mother Superior going to do to me? The reason why I write this is because of what followed. Maybe you can guess? I had to hold it up in the refectory! The clean cut piece had come from the bottom of the pot, as if it was cut by machine, so precise it was. I duly held it up and while kneeling there, I caught sight of the Novice Mistress. With my downcast eyes, saw that she got off her chair and came towards me. "Get up and go and bring the other half of the chamber!" I did just that and when I returned, the Novice Mistress was outside the refectory waiting for me. She said, "No one knows what you are holding up; it's just as if you are holding up a dinner plate." Mother Gerard gave me her broadest smile and that made me feel better. I think she felt sorry for me and whispered, "I'll get another one. Don't let it worry you."

The Novitiate year Passed quickly, so very quickly. There was plenty of work all around, a complete filled up day, everyday. The silence helped us to live the life that was expected of us. I remember the ten day retreat we made prior to our taking the vows of poverty, chastity, and obedience. During the ten days retreat, we did not work, except to clean the Chapel. We were to prepare ourselves during this retreat, to give our lives totally to God, for the rest of our lives, and to be totally absorbed in Christ, whom we would espouse. There was no kind of relationship with anyone, just service-oriented and functional. In the training of novices, one of the rules was: If we meet a man we were not to keep our eyes on him. In fact, in some religious orders, the Sisters were not even allowed to say the word 'man'. Some religious orders substituted another word. I know of an Order of Religion that used the word 'hat' for man. I have to chuckle to myself as I write this and find it even hard not to believe it myself. The Sister would answer the doorbell and report there was a 'hat' at the door. If I did not live through those archaic times, I would find this mentality very hard to believe.

During the ten day retreat, I had time on my hands. I missed all the tasks and duties that had kept me going and fulfilled my life. I was happy when I had plenty of work to do. The busier I was, the better I felt. I did every task that I was given, I was very capable of doing. I felt there was very little I could not do, at least in the domestic world within the convent. So during the retreat, I felt something was missing and as if I should be doing something!

This retreat signaled "The Canonical Year" was about to come to an end. The year had helped to lay the foundation for the future vowed life we novices were going to live. The Retreat put the final touches to "The

Canonical Year." For the novices, it would culminate in a final giving up or letting go of all our earthly possessions. Somehow, I felt ill at ease, at the finality of it all. A new life was beginning in earnest. It frightened me to just think of it but at the same time, I knew that I would manage the work in the Religious Life well. I kept telling myself I was a good worker and I would cope with it all as I had done in the past.

Sometimes, I would think of the glorious life ahead of me. To have security and that I would always be around people, I'd always have a bed to sleep in and meals at the regular times. No more worries ever, about any of those necessities.

Chapter 20

"The Vows"

The Retreat Master was a wonderful speaker and I did get a lot from his talks. I enjoyed listening to him and we had three lectures a day. He gave very, very uplifting talks. I gained a lot of knowledge and was hungry for more knowledge. He brought his own experiences of monastic life with a great sense of humor. I think it was this retreat master who told us most of the jokes that we heard, like the joke about the monk whom I already mentioned, had a mouse in his soup. Most of the talks were on the three vows of poverty, chastity and obedience.

To me, I thought obedience was so very simple. I just had to do what my Superior or an appointed authority figure told me to do. That's what it boiled down to for me. We literally had to obey. An example which was commonly quoted from religious books in the past, about the Abbott ordering one of his monks to plant something upside down, which was the wrong way but the monk obeyed anyway. It was, for him, "The voice of God speaking." I had no problem with that, I thought! It didn't seem difficult to me. I could always go back and fix it or plant it the right way, once the Superior was out of the way.

Chastity, I understood it well, when it was read from a spiritual reading book, or the Novice Mistress talked to us about it during the Canonical Year. The very thought overpowered me that one of these days after the retreat, I would pronounce my vows and I would belong to Christ forever! How did I ever arrive in this convent, and learn all that I learnt in this short time and make the grade, so to speak. I was going to be "The Spouse of Christ." I would hold my breath at the very mention of it. How fortunate I was! It was an ecstatic time for me. I was literally walking on air. I did have some doubts about my high calling or vocation but they were quickly removed when the Retreat Master would quote words like, "You didn't choose Me, I chose you", quoting Scripture. The doubts I had, or the unworthiness I felt, was from other parts of the Scripture. That just would hit me. When Father said, "You leave behind father, mother, brothers and sisters, and worldly possessions for my sake." Well, how does that go for me? I did not have any worldly goods to renounce. I did not have a family. So what was I doing here in the convent when I had none of these to give up? Sometimes my brain was working overtime. My thoughts would drift back to where I came from and where I was now. I remember trying to sort all this out in my mind as to what I had to do at that time. Choice never entered my mind. I did wonder now and then if I was in the right place. I knew that I certainly couldn't be in a better place. But . . . Where did Poverty fit in for me?

> I was to give up my mother and father,
> They were the ones who gave me up.
> I was to give up brothers and sisters,
> Where were they?
> Before I entered the convent, I had nothing.
> After I entered the convent, I wanted for nothing.
> I was to give up those nearest and dearest to me,
> But Oh! I missed them more than words can tell
> The orphanage girls were my sisters.
> Father Lynch was my only father.
> I could write to them occasionally
> But they were too far away,
> Lost and gone forever.
> I would never see them again.

Dwelling on these thoughts, the tears would well up in my eyes. I would try so hard to keep the tears from flowing but it was not too easy for me. I also felt ashamed of my crying. The Chapel was one place where I seemed to cry more easily. Trying to hide the tears in a public place, like the Chapel, was not possible. I learnt, when I was in the orphanage, crying did not get you anywhere. Tears were a sign of weakness. They were also a sign you were guilty of something that you did wrong. One of the Sisters who sat behind me in the Chapel stall probably thought the same thing. She very kindly pulled me aside when we left the Chapel and told me I should go to

confession to the Retreat master. I was not to be scared of him and I would
be able to talk easily to him as he was very kind.

I could go to Confession all right, and 'talking to him' behind a curtain
was fine, but not openly. I had never faced or talked to a man before. Even
with Father Lynch, whom I knew all my teen years, I never ever talked to
him privately, or let him see I was sad, or feeling down about anything. I
was trained in the orphanage to hide any emotions. I only knew to try to
keep a brave front always, no matter how I felt. By the way, in those far off
days 'feelings don't count', was a favorite expression by authority figures.
Who was I anyway to be talking to such an important figure as 'The Priest'?
I also knew I was afraid to talk to anyone, let alone a man, and a priest at
that. I knew any Sister could talk to the priest at any time during the retreat
but I was too fearful to approach him.

I did not belong out in the world to anyone. I didn't know if I belonged
in the convent either, but I tried to realize it was a spiritual family. God was
my Father, heaven is my real home. I would try to focus my thoughts on this
noble spiritual family. Ideally and spiritually, it was great and wonderful. I
would try to keep my mind on these thoughts instead of brooding over the
past. The past was gone. I really wished more than anything to be strong and
brave. Somehow, I knew, as soon as I started to work again, it would help to
fill the space of this quiet stillness. In this retreat, I was thinking too much
of myself and my home sickness and loneliness. I tried to resolve all these
thoughts by myself. It just worried me so much I would cry and someone
would notice me. I wished I was more in control of my emotions. The tears
would flow when I least expected them, and always in the wrong places.

The Superior, Mother Gerard, was a wonderful woman. Among
ourselves, we called her "The Valiant Woman of The Gospel'. I would
have really liked to talk to her but it was she who interviewed me to join
the Congregation. With this in mind, I knew and felt that she would have
been very disappointed in me. I was sent to speak to her one morning and I
could hardly get any words out in her presence. Each Novice who was going
to take her first vows had to have some time with her. So, no words were
forthcoming from me. I finally managed to say, "I don't think I am meant to
be here." That was not the way I wanted to express myself, or what I actually
wanted to say, but it gave me a start. That was all I was able to blurt out.
Sister Gerard reminded me the devil knows I'm on the verge of taking my
vows and is having his last fling, so to speak. The devil is definitely at work
and wants nothing better than to tempt you right now when you are on the
threshold of taking your vows. This is a trial period and even the saints did

not escape these temptations. She gave me quite a religious and uplifting talk. It helped me, at that time, to move on with my life and I felt bad that I was worrying the Superior. After all, she had so much responsibility for all the Sisters. Her life was not easy. I thought I should have dealt with my problems myself, instead of bothering the Superior with my trivialities. It pleased me to hear the Superior say one day to me, that I was a great asset to the community. I didn't understand how I was an asset to the community, but it made me feel good. I was a good worker and I could be relied on to carry out any task that was assigned to me. That comment also made me feel good. Of course, I checked the dictionary to find the word "asset".

The Religious Life was often written and spoken of as the state of perfection we were to strive for Perfection. Somehow, looking back at those training days, I associated holiness with, "Cleanliness is next to Godliness", and outward cleanliness associated with perfection. Yes, I could strive to achieve this. That was something I could really do and it gave me confidence.

I was determined to forget my childish ways and grow up. I was now a nun about to take my vows. I tried to memorize some quotations from The New Testament to help me every time I thought of the past. "No man putting his hand to the plough and looking back was worthy of me" or "God is my Father". Quotations would help for a time but I felt torn between the high ideals of Religious Life and the 'Old Maud' creeping out again. I would strive to put on the new man.

I took my vows of Poverty, Chastity and Obedience on October 7, 1950. I was eighteen years of age. It was exactly a year to the day of my Reception of The Habit. It was, as always, a great day of celebration, but carried more of a serious tone to it because of the vows. This was called 'Taking the first or simple vows' but it was meant for a lifetime. Three years later, we would pronounce our 'Final Solemn Vows'. The only change on this day that took place was the replacement of our white veils with black veils.

I read and re-read the letter from Father Lynch for my big day of taking first vows. He was so very proud of me. He said Religious Life would grow on me and "It will be yours by the way in passing." I missed him! How I wish I would see him again. I said to myself, "Remember Maud, you left that all behind you." "Any man putting his hand to the plough and looking back is not worthy of me."

The next day was Sunday. It was a continuous or extended celebration throughout the day. We were free to do our own thing, such as, spend time in the garden, read a spiritual reading book, or spend time with the sisters in the Community of the Finally Professed Sisters. It was great to be free to talk to the sisters and get to know them. During mealtimes, instead of reading, there was a long-playing record of classical music. How I loved to hear the music. It seemed to do more for me than the continuous readings. It was strange seeing all my co-novices who were professed with me, now, wearing 'black veils', instead of the white veils of the novices. It signified we had passed the "tough grade" of the Novitiate.

The free day really did me the world of good. Monday morning found us all back to our regular duties. I was happy to be back to the familiar routine again but with a sense of really belonging, because of having taken the vows. Maybe, it was more of a secure feeling, that I was now a professed Sister.

Chapter 21

"I Became a Teacher Overnight"

Nextday, after breakfast, I went to the Chapel to clean, and then I was to go to the laundry, which was situated in the basement of the school. One of the sisters tapped me on the shoulder as I was on my knees polishing the floor in the chapel. She said, "Mother Gerard wants you over in the school". As I looked up, Mother Gerard was standing at the door of the chapel with two other co-sisters. I dropped everything and left the chapel. In silence, I accompanied the sisters and Superior to the school and up to the second floor of Mother Gerard's office. She handed each of us a black apron and told us we each were to have a classroom to go to from now on. We were going to teach!!! Even if I was to break the silence, I wouldn't have been able to speak. I was dumbfounded, just in pure shock. I looked at the sea of faces, all standing to attention in the class. In two shakes of a lamb's tail, and with a wave of the hand to the children, I disappeared from the classroom and went to Sister Fidelma's classroom. I barged in the door and made a sign for her to come out. I don't remember what I said to her, but I knew I could not go back into that classroom, there was just no way. Sister Fidelma, who was professed with me, had the experience of teaching in Ireland. She had taught in the same school she herself attended. She talked me back to the classroom, telling me I could give them writing to do 'til I sorted myself out. I was not able to sort myself out. I kept thinking, "Oh God, I've taken a vow of Obedience, what do I do?" I felt like the wrath of God would come down on me. I'd be punished for disobeying orders.

Mother Gerard took over the classroom and as the children were busy writing, she brought me back in with her to the classroom. The children went on with their writing and they seemed totally oblivious of my presence.

Mother Gerard told the children I would be their teacher from now on. I could feel myself sinking into the floor and my legs were feeling like jello. It was a terrible shock to me.

I don't remember how I got through that first day as a teacher! I don't remember anything, except Mother Gerard staying in the classroom with me and leaving the room when she was called out. I remember Sister Fidelma telling me I was to act like a teacher and in no way, should I let the class notice me as someone who is frightened of her own shadow. "The children notice everything", she said. I tried to make some excuses to her, "I'm not a teacher; I don't know what is expected of me; I can't go in there anymore, I really, I can't do it." Sister Fidelma said, "Act like you are a teacher." The children don't know, but you can show them that you are. Don't ever let the class know that you are not a teacher. They will play up then." So, I continued teaching and continued to complain to Sister Fidelma and gradually I gained confidence. In the recesses of my mind, I had the terrible thoughts of being in the wrong place. The nuns did not really know about me that I had had an orphanage upbringing, and missed all these years of school. I had no family. I blamed myself along the way for not telling them. At that time, I couldn't bring myself to even mention those things. I wanted to talk to someone about but was afraid of the stigma which went with it all. I was torn in two, as it were.

I often thought of myself in school in the orphanage, with flashbacks of the classroom. How did Sister Colman teach us? She would say, "Hold your heads high, backs straight, shoulders back, and let the world know you can do it." It was six or seven years ago since I was sitting in the classroom desk and here I was sitting in the teacher's desk! As I'm writing in my memoirs and reminiscing on all that has happened to me, I wondered at times, if I'm the same person. What happened to me? How did I ever reach this level of coming up in the social world? On the one hand, I felt so incompetent and on the other, I was going to go at it. I would think of Sister Colman's words, "You girls will make it, I know you will."

In spite of the scare of having to go into the classroom every day, I gradually got used to it. The third Sister, Sister Euphrasia, also had a classroom, and she was in the same situation as I. Yes, she was totally unraveled. I saw things were not going well for her, and I tried to help in whatever way I could. In time, this helped me to have more confidence by observing how frightened she was. I was in that very same place as she was in trying to act like a teacher. I continued to teach and I must say, I eventually enjoyed preparing my classes. Not only did I pre are, but had o learn some of the material myself before I could present it to the class. Mother Gerard eventually acknowledged to me that she was happy with how I was doing in the classroom. She said, "I think you have the makings of a teacher and you appear to be getting into it more easily now." I was happy she actually acknowledged all that I was putting into it. I told her some of the subjects were difficult for me but I was learning the material before I would teach it. Mother Gerard also said; "I admire the way you went about the teaching and you're putting all you have into it. You have a good strong character and a willingness to learn. I know you can put your hand to anything and you have proved it." I did feel better about everything and gained more confidence in my teaching abilities. I must have just needed that bit of encouragement to keep me going at it.

Also, interaction with the children in my class made me realize they did not know everything and that they were learning. I used to feel when I was first put to teaching that they knew more than I did. I was putting myself down because of where I was brought up. I thought everyone was better than I, in every way, and I was even scared of the children in the beginning.

Holidays mean "vacation" in America. The school holidays came around and the children went home for the holidays. I thought this would give me a chance to catch up with my learning and studying the children's school books. Instead, we professed novices had to fill in with all the work required around the convent. The time passed quickly over the holidays and I didn't have the time to go over to the school.

In the beginning of the next school year, Mother Gerard sent for me to come to her office. School was starting the next day. I thought maybe she was going to talk to me about school and what was expected of me the next term. She began the conversation, "You know, Sister Mary Peter, you have brains that are going to waste. You are a very bright girl and I don't want that to happen by any means. I want you to use your brains, and so I am going to put you to study." I was astounded, and felt the same unworthy, downgrading feelings about myself. All I could think of was that I dare not say what I felt like saying. I had to obey. Mother Gerard then arranged for me to start my studies when school began again. I wondered how I was going to have time to prepare my schoolwork. "Trust in God", the bible said, "and he will see you through it all." I seemed to get enough confidence in myself. Having had some experience last year did help me somewhat and I did still manage to do my assigned domestic chores. I answered the many calls of the bell when I was in the convent and attended to my spiritual duties. It was mandatory to be in the chapel at 5 a.m. for the Mass and prescribed prayers and offices. Life became hectic and I did not have time to worry about my own insignificant problems. I was over busy. The Novice Mistress still kept watch over our Religious Life. I was always in trouble for rushing back and forth to the school and talking in the wrong places. I so wanted to do everything perfectly and to the best of my ability. I was exhausting myself in thinking the more work I could perform the better person I would be. I wanted to be accepted for the work I performed. We were still under strict supervision by the Novice Mistress even though we had taken our first vows.

Sister Fedelma was my first teacher. She asked me quite casually, "Can you draw a straight line?" I answered, "Yes, with a ruler." "And how about without a ruler?" I answered, "I've never tried to draw a line, what should I draw a line for if I don't need to?" "I'm just checking you out", she said. I was wondering what this conversation was all about, as no explanation was given. Sister then produced a pencil and paper and asked me to draw something in the room. I think my eyes must have been poppin' out of my head with astonishment. I was about to say, "I can't." Sister Fidelma then left the room and said she would be back in an hour. She said she wanted to see something on the paper on her return. I couldn't help but think she was a real teacher! Sister Fidelma was in my group and I certainly felt so inferior to her, but of course, she already had taught for a year or more in Ireland before she entered the community. Nothing short of a miracle, I did produce a drawing for her. It was the sewing basket from the Novice Mistress, who, in the meantime had walked in the room and knew I had to draw something. She put the basket in front of me, and said, "Draw that." I, of course, sat looking at the basket for a while and finally got started on the paper. Sister Fidelma returned and examined the drawing. "You've passed." I will start you off on drawing classes and then Sister Dominic will take you for Art Lessons. What did all this mean? That was the first time I had ever heard of 'Art Lessons.'

Mother Gerard was very happy I was able to draw. The next time I saw Mother Gerard, she told me I was to study six subjects and be ready for an examination at the end of the year. I was to go to Sister Dominic for English and eventually go to her for Art classes. I was to go every Saturday for History classes, and so on. My mind was in a whirlwind, trying to take it all in and get organized. The exam, I found out, was The English Matriculation. I had never done an exam in my life and had no idea what it entailed. I had to start studying immediately because the exam was in June and this waste just after the Christmas holidays. My history teacher was Sister Constantine and she was to teach me the English History period from 1066 to 1485. She gave me a history book to study. I did not know where to begin with it all. I felt very confused. Not having been to school since I was eleven, I had a very hard time studying. I didn't know how to study. I only had a little experience of studying for my children in the classroom. This was different. The only thing that helped me was to see other sisters struggling the same way that I was, with the study books. I kept telling myself the others had been to school and I hadn't. I kept my eyes and ears open to learn as much as I could from just listening to others and hearing their difficulties. This would spur me on, knowing it was not only I who was struggling, but others as well. At least, I wasn't alone in this. The one subject I knew very well was scripture and I felt good that I already had a good knowledge of this. It was one of the subjects I had to take, and had plenty of this in the orphanage. It helped me and made me more confident that I was more knowledgeable on something. So I could concentrate more on other subjects.

Time went by so quickly and before I knew it, it was time for me to take the Matriculation Examination. The results came out and I had passed four of the subjects and failed two. That meant I could repeat the two subjects during the summer. Mother Gerard explained to me she wanted me to be able to go to college for teaching, so that meant that if I had to get into college, I would have to do all subjects again and pass all of them at one time. Passing all six subjects at one exam means an entrance into College. I repeated the Matriculation the following year and passed. Would anyone ever know what this meant for me? To be able to study and actually pass an exam was quite an achievement. Inside, I was jumping for joy at such an achievement. I was overexcited though I tried not to show it in front of others. I think I was very surprised at myself. Amazing what one can accomplish under pressure! It was a good feeling, to know I had passed the exam and I could now give more time to preparing my schoolwork.

Mother Gerard informed me I had passed very well in Art. She said, "You scored higher than your teacher, and the highest score you got of all the subjects was in Art." My teacher was Sister Fidelma, who had taken the Matriculation Exam with our group. I could not believe it. I did not understand how that happened. What it did for me was to give me more confidence in myself. I can do it just as if everyone else can do it!

A particular college I would be attending, called Rugby, in England, was requiring students to have music ability. I had passed the Art. If I had the two subjects of Art and Music, I would get these two subjects free for the next two years of College. Therefore, I was to take music, piano lessons and learn one instrument that I could carry around with me in college. This was to be a part of the requirements for future teaching.

Sister Dominic gave me piano lessons. She was the Sister who also took me for both of the English subjects for matriculation. She was also the principal of the public school in the parish. When Sister Dominic came home from school in the evenings, she gave me and other sisters who would be going to College with me music lessons. We all had to fit in our own times for practice and I had to practice before I went to school in the—mornings. Mother Gerard said one day, "I have to almost drag them to come and practice at the piano this one, (meaning me) I have to drag her away from the piano to go to her classroom! I really loved the piano and I had to practice because I would be having free lessons at College. I did not want to miss that opportunity of a lifetime. I duly went for the music exam at the local or nearest college at the end of the year and passed. I was also accepted for College having done the Entrance Exam. As teachers were needed in the school where I was teaching (our own private school), we could only let two sisters at a time go to College. I had to wait 'til the following year. I was to go to college and start in September of 1955. Meantime, in 1953, I, with a group of sisters, took the final or Solemn Vows.

Everything had fallen into place, so to speak, and I began to realize I had done all that I had to do. No more studies. I was to keep up my music practice in between times. It was like a big break for me to be free of the pressure of having to study. I would have enjoyed continuing study of any kind, so long as I had ample time to study and not to be under any more pressure to have to meet deadlines.

I was now also a full-fledged nun, finally professed and teaching in the school. Summer Vacation came around and we were free to help the sisters in whatever assignment was appointed for us to do. I was busy in the kitchen when Mother Gerard called me out. She said there was a very irate father of one of my pupils who wished to speak to me. Mother said she would come with me, as we never went into the parlor or anywhere on our own. There were always at least two Sisters present at any outside happenings. So I went with Mother Gerard to meet this father. His reason for coming to see me—his child was being kept back in after school hours, and he objected very much to this. He intended to take the child out of the school. Mother Gerard tried to explain to the father that Sister was not punishing the child but was giving her extra attention, when all the other children had gone home. This child was having drilling in the three "R's, the child's mother knew about her staying after school and would come and get her child when she came home from work. They lived within walking distance from the school. This father of the child really scared me. I had, first of all, never been that close in a room with a man before, except Father Lynch. I certainly was very frightened of seeing a man so angry. This was my first experience of this type. It shook me up so much and sort of put a damper on my enthusiasm to give any extra help to any child who needed help. From then on, I feared men somewhat, they appeared to be so strong and overpowering.

A week before the children returned to school, for the start of the new school year, many of the sisters went over to clean the classrooms and do a kind of spring-cleaning. It took a good part of the week to do all that had to be done. On Friday morning, Mother Gerard informed me, I would be teaching the 'ELEVEN PLUS' class. The secular teacher had to retire because of ill health. It was like giving me notice at the eleventh hour. My immediate reaction was, "I can't possibly teach that class." In fact, I was aware of 'Obedience', but I almost exploded in the presence of Mother Gerard, but controlled myself in the nick of time. Later in the day, I went to Mother Gerard's office, knocked on the door and made the venia in apology for my behavior. I very reverently asked if I may speak to her about teaching the 'ELEVEN PLUS'. I told her I can barely manage my seven and eight year olds and I did not want to let my community down by refusing. Yet, obedience was on my mind. In my day, one did not question the command given by the Superior. I merely said to Sister Gerard that I was not the right person for that class because I had to study everything beforehand, to be able to present it to the children. 'ELEVEN PLUS CLASS' was the final class in the junior school. If the children passed the exam, called 'ELEVEN PLUS EXAM', they were then admitted to High School. If any child failed, she would go to a Trade School instead. I really felt the weight of that responsibility, and so unqualified for that particular class. Springing that assignment on me really did me in, and shook me to the core of my being. How? How was I going to teach that class? Was there anyone to help me or step in instead of me? There were so many Sisters better than I was in every way. No matter what excuse I came up with, it did not matter. There was no other teacher. Mother Gerard said she had tremendous confidence in me as a teacher. I put 100% into everything I did and she was confident I would manage well. It was the same thoughts going around in my head (I did not have the basic schooling. I had to study before I could prepare for the class.) There was no way I was going to escape this assignment. I was like stuck in those awful feelings of unworthiness, down on myself, remembering where

I came from. I was stuck between a rock and a hard place. There was no one I could talk to about it all. Even if I could talk to one of the Sisters, I wouldn't have been open to talking about my history. So, I had to knuckle down and get my schoolwork prepared. I was on my own again, and on the same road again, as before.

Mother Gerard told me I had a very outgoing personality. I was very talented and can put my hand to anything. These qualities are an asset in a teacher. These words to me, I must admit, did boost me to feel better, but I knew what a struggle it would be to try to prepare my schoolwork and keep on top of things. Knowing that underneath or inside of me was this knowing feeling of unworthiness and feeling so very incompetent. I wondered why I was chosen to teach this class when I was actually the last person that should have had this responsibility. I had not been to school since I was eleven years old and I missed out on all that school time. Plus, I was from an orphanage, which was a different kind of schooling from the normal schooling.

The school term began and I threw myself heart and soul into it. I figured out the main subjects I had to teach were English, Spelling, Composition and Reading. This I could manage with some preparation. Math, called Arithmetic, entailed learning the tables as a base for math. Scripture and Catechism I also knew. Thank God! This subject wouldn't require too much preparation. I would need to study and really work at the other subjects, especially History and Geography_ I spent lots of time on what subjects I wasn't familiar with and more on these subjects. As I sorted all this out in my mind, it was not such a monumental problem, as I had anticipated and worried over. I had the same class all day for all subjects, so I organized myself. When the class went for gym, (it was called 'drill' in those days) I was delighted to have some free time to prepare for the next class before they returned to the classroom.

I would tell myself this will be my last year in this school. I will be going to college to be a real teacher. I'd be qualified, so I tried to make the best of it and was hopeful for the future. These thoughts kept me going. I will also feel better about teaching when I'm a real, qualified teacher. What actually worried me was the Government Exam at the end of the school year. If any of the children would fail, I would probably think the teacher was not up to par and so would the parents.

It was a year full of anguish for me and I was afraid some of the children would not make it. The attendance at the school was good. In my class, it was the same children were absent. We knew ahead of time if a child was not coming on a particular day. There were four children who were photographic models and they missed many school days. It happened that these same four children did not pass the written test, but their scores were borderline. They were given a chance to go in for an oral examination. They certainly made a good impression on the examiners. They passed the oral exam, which meant there was 100% of children passing in the class. Excitement was everywhere. Mother Gerard was so delighted with the outcome and she contributed the bulk of the success to all the work that I had put into it. I thanked God over and over for all his help; it was nothing short of a miracle, considering the circumstances I was under throughout the year. I did gain experience and learned so much. There was one thing that struck me when I was first told to teach the 'ELEVEN PLUS' class, It was the fact this was the age I was, when I left the classroom to go to my situation job. Maybe, the fact I was on par with the children or at the same level as they were, that made them grasp the subjects better from their level. I certainly was not able to talk above them. Towards the end of that year, the previous experienced teacher, who had retired, Miss McHale, came to visit to spend some time on English, Arithmetic, and Intelligence Test Papers, advised me. These were the three subjects, if they passed, they would be able to manage any of the other subjects. I was fascinated, at that time, that there was actually a subject called Intelligence. Was that not a basic ingredient in everyone, a mental ability to work out problems? It puzzled me that it was the name of a test paper the children were supposed to do. How would I ever go about that for a subject? Miss McHale brought in previous year papers that she had at home. They were actually called 'Intelligence Tests'. I was having a fun time going through these tests with her. I then understood what was meant by the tests. Miss McHale would say, "If they haven't got it in the top story, then you are wasting your time teaching them."

Examinations were over and the children went home for the summer vacation. Religious Life continued as before. It was a great relief to leave the classroom behind, though I did miss the children. The College I would be attending in the fall mailed the requirements to me. The Superior who received the letter gave it to the sewing mistress. It was up to the sewing mistress to get the necessary clothing that I would need. I was told by the sewing mistress I had to take part in sports. It was compulsory. She was going to fit me with a skirt and blouse. I did not think. It would work. "I could never take the Habit off." After talking it over with Mother Gerard, she would discuss it with the Superior General of the Order. Personally, I was so thrilled at the thought of having to join the sports at College. If there was anything I had missed in the convent, it was sports. I had played Tennis every Saturday with the girls and Father Lynch just before I entered the community. The fact we were all so busy in the convent, with domestic work, this kind of gave us the physical activity that we needed but I missed the sports very much. That was a thing of the past, that I had sacrificed when entering. So, now I was happy to join sports at College. I felt good that sports were part of the curriculum. I had a special division set aside for my 'wardrobe' in the sewing room. At this time, life was great, and I was looking forward to it all. Sometimes, I would wonder if this was a dream. No, I was ready for College and I was really looking forward to it. I would be doing activities that I like. I would be taking music and art, free, for two years. It was an offer by the government to students after World War II.

Chapter 22

"Preparation for Africa"

The Major Superior arrived from Africa for Visitation at the convent. Her name was Sister Paula. When Visitation was held in any convent, it was expected that some changes by way of transfers to other convents would take place. I was so very secure, and not a thought entered my head that I would be transferred. Yes, it happened to me! I was going to Africa! I didn't believe what I heard. I was going to Africa! No, it couldn't be!

I had to move fast and the first thing I had to do in preparation for going to Africa was get my birth certificate. The Superior said, "Go immediately and write to Father Lynch. It will take time to get this all done." I had just mailed a letter to Father Lynch about a week ago, giving him all the news of 'me' going to College. I had never heard of a "Birth Certificate" and was curious to find out where I was born. Once I heard that the Birth Certificate would have all the information on it, I couldn't wait to get my hands on it. Mother Gerard had not asked for anything like that or for any papers when I entered the convent. I didn't know everyone had a birth certificate. I would definitely have gotten my hands on that Birth Certificate, if I had known about it. The state of mind that I was in, in Belfast, trying to look for my mother and I did not know there was such a thing as a Birth Certificate!

The Registered letter duly arrived with a letter from Father Lynch. As we Sisters were only given the letters after it was opened by the Superior, I was called to the Superior's Office. Mother Gerard handed me the letter with the Birth Certificate. On second thoughts, she took back the Birth Certificate stating she needed it to get my official papers through quickly. I left the office and went immediately to my cell to read my letter. Oh, I was so very curious to get that Birth Certificate into my hands! As the Bursar's office had to keep all the official papers of the Sisters, I thought, maybe, I will never set eyes on it.

Father Lynch wrote he had such a hard time finding my Birth Certificate—the spelling of my last name was changed from Fryers to Friars and my birthday was not November 5 but November 14. My first name was not "Maud", but 'Sarah'. Father apologized for the delay and hoped I would be happy my new country.

"Oh God, do not let me cry." The tears just streamed down my face while I prayed for them not to. I wanted to be able to just talk to Father Lynch about all that was happening. I kept my silence about it all and also for the rest of my time in the convent in England. I tried to hide back the tears. I was no doubt, in shock at all that was happening to me. One of the comments that was made to me by the Superior General was, "It was all good for me, it would humble me and that was what we all needed from time to time to keep us humble." Humility is what I needed right now, because all this College would just go to my head! This is what I needed right now, and God was testing me. So I was informed, but I was in shock!

I was happy my name was Sister Mary Peter. I didn't have to talk about my name being changed. I had also put that old name behind me. 'Maud' was really gone now, but I would have loved to have been called by my real name of 'Sarah'. I was wondering why my name was changed in the first place while in the orphanage. Later, many years later, I heard most of our birthdays and names were changed by the nuns once we entered the orphanage. They probably had their reasons, but it certainly caused many problems in later years for the orphanage girls in search of their parents.

Chapter 23

"Out on the High Seas"

My mind is in a fog as to how I got to the boat. I don't remember what the date was when we left South Hampton. I do remember the boat took almost three weeks for us to arrive in South Africa. There was another Sister traveling with me. Her name was Sister Oliver (Farrell) and this Sister was in the group ahead of me in England. We arrived in South Africa on the twenty sixth of July, 1955. I was twenty four years old at the time. The boat we traveled on was 'The Carnarvon'. We heard this was the last trip for 'The Carnarvon'. It was going to be scrapped. It had been a war boat converted somewhat for passengers to South Africa and back to South Hampton. Apparently, the boat would be scrapped after we arrived in Africa.

The excitement and novelty of going to another faraway country did not hit me at all. I remember standing on the deck of this big ship docked in South Hampton. I was watching all the people and there seemed to be crowds falling over each other. Once the relatives got off the boat, I watched the crowds getting off and the open deck was still crowded at the rails. The travelers and their families were all holding colored paper streamers that were blowing in the wind. A closer look showed me they were colored toilet rolls. On the ground, the families were holding one end of the toilet rolls while the travelers were holding the other ends and slowly releasing them 'til there was nothing more to hold. Seeing the tears of so many people who were leaving loved ones behind was very sad. I couldn't help but cry with them. At least I had an excuse for crying and no one would notice me, when so many of the passengers were shedding tears. My companion was crying also and though it was a colorful scene, it was a very sorrowful scene. The Carnarvon gave off some deafening blasts from the funnels and she slowly moved away with the little tugs alongside her. This was the precious cargo of all these people she was carrying.

The band played loud and the people sang with it, "Should auld acquaintance be forgotten" . . . and the crowds on the dockside became smaller and smaller . . . and the boat sailed on its way. So long as the people were still holding on to the colored toilet rolls, they were still connected to their loved ones.

With nothing more to look at but the wide-open sea, we all began to move away to our bunks, if we could find them. I was not in any hurry to move. I thought I could stay on deck and watch the sea forever. It was just too magnificent to walk away from, that wide expanse of water, and all out there in front of me. This was my first experience of the ocean.

It was wonderful to see so many new faces. I personally was afraid to talk to anyone because of the convent life and we did not talk to any outside person, unless they first spoke to us. So, I hesitated to meet anyone of the passengers. I was just the same shy person as when I entered and I had wished I could get out of this shyness. It was hindering me from meeting people. As time moved on, we all got used to each other and we sisters could walk and play games on the deck. At that time 'deckquoits' was a game that was played. It was not good for me to just sit demurely, like a good nun, and watch everything. It was certainly not in my nature to do just that. I was tempted to join in. I actually was longing to be part of it all. The problem was the weather began to get real warm and very hot, and not being used to the heat made the continental and English folks almost feel like we were going to faint. I was not able to spend much time out on the deck in the heat. To add to it, we Sisters were wearing serge Habits. A doctor, who was a passenger on the boat, came to talk to me down in the dining room and asked if I couldn't change into some lighter clothing. I was ashamed to tell him we only had two Habits with us and they were both serge. He offered to give me some outfits from his wife. He said she had plenty to spare. I explained to him the rules did not allow me to do that. I felt really terrible having to tell him the Rule did not allow me to do that. I only wished I could get into lighter clothes, because it was so very, very hot. If I could change into other clothes, I would then have felt free to join in the fun and sports on the deck. The other two Sisters on the boat with us from another Order of nuns kept very much to themselves. Every day I saw them sitting in a corner, always the same corner, and they would be reading or sewing. I don't think they knew how beautiful the scenery was because they didn't seem to ever look up and see the world. Maybe their life was stricter then ours. The doctor found out they were a very strict Order belonging to the Church of England and they were an enclosed Order. They were, or appeared to be, older nuns. The doctor and his wife came over to talk to me. He said: "You know, if my daughter wants to be a nun, I will see to it she joins your Order and not turn out like those two in that corner over there," referring to the other two nuns. "They don't even bid one the time of day." Another time, when the doctor came to talk to us, he said, "You two are both so young looking. Maybe it's all that material around faces that gives that impression." We did offer to tell our ages. Sister Oliver was twenty-five and I was twenty-four, He shook his head and thought we should be out getting experiences before we ever joined the Order." He said, "It's none of my business, but you look far too young to be nuns." Actually, I thought I was already old at twenty-four!

My sailing companion, Sister Oliver, spent more time in bed down in the bunk than she did outside. She was feeling so terribly ill. I was concerned because she didn't seem to be making any recovery. The usual saying was that she needed to get her sailing legs steady. The officer on the boat said he would send the doctor on the staff down to see her. The nurse also came down to check on her at different times throughout the day. I was worried for a while. When we were three to five days out at sea, mid Atlantic Ocean, passing the northern part of Spain, and we were going through the Bay of Biscay. I had heard from the passengers this Bay could be treacherous. It was well known for its storms. Very few passengers arrived for dinner in the dining room that night. Just about a handful of us were down there. I was whirled off my feet and I just stayed on the floor holding on to the legs of the long table that I was supposed to be sitting at. From my horizontal position, I watched the waiter bring the first course to a couple sitting at a small table in the far corner. I wondered what anchored them to their positions at the small table. The next time I was able to look in their direction, I saw all of them on the floor. The boat was heaving from side to side and the high waves were lashing against the portholes. It gave a very scary picture. I had a quick but real vision of us all going under but we survived—the storm—but the sea still looked green and angry and most of the few faces I saw, also looked green and pale.

The next day some of us brave ones ventured out on the deck. Huge waves soared over the sides of the ship and lashed back to the sea again. It was difficult to keep one's balance. The bow of the boat was heaving in and out of the water. I was totally carried away by my curiosity to see as much as I could of what was going on. I was not aware of the warning signs which were posted out on the deck at all times. An officer or sailor shouted to me to go back and go inside, this was no place for me.

The bad storm did not help Sister Oliver in any way. An intravenous line was placed in her and she was on total bed rest. She was too weak to even try to move. I became afraid of something happening to her and each day that passed, I wondered what would happen to her. The people kept asking me how she was doing. I had heard from some of them that if she died at sea, she will have to be buried at sea. I couldn't even think of such a thing. I was frightened for her and myself. I thought of that possibility and of arriving in South Africa without her. I continued to keep an eye on her but when the weather was cleared and there was a clear bright blue sky, such as I had never seen in England or Ireland, I just_ wanted to be out on the deck. It took about ten days to two weeks for Sister to recover enough to be able to come out of her bunk from down below.

Having spent three weeks on the ship, I had ample time to be out on the deck or hang out along the railing and watch the sea, The sea held me spellbound. There was water and more expanses of water, just never ending. I had so many questions I asked myself. Why doesn't the water spill over? How does the water contain itself? Does it have boundaries? We had many storms during our three weeks at sea, but they did not compete with the storm as the ship passed 'The Bay of Biscay.' the waves' motions were very changeable. Some days were so stormy I thought the large heavy swell of waves would be powerful enough to throw the boat over, and all of us along with it. The thought of being drowned at sea was all that I could think of in these heavy storms. To add to these awful thoughts of drowning at sea, was the fact that anyone who died on the ship, would have to be thrown into the sea. The captain of the ship had already spoken to me in the presence of the ship's doctor. Sister Oliver was at times very ill and she had everyone worried. She did not seem to be able to recover properly before another bout of illness would occur. I was told if she actually died while on the ocean liner, she would have to be buried at sea. The doctor was truly concerned about her and visited her as often as he could. I was so afraid. His words really shook me to my very being. Anytime I'd look over the railings, I would visualize the body of Sister Oliver being thrown overboard! I couldn't think of anything worse that could happen. It affected me so much that I think I was getting sick from the thought of it. I remember at one time, when Sister Oliver was a little better, I tried to talk to her about getting from the dark bunker she was in and come up to the deck for some fresh air. I was getting angry because I thought she could have made a little effort to get better. I took care of her and when the nurse would bring her something light to eat, I would feed her and wait on her hand and foot. The nurse would wash and bathe her and I would help, but I began to think she has got to get on her own feet. I was scared she would not ever reach the African Shores. I wondered what I would do if I landed all alone and Sister Oliver wasn't with me. I think all the passengers ought to know Sister Oliver was very ill. They began to be concerned about me being down in the bunk most of the time. The passenger doctor, (I think his name was McIlroy) would tell me to come out on the deck, as everyone missed me at the different games. He said I would be the next to get ill and he noticed I was not the same person. Why should two of you be ill? Take care of yourself first. Sister Oliver did begin to feel better after about two weeks and I began to enjoy life again. I think I was feeling the responsibility of it all.

It was hard to believe I was sailing the high seas on board the ocean liner, the Carnarvon, and the only sign of any other life out there was seeing other ships way out on the horizon. Generally, we could only see these ships at night because of their lights shining. People would bring out their binoculars to see the ships passing in the distant horizon out in the darkness.

In the orphanage recalling my school days, we had classes on history and geography, but as I sat out on the deck meditating on the vastness of the sea all around me, I continued to have so many questions. I remember the teacher; Miss 0' Donnell in school telling us about the sea. She brought a bucket of water in the classroom to demonstrate the earth and how it had been surrounded by so much water. The water would never spill or fall off the earth. The earth was suspended in the air and it was turning around on itself in space. I was amazed to see the teacher swing the bucket of water in the classroom. I was ready to jump up and clean up the spill. I thought the teacher ought to swing the bucket outside, and then it wouldn't matter if the water spilled over. That demonstration of the bucket of water left an indelible print on my mind. I would go outside to play in the yard and look up at the skies and expect to catch the earth as it fell out from the skies.

As I sat out on the deck of the Carnarvon, I also recalled Miss O'Donnell's lessons. I didn't remember too much more of what I learnt about Geography apart from the things I learned by rote. Having had no other experience of the outside world, I guess it was hard grasping anything in theory that was as complicated as the earth up in space. I recall Father Lynch telling me when he first arrived in the orphanage as Chaplain, he always remembered me standing all by myself outside on the grounds and looking up at the skies. He actually thought I was a little simple and backward. Father later wrote in his notebook, "Maud is very strange in ways, but she is great in sports."

I also remember learning directions by rote.

> North to the ceiling
> South to the floor,
> West to the window
> And East to the door.

I loved that rhyme. I have to mention the teacher we had in this class was Miss O'Donnell, the only secular teacher we had. We all loved her. I recall every day how we stood to attention when she walked into the classroom. She was the highlight of our day! We children did not hear of 'makeup' in those days, but looking back now, we thought she was like the Greek Goddess. She was beautiful. It was her high rosy cheekbones and perfect features. She stood and walked as if she was master of everything around. She wore beautiful clothes and really stood out in contrast to the nuns all dressed in black. All you could see of the nuns was the eyes, nose and mouth. We loved Miss O'Donnell. Later on, when I worked for Father Lynch, I found out Miss O'Donnell lived just around the corner from as. I made every effort to visit her. Without knowing about heroes back then, I guess she was my heroine!

Father Lynch was also my hero, but he was more like a father. Miss O'Donnell would say to us when we visited her in her home, "You children just saw me through rose colored glasses.

I'm just rambling on with my thoughts while I sit out on the deck. There was a passenger onboard who was a missionary teacher. He was a religious brother from some Order. I had not seen him before, but now he was seen out on the deck quite often. He introduced himself as a missionary brother and his conversations were so very interesting. He was also so very knowledgeable about the world around him. Eventually, as he became better known among the passengers, they would ask him to come together with them in the evenings to listen to him. He was a teacher and besides all the degrees, he was also an astronomer. This is where we benefited from his knowledge. He would gather with all those interested, on the deck, in the evening. The stars would be so bright and clear and he knew the names of the stars in the heavens. It amazed me I had never seen stars shine like this in England or Ireland. What I did see from the boat was "The Southern Cross." They were four bright stars that shine out above the other stars and were in the form of a cross. I was to look at this constellation of stars for many years to come, in Africa.

Chapter 24

"Some Introspection on Life"

In the early morning, I often sat outside and as we had an hour's meditation, I would try to get it in before breakfast. It was great having space to be alone and watch the sea in all its grandeur, in all its openness and nakedness, stretching as far as my eye could see and well beyond. Nothing in front and nothing behind to cause any stress, just myself at the center of this vast expanse of water. It was so peaceful but so frightening at the same time. I thought of our lives being a little bit like the ocean. We know so little about it. We really don't know what it contains, what it can offer or bring to us, or how far away the other side might be. Like the ocean, we don't know how many storms we have to face, or what a life ahead might be. We have to face the ocean of life. Deal with whatever it brings or whatever it takes away from us. I myself was not dealing very well in life with these thoughts that I had. I loved to watch the undulating waves of the sea. Sometimes they were calm and sometimes stormy. They kind of reflected my own life. I was sometimes happy and talked to God about the wonder of it all. Other times, I would question how this world really came into being and how I carne into being? I felt so infinitesimal in this vast open expanse of water in front of me and all around me. Did God really know I existed? At times, I wondered, when sitting out on the deck, all alone, and not one person in sight, if God really knew about me. Did He drop me down in Belfast? Who is my mother? Where is she now? If she would know where I am sitting right now, gazing out on the Atlantic Ocean what would she think? These questions were never far from my mind all the time. And, anyway, what was this little orphan of hers doing, traveling the wide world! Coming from nowhere and not really knowing where I'm going or what the future holds!

After being on the boat for almost three weeks, 21 days, we were all hanging out over the railings of the boat to see land again. We docked at Cape Town. We had to get used to walking one easy ground. I felt like I was drunk and my feet were gone from under me. A French lady on the boat with us, who lived in South Africa, latched herself onto us and would not let us go off the boat alone. She was going with us. "You two are far too young to be out alone and you don't know this country." We had one full day in Capetown and had to be back on the boat again in the evening. It was the winter season in the month of July in South Africa and the wind was very strong and fierce, making it difficult to walk. We Sisters had our mantles on over our Habits and they were being blown out like balloons. Suddenly, while walking along, there was a line of people coming toward us, before we realized what had happened, we were being mugged. I lost my mantle, or cloak, and with the deep pockets we had in our habits, the gang was not able to get our money. The French lady's purse was taken, but they threw it back at her and went on passing us shouting and cheering. I had been thrown on the ground when they grabbed my mantle, and they had pulled me, along with it, in the process. Fortunately, I wasn't too badly bruised. I was happy they didn't attack Sister Oliver, as she had not fully recovered. So much for my first day in South Africa!

From Cape Town, we had other week on the boat. The boat from then on had to make a few stops 'til we would arrive in Durban, the Port of Natal. Sister Oliver's system did not adapt very well to the 'on again' and 'off again' stops at Port Elizabeth, East London and Durban, which was the port of the Natal Province our final stop. We were sailing east, leaving Cape Town behind, and heading towards Port Elizabeth. This was a fearful sailing as the strong, mighty winds were like gale-winds and it was too dangerous to go out on the deck. This last leg of the journey, I thought was just treacherous. By this time, we would have been glad to get our feet on solid ground again. This part of Africa is where the Indian Ocean and the Atlantic Ocean meet. Some days were so beautiful, clear blue skies and the far stretching calm, blue, ocean. When it was like this, I would feel warm and comfortable, though this was the winter season in South Africa. I compared this winter weather in South Africa to the English summers; the only exception was the sun was clearly visible in the sky. In England, the sun was more often than not, behind the clouds. The missionary brother was still on the boat and he pointed out the geographical landmarks that we would be passing. At the bottom of the African Continent was the Cape Peninsula's Cape Point. He said this was thought to be the southernmost tip, but there was another tip, about 200 kilometers from the Cape point, called Cape Agulhas. This is where the meeting of the Atlantic and the Indian Ocean took place. It was after we reached Port Elizabeth and the boat sailed southeast to East London. The eater was like a summer's day, and continued to be beautiful 'til we arrived in Durban, our final destination.

I forgot to mention as our boat was being tugged in to Cape Town harbor, we could see, not only land, but also a mountain. It looked like a huge rock standing right out at sea. As the boat drew nearer to the harbor, we got a clearer picture. The mountain was covered with a heavy cloud, and the brother missionary explained this mountain, which was the shape of a table. The cloud which always-hung over it on all sides was like a cloth. hence the name 'Table Mountain'. It was indeed a very unique setting, and Cape Town itself was built around this mountain.

Chapter 25

Arrival in Durban, South Africa

The long-awaited day arrived. We docked in Durban, our final stop. When I came to this part of my memoirs, I couldn't recall being met by the sisters or the beautiful drive from Durban to the Mother House. I took the drive many times later, but this arrival, I don't recall. I was surprised myself that I had no recollection of any part of it.

I certainly remember the welcome we received at the Mother House. The sisters were everywhere, and one by one, each sister greeted us warmly. I did wonder where all these sisters were coming from because of the endless stream of sisters coming out of the woodwork, so to speak. I don't know and wondered how Sister Oliver coped with all the excitement on our arrival at the Mother House.

The Mother House was situated about an hour's drive from the Indian Ocean coastline, but more inland. I soon discovered this Mother House was like an oasis in a dry desert. In fact, it was a village in itself. It was self-contained and self-sufficient in every aspect. There were extensive gardens with vegetable plots with a variety of plants growing. The sisters themselves had organized it all. There were orange trees, lemon trees, and trees that were a cross between oranges and lemons. There were berries on bushes and banana trees aplenty. At one time, the city of Durban was called the Banana City. There was talk among the sisters of growing coffee very soon. Sugarcane grew for miles along acres of land.

In addition to all this growth, the Mother House had three schools on the premises: an Indian school, a Black school, and a European school. That is what they were called in those days. At the entrance to the Mother House was an African clinic. This was the reason for the large number of sisters.

They were needed to fill all the posts. I'm not sure how many sisters there were but I would think there were over one hundred.

The day after we arrived, Sister Oliver and I were shown around everywhere. It was so overwhelming and so much to take in and see. There was celebration all day because of our safe arrival, and also they added two new missionaries to their already swelled numbers.

The first time I had seen a black person was when the three men entertained us in the orphanage. I had never seen any since then. When we arrived in Cape Town, this was the first time I had seen so many blacks, hundreds and hundreds of them. When the boat stopped at Cape Town, hordes of Africans boarded the boat and were carrying heavy boxes and sacks. They were loading coal as well. There was such activity while the boat was stopped, and then they all left again before the boat continued on its way. It left an impression on me that there were so many black people. They were called blacks and whites by the people on the boat. I also learned on the boat then about the complete segregation between blacks and whites that existed in South Africa.

We had dinner the evening of our first arrival in the large refectory at the Mother House. The "silence" was dispensed with by the superior, who announced our arrival, and we were allowed to talk to one another on this special occasion. Dinner began with the reading of the Gospel, then some Irish music was played from a long-playing record. When the music stopped, we could talk. I happened to be sitting at the very end of the table, far from the top tables where the superior and her councilors sat. I didn't notice the tables behind me, the noviate tables, this was where the novices and the novice mistress sat. Suddenly a sister, the novice mistress, stood behind me just as we were allowed to talk; I thought she wanted to greet me. Instead, she wanted to correct me. She said something to this effect, "Did you know your feet were dancing during dinner while the music was playing? You wouldn't do this if you were at home, would you? So don't do it in the convent. You can see, we have novices behind you here, and they need some good example." She said it in a very subdued and caring kind of voice, but for some reason, she burst my bubble. I was so very upset at such pettiness. I could not believe that I was being corrected at all, especially on such a happy day for everyone. The entire community was from Germany with a handful of Irish nuns. They put on an Irish record for the arrival of the two Irish nuns. It is still really hard for me, to this day, to listen to Irish dancing music and sit still during that time. Of course, the novice mistress was doing her duty. My Irish feet were made for dancing!

It was both frightening and unbelievable to sit down at the table in the refectory at the Mother House and watch the blacks carry in the serving dishes, and then leave to go back to the kitchen, while the sisters assigned continued with the serving of the dishes. The blacks carried hot dishes on a big tray on their heads from the kitchen and walked around so gracefully, and I sat in amazement and wonder. I waited for a big crash to take place any moment. All my time in Africa, I saw the Africans carrying large quantities of things on their heads and they did it always so gracefully. Never did I see them drop anything they carried with dignity and grace, not to talk about balance!

A big problem for me was the language. In England, everyone spoke English. In the convent in England, there were a few German-speaking sisters who spoke English with very little accent. The sister who sat next to me at dinner on my first night in Africa offered the bread to me, and I did not know what she said. She spoke English with an accent. It was difficult to understand. What the sister was trying to tell me was that the bread was homemade. The Mother House had its own bakery. I understood *gut* (good) after another sister explained it to me. It is English with a German accent!

My first full day in South Africa at the Mother House was coming to an end. Sister handed me a letter from the mother general, or the superior of the convent. I was to go to the office at 7:00 PM or after dinner. Another sister showed me where to go. I duly arrived and was informed I would be leaving the next day for my first assignment. One of the sisters would drive me to the place of my new assignment. The drive was approximately one hour from the Mother House.

Two sisters accompanied me the following night to my new post. It was dark, pitch-dark, outside. The only light was the lights of the car that showed the way. The sisters were used to this drive. We drove over bumpy dirt roads and sometimes, I was afraid of my life that I might not even reach the convent. The convent was situated along the edge of the Indian Ocean. It was built in the shape of a quadrangle with the chapel in the center and wide corridors on all four sides with the cells or rooms on all sides. I was given a cell facing the sea. I was delighted to have a room with a view of the sea. I could now enjoy looking out at the sea with my feet firmly on terra firma.

The sister who had the cell next to me was showing me the way around the convent. It was late at night. Naturally, I couldn't see the sea, but I could hear the waves roaring and breaking in the distance. "Now," she said, "listen to me, this is important, and I don't want you to miss anything. Listen very carefully. I am going to be in charge of you!" I answered very quickly, "I can take care of myself, just show me where everything is, and I'll ask you if I need to know anything." "Oh no," she said. "The Mother Prioress said I have to be responsible for you." Sister continued on and on in the same vein 'til I almost was about to lose it. She then produced a knobkerrie from behind the corner of the closet. "See this!" she said. I nodded. "Yes." "This is called a kay-nob-kerrie, an African walking stick." She pronounced it over and over and made me repeat it. "Now, if you see anyone at your window during the night, just use your knobkerrie," she said and she made me feel how strong the handle of the stick was. It was the size of a closed fist. After I closed the door of my cell room, there was a knock on the door and I answered it. She said, "Oh, I'm so sorry for keeping you, Sister Mary Peter, but I wanted to do my duty properly, Sister." This whole dealing with me on arrival was like a drama scene. Was I really here in the convent? The sister, who came for me to show me the way to the Mother Prioress' office, made a sign to let me know that this particular sister was a very good person, but she's a little simple. One has to get used to her. Don't mind her!

Thank God, she told me that because I was wondering where I had landed. I got my instructions from the supervisor to be in the classroom in the morning, and the head mistress would show me where I would be teaching. I recall lying in bed that first night, and sleep would not come. I guess my mind had not had time to adjust. I thought about everything that I could possibly think of and wondered where Sister Oliver would be posted. I was anxious to be up and see where I was. No sleep came to me that first night, and when the call bell rang at 4:55 AM, it was partially dark. While I was washing my face, kind of lick and promise, I curiously opened the windows. I wanted to see the sea. What met my eyes was a cow's face looking right in at me! I had never been so close-up to a cow in my life. I was startled and quickly closed the window. Afterward, when I noticed the windowsill in my room, it was very low, about the same level with my waistline. Anyone (even the cow) could take an easy jump through the window! The cows roamed free around the farm school.

Chapter 26

My First Day in the Classroom

That morning, after breakfast, I walked a little ways from the convent to get to the school. All of the teachers were together. I was told which classroom I would be teaching in. Morning prayer and a few words spoken by the principal, we, the teachers, accompanied the children to their classrooms. I have no recollection of that first day or of the weeks that followed. I prepared my work for school, and I began to wonder how I was going to get all the knowledge in my head. The history and geography of this new country overwhelmed me. I had a difficult time trying to understand what language the children were speaking. I soon discovered English was their second language. I tried to figure out what language the children were speaking among themselves. One of the teachers said, "You'll never work that out, there are too many languages. You just keep to English as medium." And she added on the side, kind of jokingly, "You have just come from England so you can teach them the King's English!"

The children in this school where I taught were colored. In South Africa, the population is so diverse. There are blacks, whites, coloreds, and Asians. I soon learned the coloreds I was teaching were from different parts of the country, and some were boarding at the school. The coloreds themselves were of a mixed race of people, descended from Europeans who colonized the country, from Asians who came to work on the sugar plantations in Natal, and the local blacks themselves. The coloreds were a mixed race descended from all these different races. I sat at my desk in the classroom and looked at all these children. I was so frightened of them in the beginning. This was my first dealings with people of color.

I really enjoyed the teaching and was glad for all my experiences in England. Somehow, gradually, I was drawn to these children, and I grew to love them. What really attracted me to them was that they did not have wealth of any kind but were happy with very little. Some were really poor, and I think all of this struck a chord with me. I could identify with them. The children were so willing to learn; and in those days, there were not that many distractions, which children have today. Life was happy and simple. I found it so easy to teach them. They were soaking up all the knowledge like sponges. This school, especially my class of ten—and eleven-year-olds, would have been a teacher's dream class today. I gradually learned the colored race was kind of looked down upon as not belonging to the Asians or to the Africans, and they didn't belong to the whites. When I heard this, my heart went out to them. I was determined to give them as much extra time, if they needed it, to push them ahead in their school curriculum.

The first week of school, I had a difficult time trying to remember the names of the children. Not because there were too many children as I only had more or less twenty children in my class. They had Portuguese, Afrikaans, Zulu names and so on. I couldn't pronounce the names, so I made a big chart for myself of the names of all the children. I placed the phonetic spelling next to their names. In between classes, I would play a kind of game with them; and if I couldn't get the pronunciation, they would have to repeat the name to me. I would pick out one child and I would guess the name of that child, and I had asked one of the children to give me a star. It was like playing "memory." Of course, we didn't have stars to stick on, so the child had to put a drawing of a star next to my name. It was so much fun for me as well as the class. There was one significant thing that happened to me as I was going through the Register of Names in my class. I was stunned when I spotted my own surname in the Register. I had never before seen the name Fryers anywhere in the telephone books in the kiosks when I was back home in Belfast. Now I knew what my real name was, according to my birth certificate, it was spelt Friars. My eyes popped open when I saw that one of the children had my last name of Friars. Every day I would look at the name of friars and look at the child with that name and wondered! It was an unusual name so I thought . . . maybe, there's a connection here. Somehow, discovering this kept my spirits raised. I had this on my mind all the time. I would scan this child's face for some kind of recognition, but I had to be careful the child herself didn't observe me watching her. In a way, it was a distraction for me, but a good distraction. I thought and thought of eventually finding her home address. I also thought that when her parents came to pick her up at the end of the school term, I would try to be there to see her father. I would get a conversation going with him. I, of course, would have to get permission to do this from my superior, Mother Prioress, but how? No way was I going to make this public!

Chapter 27

First Train Ride in South Africa

At the end of the school year, I had to accompany some of the children on the train going from Durban to Johannesburg. It meant we would be on the train all night. As we two sisters were traveling with the colored children, we took compartments that were the cheapest. Because of their color, they were not allowed to mix with anyone else. We stayed with the children. There were no bunks in these compartments, so we sat on hard benches all night. The train stopped and started at different stations and finally reached Johannesburg at approximately nine in the morning. We left for the train before the official closing of the school day. I was very disappointed not to get the golden opportunity that I was waiting for, to see the father, Mr. Friars, pick up his child. It tore me up inside for this longed-for day was not to be.

On the train, my thoughts were going back to the opportunity that I missed of seeing the Friars family. The sudden noise when the train stopped and pulled in to the stations would bring me to my senses. Each time the train stopped, I would try to look out of the window, but there was just total darkness every time. The superior who sent me to travel with the other sister and the children had said it would be good for me to see the country. I saw just nothing. We traveled all night. There were very few lights outside the train stations.

What I did see on the train was scary knives coming through the train slits on the hinge side of the doors. Coming in from the passage, there were a few men in the passageway. This was toward the early hours of the morning. Thank God, there were a few strong older girls with us on the train. They were a big help in holding the door shut, while we two sisters tried to grab the blades coming from outside. We used our mantles to grab the blades and tried to hold on to them. It was impossible to keep holding onto them; we couldn't continue doing this as it was useless to try to keep a hold on the knives. Our hands were too sore and tired. We got some cuts in the beginning and would try to stop the bleeding; but when we attempted to grab the blades again, we just opened the wounds again. We all screamed in unison at times, hoping to make a noise so we would be heard. We pulled on the string or call bell in the compartment, hoping the driver or someone on the train would hear the call bell for help. No one heard us. We continued to sit and watch the blades come through the hinges of the door. As we watched the blades, we kept very quiet and talked in a whisper to one another, deciding what we should do. This continued for about five or six hours. The muggers kept pushing the knife blades through, and they could have done this forever because the blades were just in the slit of the door and not serving any purpose. I warned the girls they were not to hold the blades. They were not to touch them. They saw that it didn't help when we sisters held on to them. At one time, I really thought they had stopped, but they came back again with full force and started to chip away at the wood on the door. I wished I would have had a strong forceps or pliers to grasp the blades from inside. From now on, that would be something I could carry in my big habit pocket. I opened the window, and we all screamed together every time the train stopped at a station. We shouted "Help, Help," from the open window for as long as we could, at each stop, but to no avail. People were not going to get involved in the middle of the night. We dared not leave the compartment to go to the bathroom, even after we thought they had gone. We were not going to chance it outside the compartment. The girls were told by us sisters if they had to go and couldn't hold it, they could urinate on some of their clothes from their suitcases. In that way, we wouldn't be walking in it over the floor. What else could we do under the circumstances? We didn't know if the muggers would be waiting outside for their prey. We sisters had to hold a brave front, and all the while, we were so frightened for our lives and those of the children in our care. There were twelve children traveling with us, and we were all in the same compartment, a bench on either side. I recall arriving at about nine in the morning at the station in Johannesburg. We were so done in and so afraid of opening the compartment door, even after we had arrived.

I recall the families being at the station to welcome their children. I explained everything to them about the train journey, and they could certainly see that we were in a bad shape. The colored children were happy to see their parents, but the parents would not have got any attention at that time if they complained to the authorities.

I don't remember being picked up at the station by the sisters. I remember thinking, "How fortunate we escaped those muggers!" This was my second mugging in South Africa.

I arrived at this colored school situated along the Indian Ocean in July just one day after I had arrived off the boat. I had only got a glimpse of the Mother House before I was sent here to this school. Our convent was situated higher up on a kind of hill from the school. The large community room was generally used for all purposes and had a large bay window, which gave a beautiful wide view of the sea. I naturally looked around at all the faces of the sisters and the youngest one was in her fifties. I was twenty-four and thought they were all so very old. There was one young sister whom I saw floating around. She was not to be seen anywhere, but now and again, I would see her. She was always alone. Once, by chance, I suddenly bumped almost into her. The sister who was in charge of the laundry pulled me aside and said, "I see you watching that sister, we are not allowed to talk to her, so I'm just telling you in case you get into trouble." My immediate reaction was that she had something seriously wrong with her. I responded, "What happened to her? Why would I get in trouble?" No one had told me I was not to talk to her! Until they do, I thought, of course, I will talk to her when I meet her. Of course, we only talked in a whisper when it was absolutely necessary. So out of curiosity, I was determined to talk to this sister when and if I saw her. Why was she so isolated from the community? I also had never seen a person with such striking beauty. Her eyes were a pretty blue and her skin was so clear. Her features were so perfect that I thought (in my innocence) she might have been an angel or saint. Weird stories of saints in old books that I had read so much of, in the novitiate made me wonder if she was being persecuted, like it said in the old spiritual reading books. She was on my mind so much because she was absolutely isolated. I just couldn't figure it out. Her face was beautiful as if sculptured. She was young, I guess around my age, which would have been good company for me.

One Friday evening, we assembled in the community for the Chapter of Faults, which was held weekly. The superior announced that some of the sisters were seen talking to this particular sister. I'll call her Sister B for beautiful. The order of message had already been announced before my arrival that Sister B will be kept away from the rest of the community though still living in the convent. On strict orders, no sister was to speak to her. I kept as calm as I could on the outside, but inside I was reaching boiling point. At the meeting of the Chapter of Faults, the superior did not explain anything to us to give a reason for this attitude toward Sister B. She said, "Some sisters had been seen talking to Sister B, and some had waylaid her in the passageways." So on and so forth! A sermon followed about obedience and we all left to carry out the superior's wishes in this matter. The next day was Saturday. When I was finished scrubbing, cleaning, and polishing in the convent, I made my way over to the school so as to get things ready for class on Monday. As I was walking along, the priest who was from Ireland was the chaplain caught up with me, and in the course of the conversation, said, "I can see you are not very happy. Why did they send you to this God-forsaken place?" I was so afraid to speak or respond to him in case I would be in trouble.

Anytime I saw this priest, I was always afraid to be seen talking to him. He would come to visit the children and give them instructions on the catechism. I wasn't sure why he called this place God-forsaken. I thought it was beautiful. I guess he was not talking about the scenery.

I saw Sister B now and again. I wondered where she was having her meals and how she spent her day. I was afraid to ask anyone. As she was about my age, I felt concerned and wished I could help her, but I didn't know how I could. One evening as I was making my way from the school to the convent, I saw a car drive out of the grounds. There was nothing unusual about that. Later, I was secretly told the big secret that Sister B was driven off in the car. She was being sent back to her hometown, and she would get on the boat back to Europe. She was from one of those towns in East Germany and was of Russian origin. Looking back now in those days, the whole mentality was so screwed. It was also a terrible thing to happen back then that a sister would leave the convent. It was like an unforgivable sin. Her name was never mentioned again, and we were not told that she had left. One did not even talk about it.

Another sister, whom I will call Sister A, was the next youngest in the community and she was in her fifties. She was, in her own limited and restricted way, very good to me. She told me Sister B was taken off in the dark of night, and I was not to say a word about it. She was leaving the convent, which was a terrible sin in those days. It was the reason for her isolation from the community.

Chapter 28

Birthday Dip in the Indian Ocean

Sister A asked me when my birthday was, and I told her it would come up in the middle of the month. I was afraid to say the date because birthdays were not kept in the convent.

It was the month of November, summer in Africa, and the warm weather felt so good. Sister A told me during the week she would take me to the beach for a swim. It was going to be my first swim in the Indian Ocean. She said, "Be ready after breakfast." It was Sunday morning, and it was my twenty-fifth birthday. Sister must have known it was my birthday all along, perfect timing. I was certainly looking forward to a dip in the ocean. We walked down past the school to a shed where we could undress. There were no children around. They were on vacation during the midterm break. The seasons are the opposite of those in Europe. It was like spring break here in the States. On entering the shed, I got a terrible shock. There was a snake right before my eyes. I was fixed in the same spot and couldn't move. I had never seen a snake before and this snake was in a vertical position with its head above the wall of the shed. Sister said, "The snake has gone, so don't worry. It was only its skin left behind," and she proceeded to handle it, showing me how beautiful its colors were. I didn't move! She told me it was only the skin of the snake. Sister said, "Didn't you see the snake easing out of its skin?" Of course, I saw just a snake moving and I didn't know how busy the snake was. Then I saw more snakes creeping along, and sister suggested we go down to the beach and change there instead of in the shed.

Down by the sea, there was not a single sign of man, beast, or bird. The sea was wild, the waves were dashing, and it looked fierce and so treacherous. The weather was so warm and beautiful, and it was beginning to feel like a

South African summer. According to Sister A, the summer would be much hotter than this. Sister A took me by the hand; and together, we walked toward a part of the beach, which she said, was safe. It had rocks in the form of a semicircle, and it was like a natural built-in swimming pool. We both went in together, still holding hands and almost instantly, we let go of each other. A strong rib current swept us literally off our feet, and it seemed to me it carried me so far backward. I remember thinking I've got to go the opposite way. It was just really a quick presence of mind and fast acting. I expected to be thrown against the semicircles of rocks I had seen, and if I did, I would know which direction was toward the beach sand. These were quick acting thoughts. I fought furiously with my arms, and I knew I had to hold my breath, but it was difficult to hold my breath for long. I could not swim, and it was my first time in the sea. It just tired me out eventually. I swallowed the seawater and tried to hold my breath. I kept repeating this in order to cope and fight my way out. Eventually, I saw what I thought was the water's edge and the sand. This helped me to keep fighting some more and go in that direction to get out. I emerged from the sea and fell limp on the sand. Fortunately, after lying there, relaxing from sheer exhaustion, it took some time before I began to throw up all the seawater that I had swallowed. Gradually, I was feeling a little better, and slowly began to move from my side to my back. I kept rolling from side to side. I made some attempts to lift my head up from the sand, but I couldn't manage it. Looking back at this bad situation, I was probably in a state of shock. I felt really sick and weak. I began to realize what happened and wondered if Sister A was still in the sea. I didn't see her. Of course, I couldn't see her as I was unable to move my head, I tried so hard to get my head from the ground so I could see if she was in or out of the sea. I continued to lie there, and slowly I was able to move myself. I then began to feel so terrible because I realized I couldn't see Sister A. Each time the waves would roar and some seawater would edge toward me, I was able to watch it from where I was lying on the sand. I was facing the sea, so I'd make an effort to dig in my heels and move farther back from the water's edge. I was in fear that the sea would pull me back in again.

Suddenly, Sister A was standing next to me. I was so relieved she was out of the water. I really thought she was still struggling to get out, and I was powerless to even move so that I could help in trying to save her. It took me a good while to recover enough to be able to stand upright, and make our way back to the convent. I continued to feel very nauseated. I was longer in the water than Sister A, so it took a little longer for me to get my balance. Sister said in her strong German accent, "You scared me to death, and I would rather have died than have to go back to the convent without you. I would have been in big, big trouble, you know." We sat down for a while and tried to recover some more. A passing visitor was coming toward us as we sat on the bench, and we asked her to get us some water from the school, which was always open in those days. We both were parched. I drank the water and instantly threw it all up again. But it helped me to feel better. I was able to walk again. Sister A said she kept looking for me in the sea; there was no sign anywhere, she prayed out loud calling God to help. She herself was also in a shocked state. She saw me emerging from the sea but wasn't able to come over to where I was lying. While we lay recovering on the beach, the Angelus bell rang out. We both looked at each other, and we knew what the bell meant. It was twelve noon. We left the convent at eight in the morning. When we felt ready to walk back to the convent, we discussed on the way what we would say when questioned by the Mother Prioress. Sister A said to me, "Don't dare tell her what happened or that we went for a swim. Just say we lost track of the time."

Usually, we assembled in the chapel for some time before our lunch for "office prayer." We then said the Angelus and walked in line to the refectory. We two sisters had been missing in the chapel and in the refectory. This was going to brew big trouble! The Mother Prioress had us both in her room and reprimanded us very severely. She turned to me and said, "Sister Mary Peter, you are the youngest sister in this community and if you think a young sister is going to come in and disrupt religious life in this community, you are sadly mistaken." While she was talking, I was trying not to throw up. I felt it coming. I tried to talk and said, "I feel sick." The superior responded, "These young sisters talk about being sick. Is that the kind of mission sisters we need?" I was afraid to make the customary venia because with kneeling and then thrusting myself forward, flat on the floor, would have caused me to vomit immediately, which is what happened. Suffice to say, I was really feeling the effects of the seawater in my stomach for about two weeks after that incident.

I remained in this convent by the Indian Ocean 'til the end of school year when I was sent again to accompany the children by train to Johannesburg for the summer holidays. I returned to the Mother House before the beginning of the next school year. I thought I would be sent back to the same convent and school by the Indian Ocean. The directress of studies at the Mother House told me I would be teaching at the White school this year and of course, that meant I would be transferred officially to the Mother House. I returned to the convent at the Indian Ocean to collect my few belongings together. How I wished I could remain here and teach the colored children. They were special to me. While I was still packing there, Sister A gave me the news that a young missionary doctor who had offered two years of her life to work on the mission had died. The doctor and a friend were both from Germany. They had only been in South Africa for a week, and like Sister A and me, they went down to the sea one Sunday morning for a swim. Both of them could swim. Neither of them returned. It was devastating for all concerned, especially their families, who were so far away in Germany. Sister A and I understood the struggle they must have had, if they had tried to fight back the current. We were both reliving that treacherous scene of trying to battle the strong current. Nightmares of trying and struggling to get out of the water continued to disturb and wake me up from my sleep. We had heard of sharks attacking people in the water and possibly that is what happened to the doctor and her friend. I couldn't help asking myself the question, "How come we two sisters were spared?" This doctor would have been a more valuable and more useful person on the missions than we could ever have been. It was tragic! I recall some years later. in the 1960s, the government or the Natal Board had set up anti-shark nets in the sea to protect the beaches along the coastal area from sharks.

While in this colored school I was intrigued by an elderly German sister who held a very large class out in the open under a shady tree and taught the African children there all day long on our school grounds. The children would come and go all day long and join the class. She spoke to the children in their own language, which was Zulu. She also taught English and Afrikaans besides all the other subjects. I was astonished. Every time I had a chance, I would edge over to get a closer glimpse of the open-air class. Maybe, because I was young, it appeared to me this teacher was a hundred years old because her face was so wrinkled. I grew to love her and her unassuming humble ways, and what a treasure of knowledge she was. I found out her age was ninety-two. As far as I recall, I didn't see utensils or school supplies anywhere. I have often wondered how this little sister coped with it all. I would have just loved to be an assistant to her. This, I thought, was the real mission work. I admired her carrying out her daily duties in all kinds of weather. Where were the young missionaries who would be so by needed in these places? There was truly a great need for more schools and more teachers and helpers of all kinds.

Chapter 29

Another Transfer Where I Would
Learn to Toe the Line

In January, six months after my arrival in South Africa, the summer holidays were over. I was transferred from the colored school by the Indian Ocean to the Mother House. This is where I arrived after I stepped off the boat. The very name of "Mother House," it was the main house of all the convents, gave me the impression of a very exemplary community. I was already warned and literally and figuratively knew I could not tap dance around. I would have to toe the line. This is where I had my first meal at the Mother House when I arrived in South Africa. This is when my feet were tapping on the floor to the Irish music during the first meal. Initially, it was a good feeling to be surrounded by so many sisters. There was a beehive of activity everywhere. I don't recall how many sisters were living at the Mother House. There were approximately over one hundred. I recall that there were more than fifty young sisters, novices, and postulants in the novitiate. Some years later, the numbers were growing so fast that a new building was erected at the Mother House to give more space for the swelling numbers of vocations to the religious life.

There were three schools at the Mother House: the African or Black school, the Indian school, which was situated close to the Mother House, and the European or White school, which was farther up on a hill from the convent. It took a good twenty-minute walk uphill from the convent to the white junior school. I was assigned to a class in the White school. During the very hot weather, it would take longer to walk to the school as it was an uphill incline.

Coming to a new place was just great in some ways; there was, in fact, so much to take in at the Mother House. I didn't have time to wander around and check things out, but I could see the very large grounds from the convent windows where the novices and some postulants were tending to the chickens and yard work. Here, the sisters bred their own chickens in incubators. It was so new and fascinating to me. It was wonderful to see hundreds of little fluffy yellow chickens under the light, kept in special sections. I just loved it and wished I could work there outdoors instead of having to go to the classroom. There was so much going on and so much to see, but I had to set my sights on this new class.

On the way to the White school up the hill were several bungalows segregated from the school where the music teachers taught music to individual pupils. It was an ideal situation. The music students could go to the bungalows and practice without disturbing the rest of the school.

The class that I was assigned to teach was the largest class in the school. I think I had about fifty-nine to sixty pupils, far too many for one class. I thanked God for my previous teaching experience, but at the same time, I felt I was not in full control of this class. It was the start of a new year and the sisters teaching in the junior school had been with these children the previous years. So the principal of the junior school, who had taught my class last year, kept coming in and out of my classroom and taking some of the misbehaving children out with her. She would eventually bring them back to the class. I found this to be such a distraction. Apparently, the principal had these same children in her class the previous year and knew how difficult some of them were. It upset me to see her doing this because the children were missing out of their classes. What's more, it was the fact that she would have them sit outside her classroom, in a row, just like it was punishment for them. They were going to miss a lot of school if she kept this up. So from the start, I was in a dilemma. For a time, I carried on and just let things work themselves out. This principal was German but spoke English well. She wanted to show, both the children and me, who was actually in charge. It was so obvious to me. I did not feel free in my own classroom. It was difficult enough having such a large number. As previously, I had to be well prepared and had a tough time learning everything I had to learn for my own class. Naturally, tension grew. One particular teacher in the junior school was fairly approachable, and I tried to speak to her on this very domineering character that I was dealing with. I did not want to cause trouble but something had to be done. The teachers were all older than me and more experienced than I was, and of course I wasn't really a qualified teacher. I didn't have a chance of winning the struggle to fight this case because that's what it was coming to. Some of these children were boarders at the school, and the young sisters had to help the sisters who were in charge of the boarders by taking their turns of being there with the children after school hours. We had to supervise the children at playtime and in the dormitories. I had too busy a schedule to prevent me from being concerned about myself.

I continued on as best as I could, but I was not feeling well. I did not want to complain of being ill because it was not the way I was brought up. I tried to carry on with teaching. The illness got the better of me, and I landed in the infirmary at the Mother House. I was not able to lift a finger and was totally prostrate with weakness. The high fever and muscle weakness overwhelmed me. I was unable to eat and if I did, I couldn't keep it down. There was a nun who was a doctor from Germany and worked at the Mother House clinic. She visited the sisters daily those who were ill in the infirmary. I began to feel a little better after I was given penicillin injections (a cure for all ailments in those days). I had to have an x-ray eventually and this showed I had a duodenal ulcer. At that time, there was a treatment from Germany, jokingly called, the "roll treatment." After I had the injections, I had to roll over to the opposite side of where the injections were given and continue on with this treatment for ten days. I was glad I was having some kind of a diagnosis. To me, this proved I was not faking but actually had something wrong. One did not complain easily in the convent. We had to have something quite serious to complain about.

It's strange that during the time of my illness, I was having terrible nightmares of drowning. They continued to plague me and I'd wake up, out of the sea, in a cold sweat, just feeling exhausted.

I had a very slow recovery from this illness and had to hold on to something to help me walk for weeks afterward. I really felt bad that I, a newcomer among the sisters, was letting everyone down by not being a useful member of the community. At the time while I was ill in the infirmary, the superior of the convent was away at some religious conference. When she returned some time later, she made her rounds of the infirmary. When she approached my bed, she said something about, "What's this I hear about these young sisters? This is getting to be too much lately." I recall being so upset about this remark, and I thought about it for a long time. I was planning in my mind about what I was going to say to the superior when I met her again! The angry thoughts about what the superior said remained in my head and festered there. I reasoned, I did not bring this illness upon myself. The doctor had told the superior that I had caught something diagnosed as typhoid. She also told the superior I had a duodenal ulcer, and I would not be able to go back to school 'til after Easter. That night, the superior came on her evening rounds and said to me, "What are you worrying about? You, young sisters! I don't understand. When I was your age, I worked hard and was never sick. I don't know what has come over these young people lately. You haven't a single worry in the world. Just think of people outside what they have to contend with!" Why this illness of mine worried her so much, I don't know. Probably, it was the responsibility of her office as the superior of the Mother House and I was "the new kid on the block" as it were.

Later, I heard that a duodenal ulcer was due to worry, so that was why the superior asked what I had to worry over. I thought afterward, if I asked the superior to take over my present class, she would find out what I was worried about! I also thought, I might have developed an ulcer when I had swallowed all the salt water in my struggle to save myself from drowning. Of course, I dared not speak of that drowning incident as I had no permission to be swimming in the first place. As time moved on, I recovered and was able to go back to my classroom after the Easter holidays.

Whatever illness I had, it left its effects on me for a long time, and it was a big effort to get through the day. I would cry at the drop of a hat. Sometimes, I would have to leave the classroom to dry my tears and wipe my face before I could go back to face the class again. Maybe, looking back, it was just weakness and still recovering from the illness.

After the illness, I returned to teaching the same class of children. After spending one day in the classroom, I realized I was not having the same kind of enthusiasm or energy I was feeling prior to the illness. I couldn't push or go, go, go as I used to do. One morning, on the way up the hill to school, one of the music teachers in the music bungalows opened her door. She, Sister T, called me to come in; and she sensed I was having problems and was not doing well. She said something to the effect that she knew I hadn't been well for sometime, but she would like to see my old free spirit again. At the words, "What's going on?" I just dissolved into tears in her little room and tried to make an exit through the door. Sister T said, "Anytime you need to talk to someone, just come on in. I'll let you go now, as I know you are on your way to school." I think the fact that someone was personally interested in me is what really touched me. I pulled myself together before I went into the assembly hall, where the children were gathered before school. Every morning, when I passed Sister T's music bungalow, I was longing to go in and talk to her; but I had to be ready for the children and not just be dissolving into tears right before I went into the classroom. Sister T had been the superior in England at the same convent where I was during my novitiate days. In England, I had heard her name being mentioned many times. She was the novice mistress who just left for Africa right before I entered the convent in Chingford, England, in 1948. Sister T had been the superior in England during World War II, and would go out to Epping Forest, which was right opposite the convent to play music for the soldiers who were stationed there. As well as entertaining the soldiers, the sisters would bring them food and any necessities like toothbrushes and toothpaste, soap, etc.

Sister T had a great personality. She was warm, kind, and approachable. Though I longed to talk to her, I was afraid of getting into trouble for breaking the silence and being seen going in or coming out of her music bungalow. I was also afraid of getting Sister T into any kind of trouble as well as myself. I knew Sister was very popular and loved by everyone. I was also aware that among a large community of sisters, there would be some jealousy because I was called to the superior's office and given a warning not to enter Sister T's bungalow without permission.

This transitional time of life, not only in a new country but on another continent, was difficult. Facing a totally new world in Africa and also within the world of the convent was very trying. It was also exciting with all the new faces and meeting the domestic workers (all black people) for the first time. I felt akin to these black domestic workers, as I was in the same domestic kind of work in Belfast, Ireland. I wanted to be able to talk to them but with all the restrictions in the convent, it was not possible. Although we sisters could talk to them with regard to the work at hand, we were also forbidden to associate with them according to the policy of racial segregation called "apartheid." It was an Afrikaans word, which meant separateness. Within the confines of our convents, clinics, and hospitals, we had permission for dealing with the black people because of the fact we sisters were missionaries sent to Africa for that purpose.

With all the newness I was experiencing around me, it just added to my loneliness. I missed the familiar faces of the Irish nuns in England, who came through the journey of novitiate with me, and all those nuns who helped me in my studies or otherwise. I missed the humor and the good laughs behind the scenes. The old familiarity was gone. I tried to adapt to my new world. In the midst of all the newness and in spite of the number of sisters around me, I felt all alone. At times, I felt lost and lonely and really not belonging at all. I kept asking myself the same old, same old, but ever present questions: How did I end up here so far away? How did I ever get on this planet? Where did I come from? I would stop for a minute from my schedule and just stand and think about all the unanswered questions. Who am I, floating in this world, with no beginning that I knew of and no foothold or roots (roots, back then, were understood to be part of a plant or tree in the soil). I felt rootless! I always overcame these questioning and depressing thoughts by diving into work again, but I felt like I had weights on my feet and I was trudging along instead of walking in a brusque manner. Sister T would always have a cheery word or so to say to me in a quick passing as I walked past her music bungalow, and this to me was a help to know there was one person concerned about me. How I longed to be able to talk to her.

One morning in my school classroom, the door burst open between the two classrooms, and a crowd of children rushed in to tell me that their teacher, Sister C was sleeping and that some of the children shouted out that the teacher had fallen off her chair. It was a shock for me to see, so it was, no doubt, a greater shock for the children to have witnessed this episode. I sent a message with one of the children over to the principal of the senior school to relate what had happened. The doctor and nurse who worked at the Mother House Clinic were notified, and they got into their truck and drove up immediately to assess the situation. They put the sister out on the patio in an easy reclining chair. I don't know if the doctor knew what actually happened. As this was happening once too often, I was kind of afraid that I wouldn't be able to continue the teaching of both her class and mine. These episodes were happening frequently. Narcolepsy was what she actually had did wake me up to the fact that I was actually healthy, when comparing myself to what was going on healthwise with this sister. How I would hate that to happen to me in the middle of my teaching the class, to suddenly start feeling sleepy. Wow! Her diagnosis was made, called narcolepsy. It was the first time I had heard that word. I wouldn't ever forget it. Sister C was taken to the Mother House infirmary, and when they got word that it was diagnosed as narcolepsy, she came back to teach the same class. Sister C was now taking some kind of stimulant medication to keep her awake. That was the treatment in those days.

I continued to teach at the White school at the Mother House. I taught there from 1956 to 1959. I was solely preoccupied with the teaching while at the same time was trying to learn the subjects, which I had to teach the children. The history and geography of South Africa was interesting. I studied and acquired the knowledge of all the different races that lived in the country of South Africa. There were the colored races, previously mentioned, and they were the first class of people I taught. The colored were a mixed people of Asian and European descent, with a mixture of whites and blacks thrown in. The blacks were the majority of the population, about thirty million of them. The whites were in the minority and numbered about five million. Asians lived in the province of Natal, South Africa, and were mainly Indians. It was the Indian people who ran the large gardens at the Mother House. They also tended acres and acres of sugarcane plantations, owned by the sisters of our congregation.

So having learned all this history of the country, I was totally oblivious of the political situation. When Dr. Hendrik Verwoerd became prime minister in 1958, the rumors were flying around that the Afrikaans language was to be the predominant language from now on. Up to this time, it was English that was spoken by the white races, although after the election, Afrikaans-speaking whites were now in the majority. Some of our teaching nuns could speak and were also teaching the Afrikaans language. The majority of the nuns were from Germany, but they also spoke English and now we all had to learn and speak Afrikaans. The sisters from the northern part of Germany understood the Afrikaans language when it was spoken because of its similarity. They did not like to speak it because, to the Germans, Afrikaans sounded like "bad German." At the end of the school year, the directress of studies informed me I would have to learn the Afrikaans' language. When the school year ended, I was not assigned this year to go to Johannesburg with the children from our boarding school. I was happy to remain behind. I had those awful memories of the first night train from Durban to Johannesburg in 1955. It was even a greater joy to have some time to get my school class in order for the following year. There was one Irish sister, Sister JB, who taught in the junior classes in the same school and as we were the only two young Irish sisters, we just made our own fun.

During the holidays, things became a little more relaxed, and we two sisters would walk uphill to the school and talk about Ireland. She, an only girl, talked about the six brothers she left behind. This freedom was such a reprieve for both of us, and together we would go to the gym hall and play towing the ball or kicking the ball around. I enjoyed this so much, just to have some natural fun again. I told Sister JB I missed this kind of fun. It really did me the world of good to be out of the sight or reach of the nuns and enjoy myself with a ball! I had not had any kind of play since I entered the community. When in England, I longed to play with the children at playtime during recess time, but being in charge, I had to keep my decorum and dignity as a nun. When I was in charge of the children at playtime during recess, I would just enjoy catching the ball if it rolled in my direction with an "all work and some play" attitude. The children really had fun when they saw me throwing the ball. They didn't know how much more I enjoyed it!

In the beginning, when I first heard of the Afrikaans' language, I thought this was the language that was spoken by the black people. Sister JB, who lived in South Africa already for a few years before I had arrived, enlightened me otherwise. She also told me if I wanted to learn the Afrikaan language, she would show me where the Afrikaans' long-playing gramophone records were kept in the basement. She said many of them were very old and broken, but I may get some use out of them. I was only used to a small radio playing music before I entered the convent, so I had to learn how to play the long-playing records. A long-playing record was played on special feast days during evening meal but only one sister would handle it. I can't remember if I had to wind up the record by turning a handle and getting it to play. I literally learned the meaning of a broken record when the records were so cracked that it would play the same thing over and over again until I manually removed the needle to another place on another spot on the record. In this way, I was able to play a phrase in Afrikaans over and over until I became familiar with the expression and how to pronounce the words. Any free time I would have in between my religious or domestic duties, I would be found playing the broken records down in the basement.

When I was first told to learn the Afrikaans language, I was supposed to join a group of sisters who had been going to the classes for some years. The teacher warned me that I would find it difficult because her class was pretty far advanced. She suggested I go to an elderly sister in the infirmary, in the meantime, who would be willing to start me off; and then the following year, I would be ready to join her class. It so happened that this sister in the infirmary asked me if I wanted to learn Afrikaans. I said I had never learned a language before, and the sister who was directress of studies said that I have to learn it. It is not my choice. "Well," she said, "the Irish sisters that I know never could learn, it was difficult for them so I'm just telling you." I, of course, told Sister JB what this sister had said. Sister JB replied, "Don't listen to those sauerkrauts. It's easy for them because it's basically their language." The German sisters wouldn't agree it was in any way close to their language, especially those sisters who spoke the high German and thought the Afrikaans was bad German.

Saying the Irish sisters never could learn the Afrikaans' language just spurred me on even more to learn it. For that reason, I would show them

I could. So with determination, I started my class and surprised myself! I really enjoyed the class. I loved to learn the Afrikaans' words for table, chair, and all the objects in a room including ceiling and floor. I wrote the words on a piece of paper and carried them around in my large pocket, to pull out and learn when I had a chance. I probably progressed real fast because it just fascinated me to learn, especially when I began to put sentences together. The negative remark about the Irish just gave me that extra boost to get me motivated to learn as much as I could.

The following year, in January after the long summer holidays were over, saw us all back in the classrooms. The school year began about the end of January and I was informed by the directress of studies that I had to teach Afrikaans to my class. I responded, "What?" and then I realized I shouldn't answer a sister in that way! I stammered out, "But I can't! I don't know enough of the language." The directress replied that I should have learned enough in six weeks so as to be able to teach. She said to me, "Like all the other subjects you had to learn—you can do this too!" I was stunned and went immediately to look for my buddy, Sister JB who just roared with a hearty laugh! Then she said, "Rather you than me!" Sometime later that day, she got an idea and she said, "If I were you, I'd bring the broken records to the classroom and let the children listen to the same phrase over and over. It worked for you so well, and the children need the repetition, you know!" We two had our share of fun and laughter over this whole idea, but inside I really was actually very worried indeed. An expression I often heard was, "You learn by teaching." It was not easy for me because I had all my school subjects to learn as well before I went to teach in the classroom.

Time moved on. It was the last quarter (term) of school. The principal of the school informed me she would be coming over to my class to hear me teach. "Oh my God, help me! Oh God, what am I going to do?" I was in shock. I had never, ever had any instructions on teaching. It was all on my own endeavors. I could manage to teach, but I certainly would not be able to teach when someone is watching and inspecting me. I was given the news on Wednesday that the inspection would be on Friday, immediately after the Friday morning assembly in the hall. So after the morning assembly, I accompanied my class as usual over to the junior school. As I glanced back over my shoulder, I saw the principal following us. My knees were buckling from under me and I was just trembling. Sister JB came over to me as I entered the classroom and whispered in my ear when passing, "We'll go for a run out of this place after school. Just act like you don't know she's there!" I entered the classroom and did just that, but I was still very nervous indeed. I was to be observed by the principal on teaching three subjects: arithmetic, English, and Afrikaans. The latter subject was my big worry. When it was over, the principal thanked the children afterward, then bowed her head in my direction and left the classroom. What a great relief that was to see her leave. That was another hurdle behind me. I was able to take a deep breath. That same day another hurdle awaited me. I was told by the directress I should take the preliminary Afrikaans' examination at the end of the term. She would notify me of the date of the examination. I told this to my Afrikaans teacher in the infirmary who said, "You can do it. You have been doing so well, you know." She gave me three of the basic books required to read before the exam and offered to go through the books with me. I took the examination at the end of the year, and I passed it. The principal of my school gave me the news of passing the exam. She said, quite casually to me, "I don't know how you did it. I myself don't speak a word of Afrikaans. When I observed you in the classroom, I was amazed at your vocabulary." (If only I had known!) The principal of the school was herself South African and didn't speak the Afrikaans' language.

The principal of the school was born in England and came with her parents to South Africa when she was a child. I was of the impression that as she was brought up in South Africa, she would automatically be able to speak Afrikaans. Most of the English speakers were of British extraction. I soon found there was difference in both races, English and Afrikaans. Up to this time, I thought whites were only English white race, and spoke only English. I thought being a principal of a school, she would know both languages. In fact, at that time, I thought teachers and principals of schools were all-knowing and learned people. I counted myself at the very bottom of the ladder when compared to all the teachers.

As this was the end of the school term and the end of the year, I was very happy to have got through it all. In my mind, I was planning, during the long summer months, that I would work hard on the Afrikaans' language and the other school subjects so that I would be truly ready for teaching the following year. To have the long school break was going to be great for me because I would have more time to learn all that I needed for teaching the children in school.

One school day, the twelve noon bell rang and the pupils and teachers all went for their lunch break. We sisters sat in a small room near the kitchen for our lunch. Even though we were not down at the Mother House convent, we still held the silence and all the rituals. We had our lunch at a long narrow table, and we barely fit in the small room. After lunch was over, on this particular day, we were all told to remain seated. The principal had a piece of paper with notes that she was quoting and gave a sermon while reprimanding someone in the room. We all felt so ill at ease, and it seemed to me the principal was very angry and really upset. I had never seen the principal like this before. She was generally a very cool-headed, levelheaded, elite English person. This was not in line with her character. She kept going on about "something" and no one seemed to know what this something was all about. So to put an end to it quickly, the directress of studies, who was one of the counselors, stood up and said, (as if to say, we have all had enough). "Sister Mary Peter, please make the venia!" I did not believe I heard my name. I remained like stuck to my chair, unable to move. Eventually I prostrated myself on the floor in front of the small teaching community who were present. Then afterward in silence, we all dispersed. I was left speechless, not because of the "silence" but because of the shock and unexpectedness of the whole situation. Problems in those days were never talked about or discussed openly. No one seemed to know what it was all about, no concrete evidence presented. Outside, the directress said to me, "Just let it go!" and she shook her head as if in disbelief. I was trembling from head to toe; and my nerves were shattered, so much so, that I could not attempt to go into my classroom at this time. It was a Friday afternoon; and I knew I would not be able to handle my class, let alone, speak to them, so I did not go in. I eventually walked over with trembling legs to Sister T in the bungalow. By this time, Sister T knew what had taken place and stated, "This is the first time I have ever heard of anything like this happening!" She tried to comfort me, but I couldn't be comforted. I, whose whole life revolved around trying to please people and showing a good face and a happy exterior, was devastated beyond anything. I had always tried to do the right thing even if it was motivated or just showing me to be a good person. I just felt so bad and thought something had seriously gone wrong, and I was the cause of it all, even though I still didn't know what serious thing I had done. Although it appeared so petty to me, it was a serious complaint according to the person who reported it to the principal. I also knew it wouldn't be long before it would spread around every acre of land at the Mother House. It had such as impact on me, enough to dampen my spirits. I was called to appear before the superior the next day, for not being where I was supposed to be, in my classroom on Friday afternoon. I still recall the effect this stupid incident had on me. I was so angry even when I tried to sleep that night. I couldn't get to sleep. I always had an internal fear for doing anything wrong in the convent, so I tried to work a lot harder to be accepted and this upset my whole applecart. I was all I knew in the convent to show them how hard I had worked. I had tried to put one hundred percent into everything I did. The feelings that arose after this incident were that I was not really accepted all along. They were destroying my world and all that I had tried to achieve and build up. What was this incident all about anyway?

I continued two or more weeks in school 'til the school year closed but my heart was not in what I did. I had been dealt a heavy blow and unjustly as well. It was like a public scandal without knowing what the scandal was. Later, I slipped into Sister T's bungalow for some kind of explanation as to what had really happened to bring this on, but she couldn't give any explanation. She did try to tell me to "offer it up to Christ on the cross and with him, for the sins of the human race and for the person responsible." I got through another week of school, and it did help because I had very little extra preparation to do after the school hours on Friday. My buddy, Sister JB, came over to my classroom. "Come on, let's go for a run, for God's sake, and let's get out of here." It was Saturday morning, and she had seen some bicycles at the back in the senior school shed. Two of them were lying down flat behind a hedge, all ready for us. When I heard what she was up to, I vehemently objected to getting on a bicycle in case I would get into more trouble. I had not been on a bicycle since I entered the convent. I was also afraid of some of the children seeing two nuns on a bicycle. Wouldn't that have caused a stir? Sister JB chose the time when the children were all at lunch and they would all be going to study afterward. We walked a little distance to where the bicycles were behind the hedge. We tucked our habits up and wrapped the skirt hem of our habits into our belts around our waists, and we set off. I had not ever been out on this road before. It was so good to be outside, riding a bicycle again. Once we were outside the convent grounds, we were on a more level road that was also much smoother, though more like stones crushed and packed together, gravel road.

Outside, what a picture it was just to look at the wide-open terrain with all its different contrasting colors. This was the first glimpse (outside of the Mother House, in daylight) that I had seen of Africa. It was spectacular. We stopped at an African (kraal) home where so many of the native Africans lived and little children just stood and looked at us. Some of the women worked at the Mother House and Sister JB talked to them in English, with some Zulu words thrown in. They appeared to be so happy with their lot in life. Probably that was all they knew, and they would not have ever heard of the word poverty. There seemed to be ten or more children with no clothes on and playing with bits of sticks on the ground. Some were drawing pictures with the sticks in the soil. With a start from Sister JB, they all began to sing and dance. Sister said they love to dance and have great rhythm in them. I could have remained there with those happy, happy people and hearing their hearty laughs among themselves—it was just a great happy spirit that was noticeable among these people. I enjoyed the outing, and as we made our way back to the Mother House, they were all in unison cheering us on our way. Sister JB told me this will be a highlight in their day, the fact that we sisters actually came to visit them.

We rode our bicycles back through the gate of the Mother House and stopped to look at something of interest that Sister JB wanted to show me. "Oh my God, get down, get down." She grabbed my bicycle and put it flat on the ground. As we were crouched behind the bush, she said, "Did you see the car coming in the distance?" I whispered, "Yes." "Well, that's the mother general herself, arriving from overseas from Germany. Keep ducking girl!" she said. I had heard that the mother general was arriving sometime from overseas that day, and preparations were being made for her arrival down at the convent of the Mother House, but I hadn't given it another thought. While crouched down, I didn't make a stir until the car passed by. We both came up for air and then walked with our bicycles when we knew that the procession of cars was well out of sight. When we couldn't see the cars anymore, they were out of sight, we then jumped on our bicycles and rode slowly along the same path back toward school. We parked the bicycles in a safe place, some distance from the school, so we wouldn't be seen by the children. We walked, letting down the skirt of our habits, and it looked for all purposes that we had just come from a long walk in the grounds of the Mother House. This unexpected short outing did me the world of good and gave me something to think about. It was different and so interesting. Yes, there was another kind of world out there, kind of what I expected to see in Africa.

A few days after the arrival of the mother general, I was called to her office upstairs. I figured it was either she had seen us on the bicycles, or it was the upsetting incident in school the other day, or both! I made up my mind it was not going to affect me. I would, like an obedient, good nun, apologize and make the venia and that would be the end of that.

I didn't believe the command that I heard! The mother general informed me, "I am transferring you to our nursing convent in Johannesburg. Pack up your few things and you will be leaving from Durban Station with the school children on Friday evening. The sisters will be there on Saturday morning in Johannesburg to meet you, the train gets in about nine AM. See that all the children are picked up at the station by their parents before you leave the station in Johannesburg."

Chapter 30

Déjà Vu!

So after these orders, my mind was very busy. Déjà vu! Was I going to go through this ordeal on the train again? Did the superior general hear of my misbehaving? Is that the reason why I was being sent away from the Mother House? I left Durban in December 1959 to travel up north to Johannesburg with the school children, who were returning home for the long summer vacation. The compartments on this train were better than my first ride on the train in South Africa. We had no bunk beds, just sat all night on the straight, wooden benches. Only one knife blade appeared from outside, through the door side where the hinges were. The sister who traveled with me shouted so loud at them, and we rang the bell, at least we pulled a string, hoping for a quick response. Another blade suddenly appeared at the slit of the door where it was bolted. I was truly afraid if any more knife handles appeared, they would hack away at the door. We got the idea to take our shoes off and all of us together banged continuously on the door, so people in the other compartments would hear us. It seemed they also were afraid to go outside. The knives, or the blades of the knives, kept appearing from time to time; and eventually, we heard some talking and shouting and probably the guys with the knives were caught by the guards on the train. Then we sat quietly but kept our eyes on the door. No further disturbance at all, just silence. I couldn't believe my eyes; we were witnessing a repetition of what had happened on the last trip. The other sister who was with me jokingly said, "You must be the attraction!" It was, apparently, something that happened frequently on those night trains in Africa in those days.

Quite soon after my arrival at the convent in Johannesburg, I was put to work in the maternity hospital run by our sisters. I was mainly going domestic work, helping to serve the patients' meal trays and collecting them up when finished. I set the trays for all the meals and had them ready on the trolley to wheel them out. I filled the water carafes in each room and collected them each morning to wash them and bring them out again to the patients' rooms with fresh water. I answered the call bells and attended to the patients' needs if I could. It was repetitious work. In those days, after the mother had her baby, she remained in bed for at least a week, sometimes ten days even up to two weeks, depending on the condition of the patient. Because of this, another duty I had been given to me was a big one. Three times a day, I loaded all the stainless steel bedpans on a cart. The trained nursing sister would follow with the douching and attend to the perineal sutures (stitches). I would follow her to collect the bedpans, wash them, and put the next patients on the bedpan. This was quite a race. I would be in the process of placing the patients on the bedpans or collecting them, when the call bells would ring and the patient would need a bedpan. This would knock me out of line, like disturbing a relay race. I enjoyed the physical activity at the time or rather hyperactivity for a while, at least in the beginning. There was no pressure for me to study then, but, I eventually began to feel my feet hurting so badly. I had been wearing the same old shoes with very thin soles. I was on the floor all day, not only walking, but sometimes actually running. I had to really hurry. When I thought I was working hard and fast, I would often be told that if I wanted to be a nurse, I would have to learn to get a move on!

My former novice mistress in England, Sister M, was a nurse in this same hospital. One day, she passed such a remark to me about an errand that she gave me to do. She said, "Be quick, get a move on, and be back here at once, no dawdling on the way." I returned and delivered what she asked me to fetch. Sister then asked me to open a bottle for her. I took the bottle of juice and began to shake it. She immediately grabbed the bottle back again out of my hands and said, "You will never make a nurse, you don't even know how to open a bottle properly!" This was the same person, the novice mistress, who trained us to walk demurely and sedately, eyes cast down, no swinging of arms. They were to be kept folded under our scapulars when we had finished our work. So what was all this external training in this way for, when we literally were unable to carry it out while keeping pace with the work? In the hospital, we were always in a hurry, trying to finish the job at hand. I kept up the fast pace for most of the time. There was no way

I could get through the work otherwise. I was having trouble with my feet especially when I got out of bed in the morning. I was unable to put my feet on the floor without pain. This was a terrible predicament for me. One of the nurses I was working with on the floor noticed I was having trouble walking, and she put insoles in my shoes. She made the insoles from sponge she had in the cupboard. This remedy didn't help me at all. I developed blisters from the constant rubbing against the sponge. This sponge was a kind of rubber. Adding to this was the awful heat in South Africa in December. How I wished, I did not have these problems with my feet. I felt a burden to the community and so helpless to help myself. Fortunately, the superior came to talk to me one day and said, "You are wearing the wrong kind of shoe. I had a cubin heel and thin soles, and I was putting all the weight on the wrong part of my foot. You are going nonstop for twelve hours a day and often longer." This was all new for me, to be on my feet so long and not just walking, but running. I then wore sandals for the time being and was given a new pair of shoes with thick soles. I think sneakers in those days would have been wonderful! I was just delighted to be able to walk again and become a useful nun in the community. It was not good for me to be so physically inactive, though I could sit and prepare veggies and darn socks. In that way, I was doing something useful because the nuns and the novice mistress said, "The devil finds work for idle hands," according to the common expression in the convent. I was too active a person anyway to be sitting and darning socks. I thanked God my feet were getting better, and I could be off and running again. At this time, I couldn't help but think back to the Belfast days when I went with May Kennedy to buy my first pair of new shoes and I had no means to pay May back again, as she had helped me to balance the cost. The shoes were put aside by me, only to be worn for special occasions, though I never saw the new shoes again. I thought of how easy it was to get what I needed in the convent compared to the financial struggle I had in the outside world. Like many people in the outside world, I had to "take care of the pennies and the pounds would take care of themselves." I remember how excited I would be back then when I had enough small change to know I had saved the equivalent of change to a one-pound paper note in May's house.

I found it very easy to live in the convent, everything was readily available, and my needs were met for food and clothing. I had everything that made my life comfortable. I was never better off in my life. Though I was living in a comfort zone, I felt like being in a cocoon. I was longing to get out and go somewhere, even jump on a bicycle and go for a good long ride, or get out for a walk. I wanted to see what it was like outside the four walls of the convent. Though there were no walls like the orphanage, only figuratively speaking. I felt like being hemmed in. I did enjoy getting out of the convent every morning and walking outside to go a short distance to the hospital wards. It gave me a sense of going out to work, instead of working in the convent itself. I loved the hospital atmosphere, with so many people around everywhere, always busy, busy, busy. It appealed to me. The more I became involved in the hospital, the more I felt I am needed for the domestic work. I often wished and wondered if I would ever be given the opportunity to go for nursing training.

Though I was happy to the extent that the hospital needed me and I felt useful, I was more and more rebelling against some of the rituals and religious practices that were so archaic. I wanted to be a good religious, the best ever, but at the same time, I was rebelling against all the indoctrinations I had so wholeheartedly accepted in the novitiate days in England. Life had changed drastically and so differently from what we had so openly accepted as Gospel truth back then. I guess I was growing older and forming my own opinion of things. It was good to have my needs met, but it was the method of having to stand in line every Saturday to await our turn to ask permission from the superior for the basic necessities. "Please, Mother, may I have toothpaste? Please, Mother, may I have soap?" or whatever the need may be. Why did I have to ask permission for basic needs? In my head, I realized I ought to be grateful with the knowledge of (where I came from) and it should not have been a problem for me. But it irked me to have to ask permission for the simplest things. It was one of many rituals, where asking permissions for things was to keep us humble.

One Saturday, while waiting in a long line, I lost patience and I told the superior that waiting in line was a waste of time because I was badly needed up on the hospital wards. Also, instead of asking permission for everything, why the supplies couldn't be kept in a certain room or on certain shelves, and we could get what we needed and move on. It would save so much of our precious time. Of course, this did not go down very well. What I said and suggested had traveled to the higher superior and I was called up for my bad behavior.

The superior general told me I had lost sight of the reason behind some of the rituals in religious life. I was to get back to what I was taught in the novitiate. It was the humility in asking for permissions that was to keep us humble, and in turn, strengthen our spiritual life. I was given my penance for giving such bad example and that I was also just a hindrance to all the sisters around me. I was preventing them from leading the lives God had called them to lead. I was really being a stumbling block for them. Of course, it upset me that I was, so to speak, disturbing the peace by my rebelliousness, but I was only doing and asking for what made sense to me. Why couldn't they be more organized to make things easier for busy people? I began to think I should have kept my ideas to myself and I wouldn't get into trouble. I should be more careful of my responses and keep the silence. I knew I had to learn to accept things as they were, and who was I anyway to have a say in anything? Like I was trying to take over the job of the superior! I ought to have been contented and happy with my lot in the religious life, when comparing the life I had before to what I was having today. I was happy, yet the sheer frustration of so many things that I could not do anything about made me unhappy. I was not very subservient, and I began to think I was losing all my religious fervor I had acquired in the novitiate.

During one of those ten-day preached retreats, which we had annually, I tried to examine myself and reflect on what had gone wrong. I felt I had lost all enthusiasm for religious life. The old feelings of worthlessness and not really being wanted or accepted took over. I recalled the novice-mistress telling me the "old Maud" had to go, and I was to take on the new life in religion as "Sister Mary Peter." "Who was I anyway? Nobody knew me. Who was I? How did I ever come into existence?" Even though I was plagued with these same feelings and thoughts, and so many unanswered questions, that would keep coming to the forefront of my mind. At the same time, I was fully aware I had never had such a good life as this. I was never better off in my life before now. With a comfortable life, like I had, why was I feeling the way I did from time to time? God, who was the source of my life, should have fulfilled me and satisfied my longings. I was actually in a faraway country and when I truly realized that fact, I would travel off in my mind to nostalgic feelings of when I was out of the orphanage and working, especially the last few years before I entered the convent. As I lay in bed at night, my mind often wandered off across the continent and over the Atlantic Ocean, across the Irish Sea to Belfast, the place I left behind. My first job where I would look out at the Cavehill mountains, the River Lagan, Shaws Bridge, and the Falls Road held many memories. My orphanage friends and the place where I grew up—all these places were home to me, albeit, a home without a family. I longed to see the old familiar places and faces again that I was so abruptly cut off from, in the prime time of my life. Now, I was to go on the annual retreat.

A ten-day retreat was good for the soul and a time for oneself and for reflection. Physically, I was so tired, and I was glad to be able to rest awhile and not have to go to work in the hospital. I had forgotten that being alone with my thoughts for any length of time was not the best thing for me. Work for me was like a tonic because it helped me to forget. Unfortunately, I had a tendency to overextend myself and be so busy that I had no time to think. It was when I had too much alone time on my hands that I would feel depressed and restless to get back to work and be myself again. I had realized that I fended off my depressing thoughts and longings by ceaseless activity. The hospital certainly had more than enough work for us all. It was never ending. We had so few people to do the work. It was a handful of sisters who run the hospital and cope with all the work. In those days, the sisters not only worked with and nursed the patients. But besides nursing, they had plenty of domestic work assigned to them that had to be done. In the hospital itself, behind the scenes, we sisters did the washing and packing, and autoclaved all the instruments for deliveries, Cesarean sections, stitch removal trays, etc. Though while I was on the ten-day retreat, my thoughts often flew over to the hospital and worried about how the rest of the sisters were coping in the absence of those sisters who were on retreat. The retreat made me realize I was physically, emotionally, and mentally tired. I felt worn-out. Today, it would no doubt be called burnout, a word not in use then. I questioned myself on how I could change the way of life we led and why we had to be busy, busy, and overextending ourselves. How often, during the course of the day, did I hear the doctors say, "Why do you sisters have to work as hard as you do? Can't you hire more sisters or lay people to help relieve the work?" We sisters never talked about the work, we just got on with it. We never had meetings in those days either to talk over things so we just kept going and going. It would probably be like this forever. We sisters had no right to complain nor did we have any say in anything. The hospital was owned and operated by our own sisters. For me, nursing in a hospital required more of working together and helping everywhere and anywhere, whereas in the teaching profession, we were more or less on our own. We each had just the responsibility of our own classrooms and the children that we taught. In a way, compared to nursing, we teachers were kind of isolated. Nursing was more social, and I loved to have so many people around every day. Maybe, this was the type of life that appealed to me because I had grown up in an orphanage. It was what I was comfortable with, just lots of people everywhere, but the work was endless.

I remained in the Johannesburg Maternity Hospital from December 1959 until December 1962. The beginning of the long summer months of '62 saw many changes in the convent. Nuns being transferred from one convent to another. I was told I would be going for nursing training back to Durban, the city along the Indian Ocean. As there was a greater need for nurses in our congregation than there was for teachers, the decision was made for me to go to Durban, the coast along the Indian Ocean for nursing training.

Chapter 31

To Durban for Nursing Training

I was happy to be going for training and grateful to get the opportunity. I would, at long last, be a professionally qualified person. On second thoughts, I shouldn't bank on it. Things can change quickly as they did in the past for me. It did keep my hopes up, at least now there was something brewing in the air.

In 1963, I arrived at my destination in Durban for training, and it was recommended that all nursing students and nun students were to meet with the office personnel. Before attending classes, we had to get the admission paper work done. The paperwork was always done by the nuns in the convent. We had no say. It was the bursars and the superiors. I felt totally lost, as to what was actually required of me. Also, I had in my possession my birth certificate given to me for the first time. The sister who was the bursar handed it to me with all my other certificates. I was stunned, when I looked at the birth certificate and saw there was a "dash" in the place of where my father's name should have been. I stared at the certificate in disbelief. I was in shock! Just how was I going to show this birth certificate to anyone? I couldn't and wouldn't. Never, never! I was in such an emotionally devastating state that I felt I needed to go somewhere where I would be far away from everyone, and examine this birth certificate in detail. I sat and read it over and over and over. I had to get this paperwork done, but how was I going to disclose this information. In those days, it was a downright disgrace and shame, a real stigma. To backtrack to my time in the novitiate, when I was studying the constitutions of our congregation, I remember reading somewhere that the congregation did not accept girls who were illegitimate. I recall looking up that word in the dictionary, which read, "born out of wedlock." I pondered it over and over at that time but did not quite understand. Gradually as the years moved on, I came to understand that maybe my mother had a baby, who was me, out of wedlock. It was some knowledge I would certainly keep to myself, as I was totally naive when I entered and had no education or knowledge of sex prior to my entering the convent. And I certainly did not receive any in the convent. We did not have a radio in the convent and TV had not yet come in to being. I kept my eyes and ears open as usual to learn about everything, but I did not know I would have to have a "father" even though I knew fathers existed. So here I was faced with, and staring at, the piece of paper that gave me the first and only information about myself. I didn't like it! I was angry about it all It only struck me then, that I had all this time been wondering who and where my mother was, but never a thought of having a person called father in the picture. My birth certificate opened up a whole new picture, in black and white, and confirmed my worst fears. This was the reality, and I had to face my fears and go to the personnel office if I was to start college and my nursing career.

With much trepidation, I went for the interview to the personnel office. I dreaded the thought of it but at the same time knew I had to go through with it. I was met in the office by a very nice young girl, named Joan, who instinctively seemed to know I was nervous; and she just chatted away as if she had known me all along. Her accent also made me feel at home. She introduced herself and told me she was from Dublin, Ireland. That was a good start for me and I felt at ease with her. I didn't want to waste any time, so I blurted out my concern. The first question I had as I showed her my birth certificate was, "Do you think I will be accepted for nursing because my birth certificate shows I was born out of wedlock?" I didn't want to say that awful word "illegitimate." The word itself conjured up the feeling in me that I should not have been born. I had no right to be here at all. She said, "For God's sake, that won't make any difference at all." I felt at home, listening to her Irish accent and her assurance that only my certificates counted for the entrance. She had my exam papers spread out in front of her. I began to feel more confident as she typed at her typewriter. Then she said, "I'm trying to figure out what name is your official name?" So I began the explanation of my names. I said that probably, I would now have to go by the name on my birth certificate to make it official on my nursing papers. I tried explaining to her that I had just got my birth certificate for traveling to South Africa and that I had not ever seen the name Sarah written anywhere. This was the first time that I heard of the name Sarah. She said,

"What name did your mother call you by?" Then I told her I didn't know my mother, and I grew up in an orphanage. I told her I was called "Maud" in the orphanage. She said again, "But you have 'Madeleine' on your school matriculation certificate." I responded I just did not like the name Maud, so I knew that Maud was a derivative of Madeleine. I told her I filled in the name Madeleine. It sounded better. "Your surname is spelt differently also. "Fryers." I explained that apparently that was my real name, but I was born in a hospital, and they spelt my name wrong on the papers in the hospital in those days. I said that it was very confusing for the priest, Fr. Lynch back in Belfast who knew me as Maud Fryers. He had to try to get my birth certificate so that I would have it in order to go to South Africa. Father Lynch had a rough time in trying to get my birth certificate for me because of the confusion of names. I told the secretary I would be going by my legal name on my birth certificate from now on, "Sarah E. Friars." In everyday life, I would still be known and called Sister Mary Peter. The girl in the office who dealt with me was wonderful, and she was able, eventually, to get my legal name changed on my matriculation examination paper and all other certificates of mine. I was so very grateful to this girl for sorting my names out and for the peace of mind she gave me. I left her office with a great weight off my shoulders and happy to get all of this settled, which had been a big worry to me. Thank God, this was settled outside of the convent without the nuns knowing anything about me. With such relief, it was a big burden lifted off me, and free as a bird. I walked out of her office and felt that now I would be able to tackle anything. I wanted to hop, skip and jump.

Chapter 32

General Nursing

So I found myself starting my three-year general nursing training. As I sat in the classroom with my fellow student nurses, I wondered how I had reached this status. I couldn't have reached this ever on my own. It was what the congregation had done for me. I felt good and was grateful for the help of the sisters in getting me through my matriculation studies. Now, this matriculation examination enabled me to get into nursing training. South Africa was still having the same schooling as Britain, so my examinations were accepted here. I wished I could do something for Joan, the girl in the office, who helped me with my certificates. I was so very grateful to her. Back in England, in the novitiate, I was assisted with my studies by the nuns who were helping me when they had free time. Now it was up to me to study from my study books on my own. Now I was in a classroom where we were all learning the same subjects. I just felt great in the crowd. We had about thirty students in the class. The camaraderie was great, and it was so much fun to listen to the comments and remarks of the other students. The nursing study books were the old style, with gray black-and-white pictures showing nurses in stiff starched uniforms, carrying out procedures on the wards. We had to use our imaginations when studying the books as we had no pictures in the books to explain anything, compared to today's books, which contain diagrams, colors, and photos depicting what we had to learn. The only visible help we had back then was a skeletal, named Jimmy, which stood at the top left hand side of the blackboard. Among the student nurses, Jimmy became the focus of so much fun and laughter. To add to the fun, we had a student in our group, who was the comedian in the class. Right through our three-year training, she had been chosen to perform "one-man shows" and often would give us an impromptu performance in the classroom when the instructor left the room.

One day she went up to where Jimmy's skeletal frame was and gave her performance on Jimmy, and the kind of life he lived. It was so unique and spontaneous, and it caused shrieks of laughter in the classroom. It certainly relieved the tension of all the newly arrived students. It was the first time I had ever seen a skeletal. I was so intrigued to actually see how our own human frame was and to think that each bone had a name! Anatomy and physiology were the main subjects in the first year, and I really did enjoy the anatomy. It was like hands-on for me to actually see what I had to learn. I spent whatever time I had to spare, next to Jimmy, rattling off the names of all his bones. I did this because I knew most of the students had anatomy and physiology in high school. I knew I would have to catch up. Anne, the class comedian, made up a long poem about "Jimmy and I. How, at long last, I, Sister Mary Peter, had found Jimmy, had found my one true love. The couple was a great match for each other because she would have no permission to kiss him (Jimmy) and Jimmy was not able to function in that capacity either." I wish I could remember the exact words of the poem. We just had so much fun.

Among our nursing teachers, there was not even one English-speaking person. They were all nuns from a French order. All wonderful people, gentle, kind, and fun-loving. These nuns were to totally different from the nuns I grew up with in the orphanage. The nursing students themselves came from all over South Africa, some were from Australia. We had a variety of different people. Among the student nurses was a group of nun students about twenty altogether. We nuns stayed in the nurses' home adjacent to the hospital, but separate from the nurses' quarters. It was called the "Little Convent."

Though we nuns were away from our own convents, we still had to abide by the rules of our own congregation. All was going full steam ahead, and I was enjoying life a little, but very different kind of life. I worked hard at my studies. One afternoon, our mother general superior arrived; and as there were five of our own nuns in nursing training, she spoke to each sister individually. I thought it was a very good gesture for her to come and visit us while in training. I soon changed my mind when I heard of the real reason why she came. The accusations were, "I had not been keeping my decorum as a nun ought to and was trained to be. I was not serious enough in my training as a nurse. I was giving bad example to the young nurses in training by laughing and giggling in inappropriate places. During class, I was seen passing along jokes under the desk. The teacher had watched me passing pieces of paper to the student nun sitting next to me. There were some other minor complaints about me." Naturally, this left me feeling so bad because it was not the regular superior who came in to visit us but the top general superior herself. This was such a put-down for me that I was devastated and crushed. Was it because of me she came to visit? This really got "my Irish up," and I was determined to fight back. I felt I was entitled to respond to the accusations. There and then, I went back to the mother general. I was very angry at being falsely accused. On the one hand, the spiritual side of me said, "This is how Jesus Christ suffered, and who was I? Certainly, I was of no significance in this world, just take it all in union with Christ's acceptance of the cross, and move on. Theoretically, I knew what I had been trained to do and which way I was supposed to handle this situation. I certainly had not reached that level of spirituality. I walked back into the room and was determined to get even with the mother general. In my wildest dreams, I would never have responded to higher authority in the way I did to the mother general. I was angry at not being able to explain anything . . . and I was supposed to go about my duties without saying another word? Making the venia would clear up everything! It certainly was not going to this time. I wanted to know more specifics and where all these accusations had come from. Two of our own sisters were a year ahead of me in training, and they had reported me. These two German sisters were all out to curry favor with the superior. I heard this from other student nurses in training. I was not aware of this 'til one of the senior sister nurses in their group pointed it out to me. I had to obey in the future and report to these two senior sisters above me in rank and discuss things with them.

The two sisters were called "the two goodie goodies" by the nurses. These student nuns thought they would control me or they were trying to get into the superior's good books by reporting me to her. I recalled the same thing happened at the Mother House, when I was teaching and that was still brewing inside me, nor was it ever resolved. So full of energy and so angry, I charged into the mother general's room where I had just come out of and I demanded an explanation. She responded to me by bowing her head and proceeded to sit down. The expression on her face told me she was still in charge. This time it was my turn! I wanted answers to what she had accused me of a few minutes ago. Before I could get an answer, she asked the first question, "I want to know what you wrote on the pieces of paper that you passed around in the classroom?" I responded that I had not ever done that. In class, the student nun who sat next to me was directly out from Austria,

Sister Marietta. She was trying to brush up her English. Sister Marietta had written a question on a piece of paper. The question was, "What did she (the teacher) say about a cat?" I wrote back on the other side of her paper, "It's the guts of the cat, 'catgut' used for stitching in surgery." Another piece of paper had the question, "What does she mean by the 'art'?" I responded by writing on the other side of her paper, "It's the heart." It was very difficult for all of us to try and figure out what the French teachers were saying, and it was more difficult for a foreigner to understand. When I tried to explain this to the mother general, she of course, did not believe it. I left the room and brought Sister Marietta back with me into the room so as to confirm what I had written. I was still as angry as could be and I was determined not to let the mother general leave before this issue was resolved. Sister Marietta said, "Excuse me," and politely left the room. She returned with her dictionary in her hand, and the same papers that we had passed back and forth in the classroom. They were still in the pages of her dictionary. What a win this was for me. In those days of strict discipline, we would never, ever try any kind of pranks during class or out of class. I found the German mentality generally was to be very straitlaced and everything was black or white. Their humor was different. One of the German students herself, who was older than the rest of the students, told this to me and it helped me to understand why they did not tolerate my sense of humor. Theirs was a different kind of humor. Some of the expressions that the French nuns used during class were so funny and sometimes caused eruptions of laughter in the classroom. Of course, I would still be laughing long after the funny incident had passed. I needed my sense of humor to keep me going. It was a necessary part of life and so necessary to keep me sane, especially in this serious world of nursing that I found myself in.

I recall leaving the classroom after a lecture and being asked by another German nun student the question, "What did she mean by the 'art'?" I responded to her by pointing to my heart and the French dropped their Hs in every word they said out loud. I felt bad she had actually missed so much of the whole lesson, which was on the "heart."

I was left with the thought, if even the foreign language students could make it, then I surely would too.

I know the superiors have to be in charge of the flock entrusted to them. They are doing their duties in seeing that we toe the line. What I could not accept was the pettiness and the people who reported stories to the superior. The people with petty problems who were spiteful and mean and tried to be in the superior's favor was what got my furor. It seemed to me, whatever their motivation, they got my goat! At the same time for some reason, I was afraid of my own anger. I guess it had not ever really surfaced, only on occasions. I recall when I received the small two-by-two piece of paper from the superior in the orphanage with the irrelevant information on it, I walked outside the orphanage front door; and as the front gates were locked behind me, I became so angry. I was keeping my anger under control on most occasions, being well disciplined in the orphanage and now, also with my training in the convent. I was truly afraid of what I would be capable of doing, my feeling of real anger just made me make my steps to the confessional box in church on Saturdays. I felt I was a bad person with so much anger in me.

Here I was, in nursing training, trying to deal with a lot of things. I was carrying on with my religious prayers and practices. I was attending classes. I was working in the hospital. I was living in the nurses' home where there were so many different nationalities. I myself had so much still to learn, the names in the anatomy lesson. Anatomy was, in itself, a challenge. Jimmy was helpful. I would be seen next to Jimmy in my free moments, rattling off the names of the human skeleton. When I had to walk from the nurses' home to the hospital or to the classrooms to visit Jimmy, I would have pieces of paper with the names of the skeletal bones in my large nun's pocket. The walk gave me an opportunity to learn by rote. I would be sitting in the chapel at five-thirty in the morning for my prescribed half-hour meditation and my mind and thoughts were on Jimmy. I enjoyed thinking about Jimmy and how each bone connected to the other. (The song out today, "Knee bone connected to the hip bone, etc." would have been a great help back then.) The human frame really fascinated me. This nursing training, though difficult, opened up a brand-new world for me. I was out of our own convent and my world was expanding. I had met so many people and so many different nationalities. I had to work with the doctors and report to them when they visited their patients. I nursed male patients and had more fun on the male wards than on any other ward. For me, this was like a whole new world of men and people. I was simultaneously assimilating as much of the nursing knowledge as possible and keeping alert to anything and everything that I could learn. Along the way I was absorbing the culture of South Africa. I was delighted to have had an Afrikaans' patient to nurse so that I could practice the Afrikaans language with a real Afrikaans-speaking person. I moved on from the bones to the muscles, ligaments, and organs and physiology and was so happy when I passed the end of the first year's examination in anatomy. I kept saying over and over in my mind, "I did it!" It had been a real achievement for me.

Knowing what I know now and looking back at my behavior then, I probably had very low self-esteem. I was always struggling to keep up with the rest of the world around me and not showing the true me. If they knew me, they would treat me even worse and not think very well of me. I know now, maybe I was afraid of rejection, and that is why any criticism of me personally left me feeling devastated and that the whole world was against me. I was not trying to compete but to "catch up" and make up for what I lacked due to my being brought up in an orphanage. I did not have an education like everyone else had. I did not have a home or know what it was like to have a family. I always seemed to feel different and so inadequate. I grew up with hundreds of children, then I entered the convent where I was never alone. I was nursing, so I was surrounded by people everywhere in the hospital and nurses' home and living quarters. I was probably afraid of anyone getting close to me because I dreaded the usual questions by the nurses such as, "What did your parents do when you told them you were going to enter the convent?" "Did you always want to be a nun?" "Have you got any brothers or sisters?" When they heard I was the only one, I would get responses like, "Oh my God, how did your mother ever let you go to the convent?" Other remarks from time to time would be, "You are such a happy person, you don't behave like an only child!" "You're outgoing and bubbly!" I recall the matron in charge of the nurses' home saying to me, "You are such a live wire and so much fun, what on earth possessed you to go into a convent?" "Don't you feel restricted and confined?" These comments and remarks helped me to feel and think a little better about myself. These were positive remarks from outside that I never received in the convent.

There was a nursing convention being held overseas in England. Students who were in their first year of nursing training were chosen, but only one student from each hospital. The nurse in my group who was elected to go, turned it down because her asthma flared up. She wasn't able to take the pressure. I was chosen to take her place. What an honor! I knew myself, I was not the right person for this honor. There were many nurses in the group who were better choices. I was plagued with the same thoughts as usual, "I can't do this because of who I am and where I've come from, they can't choose me." A surprise awaited me. Mother general arrived to talk to me, and before I knew it, she was in my room and trying to help me with the speech that I would be giving. It was all too sudden for me and I myself really did not know what the conference was going to be about anyway. Mother general herself was all keyed up that one of her nuns was chosen. She praised me and tried to boost my confidence. After all I had previously gone through with the same superior and with all the complaints about me, this whole thing didn't ring true. Why was I, such a wonderful person all of a sudden, and in the matter of a week or so?

When the mother general left, I went to the directress of studies who was the superior of the French nuns and explained that I was not the right person. There were many other nurses more qualified and would be better suited than I would be. I won my case, and another nurse was chosen. I happily went to give the ready-made speech to her if it would help her. She was thrilled to do it and really looked forward to her first trip to England.

Chapter 33

The Sound of Music—My First Movie

One day, in my second year of training, Sister Marietta, the Austrian student who sat next to me in the classroom, told me a movie was coming out soon and asked if I would go along with her to see it. It was called *The Sound of Music*. I said I wouldn't be allowed to go and see it. I would have to get permission but I doubt if I would be given permission even if I asked. The superior, the local superior, and councilors were all in Johannesburg for meetings and so I was able to talk to the acting superior in Durban. The acting superiors said it was a definite no. "Since when do the sisters start going to movies?" I told her I would be going with another sister, and we both had just passed our intermediate examination. I did try my luck! Thinking I may be rewarded and she would allow me to go for passing the examination. "Mein gute! Um Gottes Willen!" was Sister Marietta's remark. ("My goodness! For God's sake!") So when the movie was in the theaters, Sister Marietta and I went to see it. I was excited as this was the first time since I entered the convent that I would see a movie. I was excited but somewhat scared. I was not to breathe a word. Sister Marietta said she would lend me some regular secular clothes, as I would be too conspicuous in the movie theater in a habit. As my hair was too short to go without a veil, I also borrowed a scarf, which I put on like a triangle over my head. Sister Marietta also paid my ticket to the movie. The Order I belonged to appeared more strict than most of the orders of nuns that I trained with as a nurse.

I recall the shock I was in as I entered the movie theater when I saw some familiar faces, (a row of our own nuns) sitting about five rows behind Sister Marietta and myself. I instinctively turned my face away from them so that they would not see or recognize me as I walked to my seat. I was relieved to be able to sit down and kept my face half covered, hopefully I would be unrecognizable. I still felt guilty for being in forbidden territory, but I was a little taken aback on seeing our own sisters present. I later heard the archbishop had given the sisters permission to go and see the movie. It was a very good clean movie for sisters to see. Archbishop Hurley of Durban and of the Natal Province, was a wonderful man, especially when he saved my skin! Needless to say, I saw *The Sound of Music* three times. Some years later, Eileen Hurley, the archbishop's sister, was being nursed by our own sisters at the Mother House, myself included. I would have loved to tell him about the predicament I was in and how he unknowingly had come to my rescue about the movie. He would visit his sister every week and what a stately man he was, tall, dark and handsome. He was an excellent speaker and a very good person, beloved by the people and by all the clergy in South Africa.

The Austrian Sister Marietta, who took me to see *The Sound of Music*, knew the Von Trapp family very well; and she told me to look out for the real Mrs. Von Trapp in the audience. She was sitting in the front row when the Von Trapp sang their farewell song on the stage. I recall people were flocking to see *The Sound of Music*. It was reported one woman went to see it more than three hundred times. I myself saw it three times. Anytime I hear the songs from the movie or even see parts of the movie, it certainly recalls those bygone days of bondage and how our spirits were set free and soared high after that wonderful movie. Julie Andrews was wonderful.

After the movie came out, the nurses gave me the nickname Maria. For a while, I would hear one-liners being sung to me, "How do you solve the problem of Maria?" or "Hi, Maria" in passing. I recall standing still on the hospital staircase to let the senior nurses pass (as was the custom) and as the matron of the hospital was coming down the stairs one day, she said, "Do you know you are becoming very popular now, don't let it go to your head." Wow! In a way, it made me a little scared, but I enjoyed it all and was having so much fun. I was, in a way, kind of scared of the two nuns who were seniors to me in rank, as nurses, and also in religion. I was always careful around them. I certainly didn't want the mother general arriving again to pay me a visit because I was acting like Maria. I came late one day for a lecture, and as I walked into the classroom, the nurses started singing in unison, "How do you solve the problem of Maria? Many a thing you know you ought to tell her, many a thing she ought to understand. Why do you come late again, MARIA?" It was good to have so much innocent fun, even the hospital seemed a happier place after the movie came out. It did something for people, to lift their spirits to another level!

The two sisters in training (previously mentioned), who were seniors to me and kept me in their watchful care in case I would slip up, were not to be seen anywhere. Then the one sister returned without the other sister. I had not heard where she went to, because it was their final year in training. They were almost finished in the nursing course. A day or so later, it was all the talk in the classroom. The other sister had eloped with one of her male patients whom she nursed. I was in shock! Total disbelief! I was left with only one in charge of me.

I enjoyed the nursing training, but they were tough and strict in those days. Kind of like the army and because my eyes were always open to learn, and I learned so much, I used to think it would be wonderful if every girl had the same nursing experience, certainly, a good foundation for life. Most nurses could fill many pages of their experiences while training back in those days. The pranks we got up to, especially on night duty. The trouble we got into and the discipline measured out to us.

During my general nursing training days, I got word from my immediate superior that as many of us as possible, who were foreigners in the country, were to become citizens as soon as possible. A date was arranged for a group of us to go to the court house in Durban. I don't remember the actual place where we went but I guess it was the court house. The reason given was that we would have to leave the country if we did not become citizens. It was a new government law. The Afrikaans people were now in the majority for some time, and it was rumored we will all have to speak Afrikaans. The Afrikaans people were in power for years but new laws were being passed, and more new laws were coming out. Some of them just to reinforce the existing laws. I do not recall the drive to or from the court house, but I certainly remember the scary feeling of standing and waiting in that cold severe-looking court house.

The ceremony was in both languages, Afrikaans and English. Everything was too sudden and too fast, and as I stood and joined with the many in the swearing in of citizenship, my eyes flooded with tears! This caused me to feel out of control. It just dawned on me that I would never see my own country again. It was like being transported back to when I entered the convent in England. I was so very, very homesick for my own native land, Ireland. This citizenship, I suddenly understood, was to be a final farewell forever to Ireland, Belfast, and all my friends back there. The letters from my friends in Ireland were dwindling over the years because we were so far from one another geographically. I decided, in my own mind at that time, that this was a sign from God to move on and leave it all behind for his sake. I tried to do just that but my emotions seemed to surface to the fore and were running my life. How I wished I was more in control of myself. I thought, back then, that these crying spells were a weakness on my part; and I was going to master that like I always did master everything else in my life, in order to cope and be like the rest of the people around me.

Another little surprise came to me, but it was actually a big surprise. In the convent, we did not see any newspapers; and during my training days, there was often papers lying around and thrown out. I would try to get a quick read if I got the time. One day, I picked up a brochure that fell from a newspaper that I was clearing out of a patient's room. The brochure was about a beautician, Eileen Friars. I immediately put the brochure in my nun's large pocket 'til I had time to read it. Every now and then, I would pull it out to look at my name. I was so looking forward to checking out this name of mine—an unusual name. I never forgot the disappointment of not following up the child that I taught in school with this name, when I was unable to pursue my quest. This time, I was not going to let the opportunity pass, especially as I was training in Durban, the same town where the beautician Eileen Friars lived. The chance came when one of the nurses was going into town on a Saturday morning. While the nurse went shopping, I visited Eileen. I related my story briefly and the reason why I came to see her. She herself was a native of Mauritius, an island in the Indian Ocean. She had married a "Friars." Her husband was killed in a plane crash, a small plane that crashed off the east coast of Africa, along the Indian Ocean. My pursuit came to a dead end. Eileen did not know much about her husband's family history.

During my training to become a registered nurse, I came to the realization that people thought of me as a strong person. I myself did not feel that way. I remember a call came through to the floor that I worked on. I had to go down to the foyer of the hospital. I was to talk to the alcoholic patient who was out of control. The matron said, "He will listen to you, and you are strong enough to manage him!" When I got down there, he hugged me and his grip was so tight, I struggled to get away from him. I expected to be punched at any moment. When he did release me, he started to preach and holler and throw his arms up in the air. "I am Jesus Christ. I have come for you. I have saved you. Come with me, etc.!" He started to scream and shout out religious slogans, and at the same time, pulling me along the corridor with him. I certainly did not feel strong enough to handle this man. In those days, there were no security guards. There was just one man, a janitor, who would be on guard to lock up at night and check around the place.

A couple of times I was called to come out and help to kill snakes. Generally, I was a brave soul. I would always tell them nurses help to save lives, not "kill." Most of the snakes were only about twelve to fifteen inches long. The largest and longest snake I saw was when I was in my first year in South Africa. I was walking uphill to the school one early morning. A huge wiggling snake took up the width of the road. There was no way I could try to pass it. It was, I believe, a black mamba. Some men were digging part of the grounds near the school, so it seemed they disturbed the snakes in the process. "So this is what a snake really looks like." Scary indeed, but I couldn't help noticing the beautiful satiny, black velvety skin. The diameter of the black mamba was roughly about fifteen to twenty inches and tapered off at the tail. I was indeed terrified! I returned to the clinic, which I had passed on the way before I got to the convent. The doctor, Sister Gertrudis, got in the Land Rover, with a few African men and she made some attempts to drive her Land Rover over the snake's head. The men would throw stones and some of the men would go after it with their machetes. Team work! And this was not the first time they attacked a snake. The snakes I first saw in the shed close to the first school where I taught were all beautiful in colors. I was warned how deadly dangerous they were. We were always on the look out for them when we went outside.

All my general nursing training was done in Durban. During these three years of training, I had many opportunities to see different parts of the city. There was something about Durban that appealed to me. It was many years later when I learned that the city hall in Durban was built as a replica of the city hall in Belfast, Northern Ireland. That was probably the familiarity of the place that made me feel at home there without knowing the reason at the time. Durban was a bright colorful city, especially along the promenade. I was astonished and really surprised to see such a well built-up city in Africa. The city was built so that most of the streets of Durban go right down toward the beach. Durban is built right along the beachfront. Also right along the promenade, one could see the rickshaw men in their very lively and colorful regalia. The rickshaws would be waiting outside the hotels on the beachfronts for overseas' visitors and officials so that they could take them for a ride in their two-wheeler carts. The rickshaws were always very popular with the tourists.

Part of my training also was to go to the Addington Hospital in Durban to the children's section for practical hands on at the children's hospital; it was a three-month stay. Addington Hospital was right on the beachfront; I got the opportunity to go swimming with some of the nurses. It was so much fun and much stress release for all of us. We nurses were encouraged to go to the beach. It was sweltering hot in summer that we were happy to go down. What was unique was that the swimming pools were built in the sea at the water's edge and this made it really safe to go in. A number of these built-in swimming pools were right along the beach. I had an excuse to go right along with the nurses without asking permission back in the convent. It was freedom for me and the greatest tonic! Many nurses applied for midwifery training at Addington College Hospital because it was close to the beach. There was always a long waiting list for nurses to gain admission to Addington Hospital.

Chapter 34

Scary Times

As I mentioned, I was always known as a strong person. When I worked in the hospital wards at night especially, on night duty, I would be literally terrified of the monstrous cockroaches running along the passages of the wards. Giving out medicines at night was a terrifying ordeal for me. The patients would have water in carafes and drinking glasses next to their beds on their lockers. Almost every room you entered would have a cockroach floating or wiggling in the standing drinking glass. I usually had to go and get fresh water at the tap because I would be greeted by a cockroach in the water. Often the patient would say, "Save your step, I have water right here next to me." But I would never mention why I was getting fresh water. In the dark, they couldn't see the cockroaches that I was emptying out with the water. If one jumped on me, I would let out a yell. Nights was a scary time in more ways than I can think of. I recall once while sitting alone at the nurses' desk in the nurses' station one night, while I was writing my nurse's reports, and suddenly I saw two cockroaches playing together in the corner of the room. I was closely observing them from a distance and wasn't aware that an elderly male patient was coming down the hallway. *Flipperty flop, flipperty flop*, all the way and as the sound appeared to be coming closer and closer to me, I was like frozen in time. I really couldn't figure out what that sound could be. I just sat motionless 'til the person almost arrived. But finally instead of remaining, I quickly escaped out the open veranda door that led to the outside grounds. I peeped in the window from outside to see the ghost of the night arriving. It was a ninety-year-old patient, who was lost and limping along toward where he saw light coming from the nurses' station. I realized after all, I was not as strong or as brave as I was made out to be by the authorities in the hospital.

While on that topic, I was often asked to accompany another nurse down to the lowest level of the hospital to where the mortuary was located. We took a man who died during the same night on our ward to the basement on a gurney. In those days, we nurses did the laying out of the patients when they died and took them down to the hospital mortuary ourselves. We wheeled the patient into the room where the dead were laid out temporarily, and the arm of the dead man next to us slipped off the gurney and hung down to his side. Both of us student nurses screamed out in total shock. We both jumped so fast and ran along the dark corridor to the elevators. Scary incidents always seemed to happen in the wee hours of the morning on night duty. Maybe it was because of that time in the morning that scary things happened in our imagination; things appeared as monsters in the dark of night.

After becoming a registered nurse, I was transferred to the maternity hospital in Johannesburg, back to our own convent in "Joburg" as it was called, six thousand feet above sea level and much, much colder in the winter than I ever remembered to be in Ireland. I fell into the daily routine as it was all familiar to me. Now, of course, I was a trained nurse with a lot more confidence in myself. There were many more nurse aids and domestic workers in the hospital than when I had been assigned there before. Though I was to oversee all aspects of the work on my floor, I could concentrate now on my patients and babies in the nursery.

I was ready for a new start. It was good to be back again among the sisters. I had a good feeling of security, but everything seemed so archaic. I was also tied to the job. We were on duty every single day. No days off and no time off during the day. If one is so tired, it is very difficult to concentrate or be at one's best. Being sisters, we certainly did not ever show any sign of tiredness or talk of how tired we were. We were religious sisters who are required to be there to show an example of hard work and loyalty. Sunday was the same as every other day. So compared to the outside secular world, we nursing sisters were working overtime every single day. With the additional help of assistant nurses, we were still short staffed. Any nurses forced or asked to work overtime cannot give of their best if they are overworked and under pressure for most of the time. The life of the patients depends on the nurses. They are there twenty-four hours a day. They are most intimately involved in their care and are doing bedside nursing and care around the clock in contrast to doctors who arrive each day and spend only a few minutes at the bedside, visiting the patients.

Chapter 35

Baby Found at Doorstep

One morning in Joburg, the chaplain of the convent arrived to say the 7:00 AM Mass. At the front entrance of the hospital, he found a black baby. This was a hospital for whites only. Apartheid existed then. The baby's head had bruises and scars and stale blood on it. We doctored the baby and kept him; and everyone just fell in love with him. The baby was placed in the nursery where I was working. The chaplain's first name was Peter and my name was Sister Peter, so naturally we called the baby, Peter. I felt like the mother of that baby and couldn't wait to go on the wards in the morning to see him. We had kept him for about six months. Then he was taken away by the social workers. Oh, how I missed him and wondered how life turned out for him.

Another day, when I was relieving the sister in the front office for a lunch break, I saw myself face-to-face with a young twenty-one-year-old man. He came for one purpose, and that was to request the hospital to look up his files. He had been born in our hospital and had been looking for his biological mother. He did not want his parents who adopted him and brought him up to know of his being at the hospital in search of his biological mother. I myself had forgotten the hospital had been in existence for that length of time. This young man left an indelible impression on me. I can still see his face, and I felt the urgency of his request. He was not leaving the hospital 'til he got the information he wanted. There were also many other people who were trying to find their biological mothers. This young twenty-one-year-old was the first person I dealt with. I'll call him John. I tried to explain the situation to him that I didn't think we had the right or permission to do that. I explained I was a nurse and did not have access to his files. He became so angry at my response. I told him the matron of the hospital would see him soon, and she would explain the situation to him. I sat down next to him in the foyer and said, "John, can I get you a drink of water or something?" "No," he rejected angrily. "I've told you what I came for and don't offer me anything else." He was on a single mission and I understood his rage. I only recall later that the matron went through some papers with him and probably, because he was of age, may have supplied him with the information. I really cannot recall the outcome. I certainly could identify with his search for his own mother. Was I not in the same position as he? If he only knew! My longing to find my mother unfortunately had come to a dead end. I had no resources, no social workers in those days, and as the convent didn't know my quest and I being so far away in Africa, the chances were nil of ever finding her. So I could relate and feel for this young man!

There was a convent in Johannesburg of Good Shepherd nuns who took in girls who were unmarried and pregnant. It was a wonderful organization. The nuns sheltered the girls from the public eye. When the time drew near for any of the girls to deliver their babies, the sisters would bring them to our maternity hospital to deliver. If there were a large number of patients waiting to deliver, I was often called on to help in the delivery room. We would all pitch in and help where we could. For the first time, I happened to assist the nurse in the delivery of one of these unmarried girls. The nurse had previously instructed me that I was to take the baby immediately after the doctor had attended to it and wheel it outside to another room. The bassinet was to be entirely covered with a drawer sheet. The mother was not to see her baby. This was the first time I had to do something like this. I was so overcome with emotion like a sudden eruption. Wheeling the baby out from the delivery room covered entirely with a cloth, and taking the baby to an empty room away from his mother was too much for me! I felt I was committing a very grave sin by depriving the baby from its very life and blood. Such an emotional effect this incident had on me that I was becoming physically sick from it all. I just could not handle myself. It was, I think, the unexpectedness of it all. "Was this the way they did it?" "Was this what happened to me?" What an experience this was for me. I thought and thought about it and could not believe what happened. I was reliving the whole scene of my mother delivering me and never seeing me ever again after that. I was emotionally drained afterward, but I had to make a big effort to go back into the delivery room again. The doctor noticed I didn't look well. I had to playact and tell them I felt sick. The nurse brought me a glucose drink to pick me up. For a long time afterward, I was haunted by this separation of the mother and child. How could any mother abandon her baby? Later, when I was taking care of the mother, I saw her weeping as if she wouldn't be comforted. Then, of course, I thought of my mother and wondered did she ever cry when she gave me up. Did she ever think of me again? What did my mother do after she abandoned me? How could she go about her work and not ever think of me again?

Today, I know that I was placed in an orphanage at the age of five and a half or six and not as a baby. I found this information when I visited Ireland in the late nineties. Up to this time, I thought I had been put in there as a baby.

In due course, I went for midwifery training at the Queen Victoria Hospital in Johannesburg. It was not far from our own convent hospital, so I would go home on my days off. This was a great training for me and an eye-opener to the real world. It was a White hospital but catered more to the poor people. I saw, first hand, how the "poor whites" lived (as they were called) when I had to do part of my nursing training out on "district nursing." The name "poor whites" was given them to distinguish them from the blacks who were poor. The "poor whites" in Joburg were of every race. There were many immigrants, mainly Portuguese from the west coast of Africa and Mozambique in south eastern Africa.

Our own maternity hospital in Johannesburg was situated on a hill with beautiful grounds and architectural descending landscapes. Flowers were everywhere, such beautiful bright colors you could only see in South Africa or in warmer climates. The contrast of these beautifully cultivated grounds, which gave an impression of peace and abundance and to see the chaos in the valley below of so many poor people in make-shift tents and poor housing, trying to make a living. Most of the people were immigrants, many of them Portuguese who settled in Johannesburg. I couldn't help seeing what was pretty obvious. We were actually catering to the rich, while the poor people were in such dire needs. Our schools also as well as our hospitals were for the children of parents who could pay the required tuition fees. I guess, from where I was coming from, i.e., a poor background, maybe it just hit me in the face. I recall after some time, asking one of the sisters in the convent, why we didn't care more for the poor? Her reply was, "Rich or poor, they are all human beings, and the rich people are the ones who are more spiritually in need." I then said to her, "We are not dealing with their spiritual needs but their physical needs and wants. As nurses, that is our profession." Sister continued, "Just think of our very presence in the hospital that in itself sends a message." I was left with my thoughts, which made very little sense from what Sister had just explained.

While I worked in the Johannesburg Hospital, we sisters had what was called visitation. That meant, the highest superior would visit the convent and each of the sisters had to present herself to her. By this time, a few of us sisters had decided to get together and talk out some of the ideas she had put forward in her first talk or sermon, which she had given to the entire community after her arrival. The talk had such an effect on me that I had to let off steam. The superior spoke on our spiritual life, which was understandable and expected; but she put so much stress and emphasis on our outward behavior, which certainly was not acceptable for us as sisters, we knew that. What I meant by outward behavior was the dashing back and forth, and rushing everywhere. The continuous hyperactivity we certainly could not give of our best toward the patients or the doctors. We lived our time on the wards in fear we had forgotten to do something, especially if it was important. We were always trying to catch up. The cause of all this was "shortage of staff," secular staff, as well as shortage of sisters. We were pulled in every direction to help out, and I would be worried that my unit would not be taken care of while I was called elsewhere on the wards. This was not just now and again but on a continuous basis. So a few of the sisters got together to let the superior know our outward behavior would not change 'til the problem of the shortage of staff was settled. We were aware she could not pull sisters from her sleeve, but she could do something about hiring secular nurses (as they were called) to relieve the pressure we were under. The word *decorum* was taught in the novitiate, and this is what the present mother general was now trying to instill in us again, which could not be achieved until we got some "help." Normally, we sisters just took and accepted everything and we worked like slaves really. A patient said to me one day, "You know, I never thought that nuns worked so hard. I thought they were in the convents, praying most of the day. You all work like a team of horses!" So the problem of overwork in the hospital was not taken care of and the mother general left and we continued as before. It felt good that we had the opportunity to have our say, even though we felt it was not accepted. It was just good to be able to get it out to the right source. The work was so hectic and there was no letting up. We were trained in the novitiate to use every minute of our time and not waste it. Now, we certainly did not have enough time in our day. We would grab a bite of food and get back to work. We'd get a drink of water and rush back to work. Many times, we would have patients in the labor wards at different stages of labor, and to keep a track on them all was not easy. When the doctors would call to find out what was going on with their patients, it was difficult to keep it straight as to who his patient was. For us, nightmares were all around. Good religious did not complain. It was humanly impossible to treat the patients the way we would treat Christ himself. That was, of course, the way we were told and taught in the novitiate. This was a situation not many people would have tolerated. I was on edge most of the time, trying to cope with impossible situations. To be Christlike, showing gentleness and kindness under such hectic circumstances and pressure was next to impossible. The mother general, who was the highest authority in the convent, had no idea of how it goes in a hospital. She was not informed about the dire need for nurses 'til we spoke to her.

The fact of the matter was, that working under such pressure and working long hours was not only bad for the nurses' health, but created a climate that was just purely dangerous. We were liable to make many mistakes. Once an error is made in the nursing profession, it can be dangerous. The impact of the staff shortage led to poor quality of care and those of us who only wanted to take care of patients had to suffer rebuffs and criticisms from the doctors and patients and others in charge. Besides nursing, we had so many non-nursing jobs to do, such as transporting patients and moving beds from one end of the hospital to the other. I would help to carry these beds willingly, and do anything to help the hospital shortage. Moving beds and furniture was the usual thing for us in my early days of nursing, and we thought we were strong and could manage almost anything. There were no workmen or janitors in those days. We nuns did the heavy labor. Fortunately, we did not have to do the domestic cleaning, but we had to show the black domestic workers what they had to do and supervise them.

Chapter 36

Happy Birthday

One night, I was working in the delivery room and assisting a patient who was at the pushing stage. I told the patient her doctor had arrived. She said, "Don't make me push, Sister, because I don't want the baby to come 'til after midnight." The doctor changed into his scrubs and walked into the room singing "Happy Birthday" to us. That was the reason she did not want the baby before midnight. I was not used to having birthday celebrations in the convent. So when the baby arrived at twelve minutes after midnight, I immediately wrote the date and time of birth, then realized it was also my birthday. So I mentioned it, and of course they were all amazed. The doctor, the patient, the patient's husband, their first child, and the nurse, all those people in the delivery room had birthdays on the same day! The news spread around and was in the local paper the next day. It was quite unique! What are the chances of this ever happening again in my lifetime?

After the delivery, the doctor drove in his car to the Dutch bakery close by that was open all night and returned with a cake for all of us. It was a great wee party and a needed reprieve from the pressure of work that night. The young mother, no doubt, still remembers that delivery. I was working in our own convent hospital in Pretoria at that time.

Most of us sisters preferred to work in our hospital in Pretoria than in the Johannesburg Hospital. Pretoria itself is a friendlier place, and the hospital was smaller. This is what made it a calmer, homier, and friendlier place. The South African people are more laid-back than people from European countries. There was a homey atmosphere here in Pretoria. I just fell in love with the place and the people.

In Africa, in general, but especially the people in Pretoria are not rushing to and fro. They are quiet, reserved, and laid-back. People mostly had time to stand and chat if you met them in the street. They made you feel like one of them. It was a difference of an hour's drive by car from Johannesburg to Pretoria. I was moved back and forth according to the needs in different hospitals. Pretoria was my favorite place. Even though summer heat was sometimes unbearable in Pretoria. There was no air-conditioning in the summer or central heating in the winter.

The winters were very cold in the morning and evening, but the winter only lasted for about three months. There were fans placed everywhere in the summer months, which was about nine months out of the year. Some places were hotter than others. I found the Mother House to be one of the hottest places I lived in. It was situated a little inland in a valley from the Indian Ocean. Archbishop Hurley once remarked, "You, sisters, will not go to purgatory. You have your purgatory right here." It was stifling, sweltering heat, and the smell of perspiration all around. I recall when I taught school at the Mother House, I would have to put a large folded handkerchief under my nun's starched forehead band to absorb the perspiration. I always brought a change of handkerchiefs in my pocket; and when washed, they would dry quickly in the heat. Most of our sisters nursed or taught in our own private hospitals and private schools. Many of the sisters also worked out in the rural areas among the Africans. I visited some of these mission places and was astonished at how the sisters could live there. It was like out in the wilds. No sign of man or beast around, though thank God, there were no beasts to be seen. Monkeys were plentiful everywhere, climbing trees, etc., especially in Durban area. The monkeys would come to the convent windowsills and sit there with their pitiful faces 'til they got the food they wanted. I sure enjoyed watching them swinging from the branches of the trees. They seemed to understand all that was going on. It was a good diversion from just work all the time. It was great to watch the monkeys taking care of one another, each of them taking turns of examining each other's backs and looking for fleas all over their bodies, etc. They were so meticulous in their search and spent hours doing this. I loved to watch their playfulness and see them swinging from branch to branch. I did not see too many monkeys in Johannesburg, or Pretoria, but it might have been because we were indoors all day; and there were not many trees left in the built-up towns and cities of Pretoria or Johannesburg.

Chapter 37

Tragic Events Thrown in with Happy Events

One incident that left an indelible impression on me was when I worked in the hospital in Johannesburg and was serving the breakfast trays out to the patients. This particular mother was very upset. She told me to take that monster (her own baby) and put it in the garbage bag. I, of course, had not had the report from the night nurse at that time, so I was curious to find out what she was so angry about. When I entered her room again to bring fresh water in the carafe, she said, "I hope you did what I told you to do." I was taken aback and tried to explain I had not had reports from the night shift yet. I would check it out. She immediately asked me for a bag so that she herself would dispose of the baby. I never saw the mother again. She left the hospital, discharged herself, and took the baby or "monster" as she called it with her in a plastic bag. There was obviously some serious abnormality with her baby that she could not deal with.

Generally, dealing and taking care of mothers and babies was a happy time. Once anything abnormal happened for example, when a mother lost her baby, it would have a devastating effect on everyone, not just the mother. One could also feel the sadness and demoralizing effect among the sisters and staff in losing a mother; it was just as treacherous as losing a baby and it happened more in those days than it does today. Many incidences happened to me. I recall being called up to help right after church one early morning to the delivery room in the hospital. The matron said, "Please go in, wash the patient, and transfer her to her room, number so and so, on the second floor." I walked in the labor room and shock of shocks, the patient was dead! The husband had just left her bedside to go home after the happy event!

Many tragic events happened over the period of about twenty years that I spent in maternity work in both hospitals. During one's training as a midwife, one learns of all the abnormalities that can occur in babies, but few hardly ever experience a fraction of them. One of the most difficult things I could not get up the courage or stamina to do was to tube feed the babies that were anencephalic babies (born without a brain). We would cover the exposed head and just leave the face showing. In this way, we could cope better. We all knew this condition was incompatible with life, but we used to feed the babies to keep them comfortable.

Besides abnormalities in the newborn, there were many medical problems. Most of these could be treated, and what a joy and delight it was to see sick or very ill babies improving with treatment. I remember being assigned to the premature nursery. We also admitted sick babies to the premature nursery. This day, I recall admitting twins that looked so different. I said to the pediatrician, "What's going on here?" "It's very simple, Sister. One of them was more greedy than the other!" the doctor replied. One twin had most of the red blood cells, while the other one looked so anemic. They were identical twins. I was so very interested to see how this situation would be treated. Intravenous fluids were set up, and blood was taken directly from the greedy baby and infused back directly to the other twin. So simple! It was wonderful to watch the doctor handling this delicate situation. I was intrigued at the simplicity of the treatment. Return the blood back that was stolen!

I will never forget when I was training as a midwife in the Queen Victoria Hospital in Johannesburg. I returned from a lunch break one day and was met by the senior nurse in charge of the students, and one of the tutors was standing next to her. I was called aside and told that I had only delivered one baby and that the second baby was still inside. How could I go to lunch and leave the mother with the second twin still inside her? Though I wasn't entirely responsible as a student in training, I felt shaken and speechless that we didn't know the other twin was not delivered. I was so gullible and believed what they told me and then, they showed us what should have been a second twin that they had delivered while we were at lunch. They delivered an elongated piece of tissue-looking substance and it was called papier mache. This was what they meant by the second twin. This was a one-time experience for me and it never occurred again. I was ready for any surprises after that experience. I remember trying to look up "papier mache" with regard to medical terms. I never found it. I had never heard of it before. The medical student on duty was measuring the length of the tissue. When he stretched it out, it measured over thirty inches long. He said to me, "Didn't you ever play with that stuff as a child?" Well, "I lived and learned."

Midwifery nursing was never dull. It would pop surprises every now and again. Over a span of twenty years, I gained so much and learned so much.

My one regret, as sisters working in the hospitals back then, was the shortage of staff. We did our duties well and worked hard, but we certainly did not have time to spend any extra time with the patients. We did what we had to for the patients, but the work was more important. We did not get connected on a personal level with any of the patients at any time.

Chapter 38

African Hospital

I spent some years in Pretoria and some in Johannesburg, in the White hospitals, then I was transferred to an African Hospital. This was run by our own sisters and was built from the money that came from our white maternity hospitals and from the German Mission Center in Germany. X-ray equipment and all the other necessary equipment for the hospital came from Germany. It was sometime during those years that I spent in Johannesburg and Pretoria, this Black hospital was built.

The hospital was situated in Natal, close to Durban and close to our Mother House. The first time I saw where the hospital was located, I was spellbound at the splendid view from all angles of the hospital. There were undulating hills of different shades and colors and mountains in the distance all around. The scenery I was gazing at was called the Valley of a Thousand Hills. It stretched for miles all around. It was just too magnificent to describe. So breathtaking! When my thoughts fly back to Africa, I visualize this scene of the Valley of a Thousand Hills. Somewhere between my moving around, I recall having a short stay back at the Mother House. Sister Gertrudis, who was our medical doctor, took me to see the clinic. I had a good picture of what was being done at the clinic. The clinic was situated in the grounds of the Mother House. In fact, when we would line up to go for prayer service to the chapel, we would pass the clinic and the patients would all be sitting around outside on the ground, with either breast-feeding their babies or waiting to be attended to by our sister nurses or the doctor. This kind of work so appealed to me, and I was energized and ready for action. This is the real work for the poor! Hordes of Africans would swarm around the clinic, and I wondered if the nurses ever got to see all the patients, but they did.

Many of the patients walked for miles and miles to get to the clinic. Some of them had very serious medical problems, some that could not even be diagnosed. I saw some people arriving at the clinic with very swollen legs and feet (elephantiasis) and their skin was so thick, like an elephant's skin. I was amazed they could even walk, let alone walk for miles. I was present for the birth of one of the patients at the clinic and gaped in shock and surprise to see the same patient up and walking shortly afterward, carrying her baby straddled on her back and heading for the road home. All these scenes were an everyday occurrence at the clinic. I couldn't help but compare this delivery to the deliveries in the White hospitals. Any African patients who came to the clinic and were unable to be treated at the clinic because of the seriousness of their illness or whatever the reason, would be driven to the hospital in the clinic ambulance or in the Land Rover. It was a real eye-opener to me and just marvelous work on the part of the sisters and staff (This was the Land Rover used to ride over the snakes that I mentioned earlier.) The sister, Sister Gertrudis, who was the medical doctor at the Mother House Clinic, asked me one day if I would like to go with her for a ride. I was somewhat free-floating at that time. No sister traveled alone. She had to have a companion with her. So the doctor, Sr. Gertrudis, took me along with her and gave me the history of the land as we rode along. It was a very hot, humid day in the summer. As we drove along the road, the dust was rising up behind us; the air was thick and heavy, and no air-conditioning in the car in those days. Sister said there is very little rain in the country; hence, the dust everywhere. The summers are very dry. We were driving along dirt, making shift roads, and stopping at some of the kraals where the native Africans lived. The kraals generally had some kind of fence to keep the animals from straying. The fences enclosed livestock, goats, dogs, chickens, etc. This particular kraal where we stopped had so many people, babies, and children. I couldn't help wondering where they all lived. Sister said they slept on the cement floors inside their huts. The shapes of the huts were round, so more people could fit in. Some did sleep on mats, which they rolled up during the day. In the center of most of the huts were large cast iron pots, which were used for cooking. No knives or forks were used. Generally, the people cooked maize or rice; and I saw a big cast iron pot of what looked like porridge, which is what they have for their meals. All sit around the pot and eat with their fingers. It is all so natural but it is such a different culture. Everywhere we went or stopped, Sister knew most of the people. What a joy and delight showed on their faces when they had the Sister (doctor) visiting them. Sister would remember everything about them and their children.

Of course, she was fluent in Zulu and spoke in Zulu to them all the time. On the dirt roads, there were many people, usually women carrying heavy bundles on their heads as they walked along in their bare feet. I saw very few wearing sandals. Even the children are trained from very young to master the art of carrying heavy pots and large jugs of water on their heads. Often the women would have their babies on their backs while at the same time, carrying enormous bags or bundles on their heads.

There was no running water in any of these huts or kraals. The water had to be fetched from the nearest large building such as a school or hospital. Some had to pump the water from a well if it was nearby. Most of the women were at home taking care of their livestock and their children, while their husbands were in the big cities working in the coal mines and diamond mines.

Kimberley was the diamond mine, but there were many other towns and places where the men had to travel to get to work in the mines. The men stayed in these mine locations while working, and it was often months and years before their men folk would come home from the compounds. Women stayed home to be responsible for everything.

We arrived at our destination, which was a leprosarium. Sister had packed the car before we left with medicines, mostly sulfur drugs, with boxes of old sheets and cut up sheets for bandages, some kind of oil to lubricate the wounds or lesions of the skin. All the medicines were from Germany. I have to admit, when I saw these lepers, I was just petrified; I was afraid I would catch the disease. I remembered learning about this disease as part of my general training. It was called Hansen's disease, but I had never given it another thought. Here I was face-to-face with it, and it scared me. I kept my distance but when I saw the doctor talking to them and touching them, I was edified. I had never seen such gross deformities, especially of the hands, feet, and limbs. Sister mentioned that if my immune system is strong, I won't catch it. All I wanted to do was get out of there as fast as I could. Later, I thought how selfish I was, thinking only of myself, when these poor people actually needed other humans to help them.

I sat in the car for the return home to the Mother House. Perspiration was exuding from every pore. I was sitting in wet clothes, which was partly due to the intense heat and the effect of the terrible fear when I saw the lepers and smelled the foul odor when I arrived. I remember I was longing for a drink of water, just to moisten my dry mouth. The dust was everywhere. If we closed the windows, it became stifling inside the car; and if we opened them, we got all the dust coming in. How I admired this sister (doctor)—so selfless and serving humanity all day long, in the clinics and elsewhere, just doing her duties. In the heat of the day and every day. Sometimes, when the doctor would try to leave the clinic for a lunch break or for prescribed prayers at certain times throughout the day, the bell would call her back to the clinic again. She was selfless in her service of these poor people.

Later, I was transferred to the African Hospital in Durban. There was a totally different atmosphere from the White hospital in Johannesburg that I had just left. Once I got into the everyday routine and became familiar with the schedules of the hospital, I realized that there was a different atmosphere. There was the normal pressure and tension of any hospital experience, but there was no dashing and rushing about as if the entire running of the hospital depended on me. What was just wonderful was the fact that each sister was able to take off for half a day! We could be called back on duty if we were needed, but we had to make up the free time later when things grew easier in the wards. It was a kind of culture shock for me within Africa itself, to be transferred from the White hospital to the Black hospital, but the nursing sisters who were there many years before me would enlighten and instruct me. One of the sisters, who worked in the administration and admission office, was very helpful. She spoke the Zulu language fluently. She herself said she still was trying to learn the language. It was not easy trying to find an interpreter every day because we were dealing with so many different patients all day long. This hospital was also a training school for nurse aids and registered nurses and very many of the trainees spoke enough English, which was a big help indeed. The problem with the languages was that some Africans spoke other languages. Depending on where they came from, some of the Africans spoke Afrikaans (the white man's language) and some spoke English.

In the beginning, it certainly was a challenge for me, but I got used to it all. Even the names of the patients were so difficult to try and remember because I was having a tough time trying to put a name to a face. All the black people looked the same to me anyway when I first saw them, but I became used to the faces and of course, carried a notebook with the names in my large nun's pocket. The Africans had their own African names but they had also English and Afrikaan's names. Names like Pretty, Beautiful, Adorable, etc., were given to them at their birth and usually associated with and around their birth. Often the name given to the baby was taken from the first person at the birth or some incident that occurred surrounding the birth, or some person present given at the birth.

I remember the sister in the admitting office calling a student nurse and myself to come down and take a patient up to her ward. The student nurse was to admit her as part of her training. The patient's name was Psychology. Now this threw me for a loop, and it took me some time to understand this was the patient's name. The sister actually knew this patient and remembered when this patient was born and how she came to have that name. The story was that the baby was very ill when she was born and was placed in an incubator. When the mother was able to get out of bed for the first time, she saw the doctor standing next to the incubator with his hands to his chin, as if he was thinking very hard on this case. The mother's relatives looked up in the dictionary and found psychology was the study of the mind. So the baby was given the name Psychology. She is now ten or eleven years old. The admitting office had so many difficult times trying to even just find out the age of the people who were admitted to the hospital. The patients would try to help by going back in history to give the best guess of their age. For example, they were born on a specific occasion or between certain historic occasions, or when a church was built, and when a child was born around some particular event. There were numerous challenges, and so much fun and learning came with it all.

I loved to go over to the African hospital to be there by seven in the morning. I would walk into the ward of about twenty to thirty patients and be greeted by song. The patients, who were able to get from their beds, would dance and clap their hands in the center aisle. Many of the sisters would join in the dancing with the patients but, in the beginning, I felt quite inhibited. Coming from Ireland where I could get up and do the jigs and hornpipes, it didn't take me long before I was up swinging and dancing with them. Music, rhythm, and dance were so much a part of their very being. Where (nursing in a White hospital) would I get such a hearty welcome of music and dance so early in the morning?

If a patient in the ward was very ill or if a patient died, the other patients in that ward, out of respect, would keep the silence; and they would help the other patients when necessary. I often heard the sisters saying they loved to work with the Africans. I heard the teachers saying the same thing. Now I understand why they did. I was very happy in the Black hospital and wished to stay there. These people were really in dire need of care, medical or otherwise. Every day, the clinics were full of sick patients and the hospital was always full. Many of the patients would not sleep on the beds. They would rather lie on the floor. Sisters explained they were used to sleeping on the floor all their lives and many of them could not get used to the soft beds in the hospitals. I saw some of the most critical patients who were very ill, many of them just undiagnosed. There was no diagnosis for them. There was tuberculosis, typhoid, cholera, and many with diseases peculiar to Africa, like tropical diseases. AIDS was unheard of back then, but no doubt, there were many patients who had it and patients just lay there, looking so emaciated and dying. In this hospital, I felt I was needed because the patients were so very ill.

All the mission hospitals had the same problem, that of shortage of doctors. It was as if the sisters were acting as doctors as well as nurses. Most of the time, we had no option but to treat the patients as we saw fit.

One of the nursing sisters said to me one day, "You will see many awful cases here, but one has to prepare for the worst." She said when she herself was new in the hospital, she thought she couldn't stay, when she saw some of the terrible situations and conditions the patients were in. "You know, you just have to steel yourself and face the terrible situations." I thought, well I could probably handle most situations and face each day as it comes. I was doing fine 'til one of the student nurses called me in to see a pot full of wiggly worms that a child had just passed. She said, "I'm supposed to call the sister to check it!" This was the first time I had seen such a specimen! I was petrified and at the same time I didn't know what I was supposed to check. I also, at the same time, did not want to show my ignorance in front of the student nurse. Then the nurse said, "Sister, I think you are supposed to count the worms." I said, "What!" She was right! I also had to look for the head of the worm. It was a tapeworm, and it was so long it filled the pot. I was truly scared. Many of the patients who were children were admitted for some illness, but all of them had to be dewormed. There were special medicines for different kinds of worms. One of the saddest cases I witnessed in the hospital was that of an eleven-year-old boy lying in bed, very ill, and was unconscious. One of the sisters called me to look in on him, and she forewarned me I was to expect the worst. I was horrified at the picture I saw. All kinds of worms were crawling over him and coming out of every orifice of his body. His eyes, ears, nose, and mouth were eaten away with worms. Fortunately, the boy was unconscious. This ungodly sight was so horrendous. Everything I experienced in my nursing days after that terrible experience was much easier to handle. Many times, I would hear remarks in the hospital, "So much suffering and so little comfort for them." The patients themselves had an infinite amount of patience and that was what amazed me in spite of their terrible conditions. How often did I hear the sisters saying, "God, they are so very patient and accepting of everything."

One could learn many lessons from them, such as the fact the Africans accepted and took life's dealings, or whatever came their way, as a natural part of life.

Snake bites were a common diagnosis of many admissions to the hospital. I had heard if a snake entered the hut on the night of a couple's wedding, it was a good omen, sign of fertility for them both. Treatment depended on the type of snake that had bitten the patient. What a different world existed here in this mission hospital. The name of the hospital in the Zulu language was Osindisweni, pronounced Oh-sin-dis-wen-ee, which meant, "the place of healing."

One of the many customs among the Zulu people was to have special ceremonies for the males who come of age. So generally, at the age of thirteen, the boys would be circumcised. This removal of the foreskin was not done under very sterile circumstances. We would have patients admitted to the clinics, or hospital, with septicemia after the surgery. This was a very painful ordeal and consequently, a very painful treatment. I often thought of the circumcisions that were done in our White hospitals. I could never understand why the Jewish rabbi, or whatever the person was called, perform the circumcision on Jewish boys. I think he was called a "montel", who only did circumcisions in our bris room. I used to think this procedure should have been done in a hospital under sterile conditions. Here, in the mission hospital, it was pitiful to see these septic conditions that often could not be treated but had deadly consequences. Of course, this was all part of the African culture and rituals that had been part of their lives for centuries.

The country of Africa grew on me, and it was such a magnificent wide-open country, unpolluted and unspoiled. In the summer, there was almost always a clear blue sky every day, hardly a cloud to be seen in the sky. At night, when the darkness descended, the stars shone so clear and bright and there seemed to be millions and trillions of stars. No electric lights to spoil the heavenly view. When the moon shone over the river, which flowed along at the bottom of the convent of the Mother House, the place was like fairyland, it would have made a romantic setting for any new couples. Often, when there was a wedding in the village or a place nearby, the silence would be broken by the celebration, somewhere down the river, of heavy beaten drums by the Africans out in the darkness. These celebrations would go on for hours and often through the weekend. It was sometimes very hard to get some sleep while the drums were beating at night.

In place of a dowry, a woman or young girl would bring livestock to her husband; the big offer would be a goat. Usually, for any big celebration, a goat was killed for the feast and cooked out in the open, similar to a barbeque here, was called "braaivleis" in South Africa.

Africa, with all its beauty, had many problems. Some were due to the climate of very little rainfall. Then again, we would have the monsoon rains. After months of drought that left the land dry and parched, the deluge of rain would wash the soil away. The cars and ambulances would get stuck in the wet mud. Any stagnant water would just breed mosquitoes. I can't forget the time when the nearest village, near the Mother House, which was called Verulam, became infected with mosquitoes. A factory had piles of wood stored in water and the water was not changed, so mosquitoes multiplied and were all over the hospital, the clinic, and the schools situated on the grounds of the Mother House. It was a terrible time for everyone. Parents got word of the mosquitoes, and they came out to our boarding schools and took their children back home. We all had to sleep under the mosquito netting. This didn't help at all as the mosquitoes got in and under and drove us all berserk. We always had mosquitoes in South Africa, but never to this extent and it took months before we finally got rid of them, though not totally. Due to poor hygiene and no running water, many of the people suffered from cholera and typhoid, which was very common. Certain parts of Africa would have outbreaks of malaria due to mosquitoes flying around everywhere and just "waiting in the wings," so to speak. A bite from the female *Anopheles* mosquito would cause malaria. Any person who got malaria was never really totally freed from the disease. They would suffer from recurrent attacks of the disease like chills and sweats and breaking out in tremors anytime.

Probably because of the extended amount of poverty and disease throughout the country, a lot of violent crimes took place. The African people were exploited for centuries. They had years of slavery by the British, the French, the Arabs, and Portuguese. This country of Africa was where the great slave trades began. Slaves were exported to the sugar fields to grow sugarcane. We also had sugarcane fields all around us. Acres and acres of sugarcane grew well in and around Durban. I read somewhere that the slave traders meanwhile made great chunks of wealth from this cruel trade. Africa had rich mineral resources as well, and the slaves, mostly African men, were sent far from their families to work in the mining fields and to live in adjacent compounds owned by their masters. All of the above-mentioned reasons were major contributing factors in the history of Africa's poverty and disease.

The present existing factors were listed in an article I read, stating that the poverty and disease were due to the Africans having so many bloody conflicts among themselves, the women have too many children from different men, too many droughts in the country, and the Africans generally are uneducated.

Many families were separated when slaves were exported to America, to the southern United States, and to the Caribbean to work in the cotton fields and to work in other countries.

Missionaries from different religions and different countries have done and are still doing their part in helping relieve some of the poverty-stricken conditions. Many Africans from mission schools were sent over to the colleges in Europe for higher education. Some girls traveled from Europe, but especially from Germany and Ireland, who would make the sacrifice to spend at least two years on contract helping the missionaries in Africa. Today, there are many people from different countries, among them, doctors, scientists, physical therapists, nurses, and many medical teams offering their time and talents to go to Africa. Many Christian groups organize trips to Africa from time to time to help in whatever way they can. We used to hear in my later years in Africa that missionaries should not establish roots in any place. They are there to be present to the people in their time of need. When the people have embodied the Christian values into their culture and they have become autonomous, and if the missionaries see that this is being realized, only then can they move on to where the needs are greater. Of course, some continued support would be needed in the local churches or establishments that the missionaries would then leave behind.

Seeing such mass poverty in our own area of work was unbelievable. Watching a continuous stream of Africans making their way to the outpatient's clinic or the local clinics, "satellite clinics" as they were called, every single day and knowing that many had come from afar, walking for miles and miles to get help. I always liked it when I passed an African in the dirt roads. They would greet me or anyone passing by with such joy, obviously so happy to have met us. In the beginning, I often wondered why they would not greet us 'til they had already passed us by. They would then turn around to us and acknowledge us with a Zulu expression, meaning, "We have seen you." They would bow and sometimes shake hands if they were meeting us for the first time. Shaking hands in the usual way was the African custom. While they would clasp the hands, they would keep hold of your hands and without letting go would grasp the thumbs and go back to the original handclasp. It kind of gave the feeling that you were getting a double welcome!

What was such a pitiful sight was to see so many children with *Kwashiorkor*. It was called *Marasmic kwashiorkor*. It occurred in children, generally over two years of age when they were weaned from breast-feeding and were fed starchy foods. So the lack of protein in the diet caused the protruding ribs and the bloated bellies. It was hard to treat this serious nutritional disease. We had to start gradually with diluted milk by mouth; small frequent feedings around the clock until a balanced fluid and electrolyte balance was restored. A slow intravenous of protein plasma was the treatment given in my last years there. Sending the child home required a follow-up check and supplies of increased dietary allowances to correct the mineral and vitamin deficiencies and restore good nourishment. Ongoing education concerning the importance of good nutrition was important so that the children would not go home and be exposed to the same poor nourishment. Mothers often came to the clinics to deliver their babies. Many times, they would be hanging around for days awaiting the arrival of their baby. This was a great opportunity for the nurses and sisters and those who were not nurses to spend some of their time showing the Africans how to knit and sew, and even to make use of a little patch of garden, however small, to be able to grow something for them. The time was well used. I think most of the Africans would come to the clinic early when they heard by word of mouth all the things they could learn while waiting there for their babies.

There was an elderly gentleman who lived at the clinic and was hardly able to get around anymore without assistance. Hence, the sisters kept him at the clinic. He lived at the clinic for many years and was known by everyone around. No one knew his age or how old he was when he died. His body was put in a cloth and strung unto a bamboo stick. He was buried near a little river not far from the clinic. I went along for the funeral. Sister was driving the Land Rover, and when it came time to get out and carry the body, the African man and Sister put the bamboo stick over their shoulders and carried the body. All went well until crossing the river, and they both slipped and fell into the water. It was hard to get one's balance after that and the body, which had also fallen in, was much heavier as it was wet and carried more weight now. We were not disrespectful but we were hysterical with laughter and the more we tried to get out of the wet mud, the more we sunk into it. I was not much help as the whole picture seemed really funny to me. Anytime, when I tried to be of any assistance in helping to relieve the men of their burden, everything would just become unbalanced and made things worse. We eventually arrived at the place, which was already dug up and prepared ahead of time by the men from the clinic. We placed the body in the prepared grave, and together, we helped to throw the soil back over the body. He was an unknown person, no family. Only the sisters cared for him and gave him a burial place. It was very sad, and I'm sure he found a home with God, where his spirit soared way above the clouds in heaven.

Darkness descends very quickly in Africa, especially in the winter. By the time we had buried the body and made our way back to the Land Rover, it was pitch-black. We were guided solely by the lights of the Land Rover. I used to think because of the pitch-blackness everywhere, this was why Africa was called the Dark Continent. The "Dark Continent" was the name given by the Europeans who realized they had very little knowledge of Africa, especially as the Sahara Desert was so vast, and it hindered them from reaching land. The Arabs were already in Africa for centuries and had traveled along the Indian Ocean to do their trade long before the nineteenth century. A common expression in England when you wished to get rid of a person was, "Go to Timbuktu" (Tombouctou), or "I wish she would go to Timbukta." I often heard this expression in England, but I never knew where Timbuktu was. It conveyed the idea of being as far away as possible. The expression was used a lot in Africa among the English-speaking people. I looked it up in a history book and asked one of our teaching sisters where exactly this place, "Timbuktu," was located. It was a town in western Africa, in Mali, which was the capital of Timbuktu and it was here that the great trade center began. It was here, in Mali, where the Europeans as well as other peoples began the mass deportation of black Africans to other continents and other countries. The religion of Islam was well established long before any missionaries of other religious denominations arrived to spread the word or gain converts or whatever their mission.

The nearest village to our Mother House and the mission hospital was called Verulam, named after Lord Verulam in England. The first time I went to the village of Verulam, I was astonished to see so many Muslim people. The place was a beehive of activity, with Muslims buying and selling their wares at the marketplace. This was the first time I had ever seen Muslim people. They wore long robes and had their heads covered. Well, we sisters didn't look much different. Our heads were covered and we wore long robes. I recall being at the marketplace in Verulam, one Saturday morning. About midday, a booming voice came over the village. It was the call to prayer for the Muslim people. It broke above the noise and babble and roar of the marketplace. I think there must have been a megaphone on the top of the temple spiral and the voice boomed over the entire village of Verulam. The Muslim people immediately fell down on their knees and prostrated themselves in prayer. All were turning toward Mecca, the birthplace of Muhammad. This they did many times throughout the day, every day. It was strange for me to witness all this in the beginning, but I got used to it after being on a few trips to the village marketplace where I accompanied the sister to do the shopping for the convent, as well as the schools and the clinics and hospital. The Mother House was like an oasis in a dry desert. In Verulam and in Durban, which was the nearest town, we sisters often accompanied the sister who was shopping or going into the town of Verulam for some business purposes. I loved to get out and see this new world outside the convent. Apartheid was in existence then but living at the Mother House we were not that aware of apartheid, as we were all different races in there together. It was when we left the convent to see the world outside that we became aware of the divisions. All the benches were marked, telling you where you could sit. Segregation of races could be seen everywhere. All the signs were written in English and Afrikaans: Whites, Blankes, Blacks, and Swarte. One had to look for the sign before one could sit down. Even certain areas were cordoned off where only whites could go. Even along the beachfront of the Indian Ocean, special sections were marked off. I thought of the vast expansion of salt water in the Indian Ocean, even these waters had to be segregated.

Chapter 39

Transferred Again

I don't recall when I was transferred back from the warm colorful climate of Durban in Natal at the African Hospital, to the colder, higher altitude of Johannesburg of six-thousand feet above sea level. Here in Johannesburg, I was back working in the maternity hospital, "whites only." The contrast from the Black hospital to the White hospital was night and day. The climate of the hospital was more rigid and cold, like the weather outside, at least that was how I felt it to be 'til I got used to everything again. I missed the general, warmer atmosphere of the Black hospital and the colorful scenes of nature outside and the wide-open spaces of Africa. Here I was confined to brick walls and skyscrapers. I missed the African people very much. It was a totally different world I had left behind. But missionaries did not get attached. They had to move on to where the need was greater. I had to obey and go where I was sent. The need for nurses was the problem in this White hospital, but the real needs were in the place I had just left behind! It took me some time to become adjusted to my new assignment. I had worked in this hospital before and here I was, back to the same mad dash rush of work, just as I had known before. I wished I had been sent to the hospital in Pretoria, an hour's drive from Johannesburg. I experienced the hospital in Pretoria to be homier! But I had to "put my hand to the plough and not look back." Not an easy task.

It didn't take long for me to fall into the routine of the hospital, as I had been here before. The continuous business left me with little time for feeling sorry for myself, but I missed the African Hospital. It was a very different atmosphere here, just one of super activity. Many days, we remained in the hospital all day and sometimes into the night. The sisters in the convent who worked in the kitchen and laundry and garden were able to get to the chapel for the prescribed prayers throughout the day and to attend meals regularly. Nurses here had to fit in their own prayer times when they could find the time. Often, it was late at night when we tried to squash in all the prescribed prayers that we had missed during the day.

Chapter 40

Big Changes and Surprises

This was the nineteen sixties and big changes were happening everywhere. We sisters got wind of it here and were mostly hearing it from the doctors and patients. As there was no television at that time in the convent, there was a radio, but it was only the superior in the convent who was allowed to turn the radio on and off. We had a portable radio that was carried into the community recreation room where we would assemble to darn our socks or do embroidery. The superior would carry in the radio, turn it on, and no one spoke while we listened to the world news at 1:00 PM. The news finished, then it was promptly turned off by the superior. Most of the news we heard we did not understand anyway as we did not know what went on in the world outside. The major changes at that time were many. Chris Barnard performed the first heart transplant in Cape Town, Dr. Hendrik Verwoerd was prime minister, and the name of Nelson Mandela, head of the African National Congress was among a group of eight who were sentenced to life imprisonment. All black workers had to carry a pass and were jailed if they did not carry it. This, of course, affected us in the hospital as our domestic workers could not come in to work. The money changed to the decimal coinage but this did not mean anything to us who did not ever handle money. It seemed there was much upheaval outside in the world. There were marches, demonstrations, and we heard something about the civil rights movement.

Then came a change, which affected us nuns particularly in the convents, Vatican II was presided over by Pope John XXIII. The expression that Pope John "opened the windows" in the church and talked of changes was everywhere. In our maternity hospital, doctors were bringing in their own fetal monitor machines for the first time. They were kept in a very secluded place, and we dared not touch them. They were only to be handled by the doctors who owned them. They looked like a TV machine. I would stand in amazement and stare at them, wondering how on earth they worked. I did not dare touch them at all! I recall when a doctor connected his monitor to a wall socket and connected a disk or something to the patient's abdomen. We were all standing around in awe, like the movie *Out of Africa*, just gazing in amazement and wonder. I kept looking at the back of the machine to see how on earth the picture came through to the front of the monitor. How did this monitor show up on a screen and see what the infant inside its mother's womb was doing? We could actually hear the heartbeat. Marvel of marvels! I was truly intrigued. Up to this time, we had used a stethoscope to listen to the heartbeats. From this, we could pick up any irregular heartbeats or brachycardia (slow heartbeat). What a wonderful invention. The doctors who belonged to a certain group were all allowed to use the same monitor. We got used to them, but we nurses had no idea what the readings on the monitors were all about. We still used our fetal stethoscopes to do our own checking of the babies' heart rates.

What was a great bit of news in the 1960s in Johannesburg was that we woke one morning to find two inches of snow on the ground. When I came downstairs and walked toward the chapel, I saw some sisters out in the yard, making snowballs. We had two nuns in our convent who were identical twins. They were born in South Africa and were Afrikaans-speaking nuns. This was an unusual finding, especially in the "Nuns' Habit." The excitement of seeing snow for the first time in their lives was so unique. They were like children out in the yard. Most of us Europeans had seen snow, but this was a first in South Africa for all of us. The call-bell had rung as usual at 4:55 AM, and we were to be in our chapel stalls by 5:15 AM. All of us sisters joined the twins in the first snowball game. Pope John XXIII would probably have let us stay out and dispensed us from our religious duties. Pope John would have said, "You Sisters need more fun and joy in your lives." And "All work and no play make Jack a dull boy."

Another incident or event that happened was Gary Player and his wife, who were expecting their fourth baby, flew back to South Africa from America to have it. I felt so honored to be the nurse on that case. They were on a golf tournament, and she just got back in the nick of time. All the Player babies had been born in our hospital in Kensington, Johannesburg.

It was also in the 1960s that Swaziland became independent of Britain. The tribal leader there became head of state. It was King Sobhuza who ruled the little kingdom of Swaziland. The reason I mention this was that our sisters had a school in Swaziland. I went there for a holiday one year and some of the king's children were attending the convent school. He had hundreds of children. It was like a miniature kingdom. I recall once when I went to go out for a walk, one of the sisters said jokingly to me, "Be careful the king's soldiers don't catch you." The true story was that at this time of the year, the king's soldiers would roam the streets looking for pretty girls to bring home to the king. The girls were afraid they would be caught, so they were afraid to go out in the streets at this time, summer time! The king had about one-hundred wives, and we visited the king's little kingdom or village. Each wife had her own little hut, and it was great to see this whole set up. Swaziland was situated to the east of Johannesburg and close to the Indian Ocean. I vaguely remember hearing of the customs of the king's soldiers had to fetch seawater from the Indian Ocean, so that the king could bathe in salt seawater once a year for purification or ritual purposes before taking on any new girls.

Swaziland is truly a beautiful country with many different landscapes. I enjoyed my little holiday there. It was very educational as well. But then, I went back to the hustle and bustle of Johannesburg and hospital life again. I missed the wide-open and beautiful scenery of the African countryside. Nursing had opened a totally new and fascinating world for me. It was a great education also and it was good to be back in nursing. I really loved it, and it was such a reward and joy to take care of patients. In this field of nursing, one can accept the normal hectic atmosphere of busyness and activity. To take care of patients and to meet their needs was something that fulfilled a need in me as well as my finding my vocation in taking care of others. I enjoyed being needed. I was truly happy when I was needed. To be busy was the greatest outlet for me. I had no time for self to come into the picture. In this way of life, keeping up with the novitiate teaching of putting oneself in the background, so that in a way, self did not exist. The work itself helped me to do just that.

Unfortunately, as time moved on, many of us nurses were feeling the consequences of the hectic super activity that occurred every day and the work never let up. I was not able to give my best care to the patients, and I myself was not able to push myself any more. It was as if I had to drag myself out of bed, drag myself up to the floors of the hospital, struggle to get through the work and on top of this, do overtime or double duty, like PRN, whenever it is needed.

I recall the sister who came to South Africa on the boat with me, Sister Oliver, being assigned to the hospital in Pretoria. She was not working in the hospital for long as her health was not good. I recall seeing her sitting in the hallway on the windowsill, unable to go any further. When this sister gave in and admitted she could not work the way we did, then I knew that pretty soon we would all cave in as we were unable to keep up that speed forever. This particular sister was the one person who never gave in and worked so hard and at such a speed, she was fast. So if she could not continue, then we did not expect to be able to keep it up either. Besides the regular non-nursing duties and the nursing duties, it was all just too much. Not to mention the responsibilities that went along with nursing. I often wished one of our hospitals would close down, so we would all be together in one hospital and not be spread out so thin.

Chapter 41

Habit Changes—the Good and the Bad

The 1960s saw many changes, especially for us sisters. Transition began with the nun's habit. We all had to have the habit shortened to two inches above the ankle. Few accepted the change. Most older sisters were resistant to any change. This two-inch deal caused some real arguments and discussion, and it was unbelievable that such reactions arose from some sisters whom we thought did not have a point of view or a thought on anything. Looking back, this beginning of change was really such a serious matter for most of the sisters, but it was quite funny as well. Any onlooker would have been able to see the sisters as real people, with feelings just like the rest of the world.

For many sisters, this was a major change and especially when the veil, which had so many pieces of material around our faces was changed to a simple short veil. Some sisters were not able to make the change, so they kept the old look. The old habit made us look like sexless human beings with only two eyes, a nose, and a mouth showing. What a view did we show to the world outside! Many people in the world did not agree with the nuns making changes. This surprised me. They were used to us and couldn't see us any other way. I hear someone say once that he thought we sisters were praying all day that we were of another world. I think the negative view, which we sisters gave to the world outside was partly due to the way we were trained. The focus of our training was mainly on our external behavior at all times. This external training was so drilled into us. The way we walked, the way we talked, the way we sat down, the way we placed our hands when not using them. This, together with the way we dressed, all covered up, must have made a negative impression on many people.

No wonder we appeared as sexless human beings to so many people. So a glimpse of seeing the inside of a convent during this time of change would have conveyed the true reality that we were fully human.

There were many changes that took place gradually over the years in the sixties and seventies, but the most drastic change, I think, was the simplifying of our habit and veil. Naturally, the older sisters found it very hard to change into a more modern look. It seemed modern in those days to us sisters at that time.

Change is never easy. With the renewal of Vatican II, it seemed so much came together, all at once. Changes in the Mass, which was in Latin from the time we learned to read. The vernacular that we knew by heart was changed to English. The discipline that was part of our everyday life was gradually being thrown out the window. It was like an overnight change, and it was hard to let go of the familiar structures that had been part of our lives since we entered the convent.

I was eighteen years old when I received the religious garb or habit, and now I was in my thirties. Our way of life has changed. For many, it was like losing their security blanket in losing their external rules and regulations. It was like a big intrusion and disruption. Not all sisters were affected the same way. When I got over the initial changes, I was just so happy to feel free to be myself; and the fact that I did not have to concentrate on how I walked or how I talked and if my hands were hidden under my scapular when not in use and downcast eyes. I felt so free. Naturally, there was some degree of anxiety and tension for a while in the convents after the Vatican II Renewal. Letting go of the familiar structures of many years, and it was many, many years for some of the sisters, was somewhat frightening. Their whole world seemed to fall apart. I was happy to have all aspects of religious life simplified, though change was mainly external in the beginning.

A big change in our nursing communities was the "time off." A suggestion was made that we sisters were to get a few hours off each week. That idea of two hours off a week sounded so wonderful. Of course, like the two inches being cut off the hem of our habits, this idea was not accepted at all. Some of the responses I heard were "Since when do sisters take time off?" "That is certainly not appropriate for us as religious sisters." "We have to remember who we are," and so on and so forth. All I could think of was if I would get a few hours off a week, I would want to do a lot of things that I don't get time to do because of the frantic pace we sisters kept going at all day long and every day, and Sundays as well. I thought it would be just wonderful to have time off and then at times I would fall back into the old guilty feelings of even thinking along those lines of wanting or having time off. Self-effacement! How often did we hear those words from the novice-mistress and from spiritual reading books? I was determined to do and carry out what I was taught. I tried to be faithful to the external dos and don'ts, and I kept the external rules and regulations very well. One of the frequent sayings was, "Keep the rule and the rule will keep you." So a lot of guilty feelings I had for actually thinking about myself actually planning what I was going to do when I got those two free hours a week to myself. I felt selfish in my thoughts and felt "I" was in charge, instead of me being subservient and under the authority of the superior; I should be childlike and dependent, and so on and on went some of the conflicts in my mind. Change was taking place in all aspects of our lives. I liked what was happening, but I was unsure of so much of the change. Everything seemed topsy-turvy and our whole basis for religious life seemed to be pulled out from under us. At least, things seemed to be heading that way.

I had grown up in the orphanage of keeping rules and following along with the rest of the herd. We dare not step out of line because we feared the awful punishment that we brought on ourselves by disobeying or disrupting the routine. In the religious life, I think I continued on the same path with the same subservient and conditioned lifestyle; everything was paralleled in religious life. I was continuing the same pattern. There were one or more people in charge in the orphanage, and there was one person in charge in the convent, the superior. The only rule of life I knew was childlike obedience and dependence. We would not dare or dream of questioning the rules or the authority. These were our way or means to salvation. All my life, I was conditioned to fear authority, and I always felt inferior to them. I would keep away from superiors and only approach when I had to for permissions, etc. Though I had some very nice and good superiors, I still felt awkward in their presence. Gradually, over the years, the tension lessened and the changes that were now taking place under Vatican II helped me to breathe easier, though, I felt on shaky ground.

Chapter 42

Home Leave

Time moved on, and we had to learn to adapt to many changes. The greatest change of all was the news that the sisters were now allowed to go home and visit their parents for the first time since they had entered the convent. For many of the sisters, it had been a lifetime in Africa, over periods of twenty, thirty, forty, fifty years and more. It is hard to explain the anticipation and excitement and the apprehension that some of the sisters felt in seeing their families after so many lost years. Of course, the sisters would have photos and letters from their families. Many were not prepared for the changes that had taken place over the lost years of not even seeing them. In those days, people did not make phone calls, especially from Europe to Africa, or vice versa.

I recall being on night duty in the hospital in Johannesburg, and a phone call came through to the labor ward. It was from Germany and it was the brother of one of the sisters and it was 3:00 AM when it came through. I was not able to call the sister as she was of course sleeping in the convent, a different building from the hospital. I wished I could get to her, but there was no way I could contact her. Besides, there were only two of us nursing sisters on duty in the labor units, and we were having a baby boom that night. Being allowed, phone calls were just great, but I saw some sisters who were hardly able to talk on the phone to their relatives. The tears were also flowing in abundance as they talked. The joy was so great! The sisters who were in the convent the longest went home first. Some did not feel like going home after so many years away. The choice was theirs. When my time came around, it was 1970. At first, I thought I would not be allowed home, as I had no family and no home to go to, but I hoped I would not be asked too many questions about who I had left of family in Ireland. The superior said to me one day, as it was my turn to go home, "You don't have many people or family to go to, do you?" I knew our letters were censored by the superior. As a rule, we did not talk about our families either in those days. So the superior did observe that I did not write home on the prescribed months when we had permission to write home. As to families, the answer I gave to the superior was, "I have lots of cousins over in Ireland." I was afraid, if I had said I had no family that I would not be able to go to Ireland. I was longing to see all my friends that I grew up with and couldn't wait for my turn! I wrote to Father Lynch as his was the only address that I could contact. Thank God, the superior did not have to read it as by now we were allowed to close our letters after we wrote them. "Thanks to Pope John!" So it was my turn to go home. The joy and the anticipation of it all; I could hardly wait to see everyone, and there were many of them to see. The airmail form was lying on the table in my place, and I could not wait to open it to see what Father Lynch had written in response to my coming home. I had to wait in order to write again and tell him the exact time when the plane would arrive in Belfast. The very name "Belfast" was music to my ears. I couldn't wait to see the town again after twenty-one years away.

I was coming home! I was going to see the only man who meant everything to me. He was *the* significant figure in my life. I was going to see the orphanage girls who were like sisters to me. I would see the orphanage again. I was already making plans to go to the orphanage and this time, for certain, I was going to investigate my family, well, at least, my mother. I had great hopes and could hardly contain my joy at the prospect of what was ahead for me. I was planning to visit the house where I had my first domestic job. Above all, I wanted to walk the streets of Belfast again and recall the old times. My hopes were high. I found myself up in the air, in an airplane, for the first time. It was exciting, but I was scared of the airplane falling from the sky. I felt out of control. I was surprised that I actually became sick because I was a good traveler otherwise. I arrived in Johannesburg from Durban, and in Johannesburg, I was to board a plane to Amsterdam. I thought I would be having a single flight to Amsterdam and didn't know the plane would have to come down for refueling. Each time the plane landed, somewhere in Africa, I was sick. Each time it took off again, I was sick. I don't recall the name of the places where I landed in Africa. I only remember the awful heat and suffocation while at the airports. A drink of water would have been most welcome, but I would have been happy just to moisten my lips. I remember looking at my watch and seeing 2:00 AM.

I was afraid to move around the airport from where I was standing. The heat was unbearable, and I wondered how anyone could live in this deadly hot atmosphere. If only I could find water. We were all standing packed like sardines at the airport, and I couldn't understand the languages that were spoken. This was my first stop, and my second stop was worse also because of the terrible heat and standing for so long. My legs felt as if they didn't belong to me. I couldn't feel them while I walked. I was happy to get on the plane again and get something to eat and drink though I thought I might be better off without anything in my stomach. I duly arrived in Amsterdam and had to have help in walking. I was taken in a wheelchair to the waiting room of the airport and was advised to sit with my feet up. I sat on a chair, and the only place where I could put my feet up and keep them elevated was on an ashtray stand. I arrived in Amsterdam at 7:00 AM, and we took off for London at 7:00 PM. After having my feet elevated for a while, I would try to put my feet on the ground now and again just to test if I could walk. What a scare it was for this to happen to me. I did not know it was because I had my feet hanging down for very long hours in addition to the heat. In those days, I had traveled for about twenty hours or more on the plane, and I dreaded to board another plane for fear of the same thing happening to me and I wouldn't be able to walk. Before getting off the plane in London, I tried to help a mother who was struggling with her three children, and I was one of the last to get off the plane. I was able to walk this time, though very slowly.

As I was waiting in line at the London Airport, my name was called. "Will Sister Peter come to the Enquiry," or whatever it was called. I felt awkward in walking up in front of all the people waiting in line. I thought there might be a sister calling to see if I had arrived. I got to the desk and was handed my ticket. I had left it on the seat on the plane when I stopped to help the mother with the three children. I sat next to them on the plane; I was lucky to get the ticket back. I do not remember anything more about how or who met me at the airport in Belfast. I was just enthralled to hear the Belfast accent again. It was strange hearing it after such a long time. "Did I use to talk like this?" I loved to hear the Belfast accent, and I could just listen and listen forever to the people talking. I was back home! It was 1949 when I left Belfast, and this was 1970 when I was returning for the first time after being away for twenty-one years. I couldn't help looking back on all that happened to me over twenty-one years. It seemed an awfully long stretch of time.

Chapter 43

Back in Belfast

I was staying at someone's house, which was owned by a friend of Father Lynch's. I had known her before I entered and was so happy to see her again. She was not from the orphanage but had been a student at Queen's University and stayed at a convent residence where Father Lynch was the chaplain. That is how I met her. People change over the years and as this person had lost her husband and life took its toll on her, I discovered a totally different person. I knew I was not welcome. Thank God, I had Father Lynch's telephone number. I made quite a few attempts to call him, and by the third day, I got him on the phone and asked him for a telephone number of any one of our girls. He gave me some numbers, and I immediately called "Brigid" (not her real name). I remembered this girl very well as there were five sisters in the orphanage during my time, so I hadn't forgotten them. I wanted nothing more than to see as many of our own girls as possible. I only had ten days of vacation at that time, so I had already wasted three or four days before I contacted Father Lynch on the phone. The girl whom I was staying with, I'll call her Melinda. She was planning to go out for the afternoon. Before Melinda left the house, I was given instructions to keep the doors locked; and as she was responsible for me, I was warned not to leave the house at any time when Melinda left the house. I had my suitcase packed and ready to go! I called Brigid and told her my predicament. She said, "Stay there, I know where Melinda lives and we'll come and get you."

As I was afraid to leave the door open after me because I had no key for the house, the plan was that I would throw the suitcase out the front window from the parlor below. Brigid and her husband drove up. I had been watching for them. As soon as I threw the suitcase out the window, Brigid's husband moved toward the window to pick up the suitcase. I shouted, "Wait!" I was going to jump on top of the suitcase as the windows were high and I would have a shorter jump. What a relief to get into the car and with someone who was like family to me. I breathed a sigh of relief! Brigid said, "I must confess, I've never seen a nun climb out a window, there's always a first time for everything. And well, Maud, how are you, it is great to see you. How long has it been?" We talked and talked and talked and laughed and cried, and yes, I was home. My name was "Maud" again after twenty-one years away. It was all very strange indeed but I was home.

Chapter 44

To the Orphanage Twenty-first Birthday Party

I didn't hear or see Melinda again. I had a busy time for the remaining days. The orphanage was informed by Brigid that I was on home leave, and it was twenty-one years since I had left Belfast. The orphanage, as well as our girls, got everything together for a coming-home party. It was great fun and good "crack" (fun). It was so good so see everyone again and hear their stories. May Ferris (Kennedy) was there, and I hugged her so hard and wouldn't let go. She was the person who took me away from my first job and helped me when I was desperate and destitute. Oh, how I had missed everyone! The party was called the twenty-first birthday party. It was to honor the twenty-one years I'd been away. I thought, that now because I was a nun, that I would have better luck talking to the superior of the orphanage this time around. The same old questions, "Sister, do you know how I got here to this orphanage? Does anyone here know or remember if I was placed here as a baby or when I came here?" "Which sisters were here in 1930s that would remember something about me?" "Sister, don't you have a book with some information as to when we all got here? None of us know anything at all about ourselves" "Sister, the fact that I'm now a nun, can you not tell me something. I'm a mature person now and I can accept whatever you tell me no matter how bad it is . . ." All to no avail! My convent discipline and self-control was gone in a matter of seconds. I asked the sister why no one would give us the information we so desperately sought. We were all older and ready to accept it whatever the news, good or bad. Why, why, why?

Some of the girls, who had never left Belfast, had some information, which they got in a roundabout way. Brigid had four other sisters and her older sister remembered when they were placed in the orphanage and where they came from, but most of us had no information at all.

I knew my real name, which was on my birth certificate, and I thought I'd give it a bash at calling people from the telephone booths in the streets. As I mentioned that I was always known as "Fryers" in the orphanage, I discovered the spelling of my last name was "Friars"; and if this is the spelling on my birth certificate, then this must be correct. So now, I could start calling any person in the kiosks with the last name of "Friars." My heart was beating so fast when I actually got through on the phone to somebody with that name, thinking that maybe this is actually a relative. I made contact and this was just great. I was invited out to their home. No one living in the house had any inkling of me, and it was a lost cause. I kept on trying but all to no avail. It was very frustrating for me as this was probably my one and only chance of finding my mother dead or alive! My time in Belfast was about up, and I would be returning to Africa. I just felt like I was a youngster back in Belfast, and I had never left it. I still had the sheer determination to go full force in pursuit of finding my mother. At times, I would tell myself that I'm a grown woman, thirty-nine years of age, and I shouldn't be acting like a child looking for her mother. I felt and knew it was all childish behavior. I would remind myself that I am a nun, and I should have grown past all this childish behavior of looking for my mother. But the urge was very great and so little time to look for her.

One of my many desires was to visit the familiar spot I used to visit when we started the club for the orphans in College Square, right close to the technical college in Belfast. After WWII, the government was offering free classes, so I availed myself of the opportunity at that time. I went for the cookery classes so I would know how to cook when I got married. In those days, that was important. I knew, if I arrived at the Technical College, I would find my way around and visit the people I used to know. There were many small shops in that area, but the shop where I used to go and buy bread and jam, milk and butter for the club was one of the places I wanted to see, especially Miss Savage who owned the shop and who would give me any leftovers at that time if she had them. Father Lynch gave me the money. Sometimes, Miss Savage would give me a small tobacco packet to give to Father Lynch. All these were memories now, and I was expecting to find everything and everybody still there, as in those days twenty-one years ago.

Chapter 45

Belfast Had Changed

Coming from Africa, I was completely unaware of the troubles in Northern Ireland. Here downtown, I was walking over stones from fallen buildings; there was rubble and debris everywhere, just a gray-looking place and the continuous drizzle of the rain just added to the sad-looking state of things. It all appeared so bleak and shabby. There were foot patrols of British soldiers everywhere. I could not find any roads leading anywhere. Once I asked the first soldier I saw to help me find where I was and he directed me to a huge fenced-in place, like a mall surrounded by a makeshift wall. He said, "All the shops are in there, Madam, but you have to go through security when you go in and when you come out." It was just as he said, and it was the first time that I had ever had a scan or been palpated to see if I had any kind of weapons or such like things on my person. I was scared inside that tent, but I just walked around like everyone else, looking at the whole setup and wondering what was going on in the world, at least my immediate world around me. Over the loudspeaker came a warning that the place will be closed at 5:00 PM, and we were reminded of the curfew. I went toward the exit and again through the bleeps of the scan and palpation, and my purse was checked. I walked out of that place and wondered why I hadn't checked all this out beforehand. The people had disappeared very quickly, and I hardly saw anyone in the streets. I felt so utterly lost and confused. I went back to the shopping tent to ask one of the guards where I would be able to go to find a bus that would take me home. "Sorry, Madam," he said. "There are no buses after 5:00 PM. Do you know about the curfew?" So I thanked him and just strutted out of the tent again. Outside, I began walking, I began to feel like crying, and I just felt lost and alone. The rain was just "falling softly" as they say in Ireland. I had the sense of not knowing what had hit me. All was strange and weird in Belfast. It was not the Belfast I had been looking so forward to seeing and for so long. It felt so good and kind of free the first time that I had donned civic clothes in Ireland, instead of the religious garb. Now, I wished I was back in the habit and back within the security of the convent.

Once during my time in Belfast, my friend Jean and I were house-arrested; we remained in the house for three hours. Eventually the police returned to question us further. I was somewhat suspicious to them coming from South Africa. The police then escorted the two of us from the house to our car. They had, of course, fully examined our car while we were inside, and we were scanned and checked before we ourselves were allowed back in the car. As Jean drove off, the soldiers were standing guard outside the house, armed with their rifles. A wee bit down the road, and as I thought, out of sight, I exclaimed, "What on earth was that all about?" Sheila muttered, "Don't say anything." I saw the British soldiers were patrolling the streets, standing at almost every corner of the streets on the Falls Road. The British troops had forts strategically set up, especially set up in west Belfast. An array of jeeps could be seen all over. As we left the Falls Road, we were making our way toward town when we were stopped by one of these jeeps, and again we were scanned and checked out. Jean drove me to town. I was horrified to see there was no town, only the rubble and debris and broken glass and tumbled-down brick walls. A disaster zone! In place of the town was a huge tent set up where people could go and shop. Again, I had to go through the scanning and personal checking points at the entrance and exit of the shopping center within the makeshift temporary tent. I told Jean I would just love to ride the bus back again. I longed to ride the buses, and I longed to ride my bicycle around town. This was the only means of transport in the forties for working classes, besides walking everywhere, so I wanted to experience all the simple joy that I had back then. I wanted to rekindle the old days as I remembered them. I wasn't aware there were no buses after 5:00 PM, so I was happy to walk home. I asked directions from the security guard at the exit, and I made my way walking along the road, this gave me a chance to gather my thoughts and see Belfast close up from the streets. I had forgotten about the twilight in Ireland. It is bright up 'til 10:00 or 11:00 PM. In Africa, the darkness descends early, especially in the winter season. There is pitch-darkness about 4:00 PM in the evenings in Africa. I walked all the way to the house where I was staying and only had to ask my way once from an elderly woman carrying a load of shopping bags. When I asked her for directions, she replied, "Oh, Luv, it's a fair bit you have to go, you know, it's a wee while along but sure you'll be flying along in no time, your legs are younger than mine!" I walked along beside her as far as she was going my way, and then I was feeling sad to let her go as I made my way back alone the rest of the way. I very much enjoyed listening to her Belfast accent along the way, and it really only began to sink in that I was actually home and actually walking the streets of Belfast. Outside of the town, as I walked the streets, I could see the Black Mountains in the distance and this was the Belfast that I remembered. When I reached the bus depot, I could see the buses and the trolleys that the drivers would change. And how we loved to swing on the trolley wire when the bus conductor would have to swing it from back to front when he changed the direction of the bus. We would jump on the trolley ropes then and swing around with him.

The following day, I walked the streets on the Falls Road. I wanted to be alone and to take in all the places I used to know. I wasn't going to let the soldiers keep me back from seeing my old familiar haunting places. I walked from Donegal Street, up the Falls Road, 'til I came to 1 Inkerman Street, just off the Falls Road. This was May Kennedy-Ferris's home and my home when I had no job and no place to go. I stood and gaped at all around me. There was no Inkerman Street. It had been demolished and high-rises were in their places. I missed all the little side streets that held many memories for me, and I wanted to see those places again. I should have realized as I walked up the Falls Road, seeing the Divis Flats coming closer and closer, towering above everything, that things had changed. These flats were an eyesore and not in keeping with the familiar homesteads all around. So much change and seeing the Belfast town in daylight was like a ghost town. The names of the streets on the Falls Road were always so fascinating to me because they were not Irish names, but foreign names. Later on, in my following trips to Ireland, I learned most of these names were given after the Crimean War. Names like Bombay Street, Balaclava Street, Kashmir Street, Cypress Street, and Bosnia Street. One could not forget those names precisely because they were different. Such big names for tiny little side streets off the Falls Road. The people who lived in these areas all worked in the local linen factory in the old days, in the beginning of the twentieth century. May Kennedy-Ferris was very proud of the fact the nun Sister Coleman, who was principal of the orphanage school, had actually lived in 1 Inkerman Street. They were a very noted musical family in those days, early 1900s. I was heartsick to observe that what I longed to see was now lost and gone forever. I longed for the good old happy days of that simple way of life. How, back then, the people would all be out on the streets talking and chatting, and everyone knew everyone and all the goings on in that little area. It was like being back in the WWII era, but the people and places were no more. I couldn't help wondering why life had to be like this: bombings, killings, and shootings everywhere. Why does Ireland had to suffer like this and for what? A little piece of land? The whole scene had such an effect on me, I couldn't contain my emotions. I walked down the Falls Road and wept as I'd never wept before. I was glad to have a large white nun's handkerchief in my pocket. I couldn't help feeling the loss of so much, especially the people whom I knew so well back then. I thought I could just walk in on them as in those days of yore! Here I was, living in Africa, where the needs of the people are so great, where we missionaries tried to meet the basics of food and clothing, etc., and education and to contrast this scene in Belfast, where the beautiful country of Ireland is being torn asunder. Why, instead of pulling down and destroying a country, could the soldiers not be sent to build up the country!

I spent one day at May (Kennedy) and her husband, Davy Ferris's house in Downpatrick. This was the place where they had been relocated during the time of the troubles and the demolitions of their Falls Road home. This house was larger than their Inkerman Street home and much brighter. I was able to look out the window and see Downpatrick, the little town situated in a hollow valley; and the green, green hills of Ireland, spreading far and wide. It was just like being home again to be in May and Davy's home. My time there was limited. They said, "Maud, the next time you come home, come and stay with us." I, of course, could only think of the present, not of the uncertain future. For my part, I just wanted to sit down and talk right now, where I was, and reminisce on the old days, and tell of all that had happened since I had entered the convent in England and since they, May and Davy, had settled, married, and lived through so much turmoil. After twenty-one years, there was a lot to catch up on. Instead, May and Davy's conversation were so taken up with the political scene in the North of Ireland. The conversation seemed endless about the troubles and about the republicans in the forerun, Gerry Adams, Gerry Fitts, Bobby Sands (who later in the 1980s had died in the hunger strike in Long Kesh, one of the jails in the north of Ireland). I had often heard the remark that the Irish are great at talking politics but not talking about their feelings. The conversation in May's home was mostly on the political level. Time and distance had changed us all. I wanted to change the topic and give them a broader picture of what was going on in the world, especially in Africa. It was not to be, as the people were so intensely caught up with the present situation, just like a civil war, and their interests were so focused on the politicians who were rising up in Ireland to be the future fighters for real peace. I could understand their concerns, and wished I had known more of the past and present history of the north of Ireland. I failed to follow their conversations and did not know any of the names that were mentioned. I was aware life had changed in a very big way. May and Davy had changed, and I was living in another faraway distant world of Africa. So I left May and Davy's house with a feeling that I had not connected. We had all grown in our own different worlds. The other girls from the orphanage, whom I met at the twenty-firsty party of my coming home, seemed to all talk on a level that I did not understand or follow, so I felt out of it.

So it was in 1970, I took my first trip home to Belfast, and now, after my visit home, I was to plan my return back to Africa. I had enjoyed the anticipation of going back to see Belfast and all my orphanage friends, but the elation sobered down gradually at the awful reality of what was happening to Belfast and all the people, especially those whom I used to know during the 1940s, especially the WWII period after the war was over. I felt the joy and jubilation at that time, of living again without the fear of bombs dropping. I did realize that returning to places after time and long separation had certainly changed my perspective on everything. It was sad for me to leave. It was an immense letdown, and I did not accomplish my one quest, which was to find my mother. I doubt if that chance will ever come my way again.

As I sat by the window of the airplane on my trip back to Africa, looking down at the beautiful green, green hills of Ireland, I recalled the arrival of that tremendous moment of seeing Ireland on arrival after such a long time away. It was a huge contrast to the brown dried-up hills and plains of Africa. A heavy sadness came over me when I realized I may never see Ireland again. Ireland was lost to me, my friends were changed, and many were scattered all over and settled in different countries. I did not belong in Ireland. I belonged in Africa. I could have wept forever. Father Lynch, the one person more than anybody that I longed to see and talk to, was only available once on a passing-through basis. Ireland was now a different world to me, and I would have to deal with the total loss of that beautiful country and all that it once held for me. I was totally oblivious of all around me on the plane, my mind was so far away. My lungs still held the wonderful fresh Irish air that I had inhaled deeply before boarding the plane back to Africa.

It was a very long journey back, stopping at least twice in Africa where the heat was unbearable; and again, we were packed at the airport, huddled like sardines. I was emotionally drained and tired. My thoughts were of Ireland, and I thought I would never see Ireland again or even want to go back to see it. I had mixed feelings. Ireland, I thought, held nothing for me now. The Belfast that I knew was gone forever, along with my friends, and the hope of ever finding my mother was also gone forever. These thoughts were very depressing. I knew, in spite of all these depressing thoughts, I would get over it all and be my usually bubbly self once I got back to work and duty on the hospital wards.

Chapter 46

Back to Africa into a Ten-day Silence Retreat

I knew my experience over the past years was to throw myself into work, and this work was my savior. In the convent, we had an annual ten-day retreat. It was just the beginning of the retreat at the Mother House when I arrived, and I was to join in the retreat before I returned to the hospital life. I went right into the ten-day retreat, which had begun the day before my arrival. In one way, it was good because silence was strictly kept during the retreat. In this way, I did not have to talk or give an account of my home leave. It was good up to a point because it gave me a chance to settle quietly back into the convent life while on retreat.

It was the custom, when we were in the chapel, to sit facing one another for songs and official prayers so we were seen by all who were present. The talks of the retreat master just seemed to trigger off so much emotion in me. Every talk just raised a storm of emotions that I could not control. I recalled the novice mistress saying, "Just control yourself, and remember you are now a religious sister." "Feelings don't count, etc." I felt totally out of bounds and not in keeping with what was expected of me. I thought I was a strong person and this was not in keeping with my usual strong character. My name was Sister Peter, and how often was I told I was a true rock that could be depended upon to help in any circumstance. Peter meant "rock" in the New Testament. I felt my whole foundation was on shaky ground, and I was very helpless.

For some reason, as soon as I entered the precincts of the chapel and the silence I knew I would not be able to hold on to my nunlike composure, emotions would well up in me each time. It certainly did not help to have a whole community of faces looking across at me, being in such a conspicuous place as well. Leaving the chapel would have caused more disturbance and drawn more attention to myself. So I tried to sit through the talks and keep my handkerchief over my eyes. This handkerchief helped to smother my sobs somewhat. It was a terrible feeling to be so out of control, so strangely out of control for me that my whole foundation was shaken to the core. This crying and sobbing was so out of character for me also, and it just left me feeling as though I was acting like a child. Try as I may, I could not get control of my emotions. I was so upset with myself for allowing this to happen. I eventually tried to tell myself the retreat will soon be over and I will feel better once I get on the hospital wards and have plenty of work to occupy me the whole day. There was no other way I knew to help myself, and to get over this emotional trauma, and to deal with the loneliness. Being overtired definitely caused my breakdown, it played a big role.

During the ten-day retreat, we were allowed to make an appointment if we needed to talk to the retreat master. I had never done this before. I longed to talk to someone, but who? One of the sisters approached me and suggested maybe I ought to go and see him. I knew in my head he would not be able to help me, that he would give me spiritual talks, and I was taking in very little of the talks at this time. I was just in another world, my own world of terrible loneliness, feelings of worthlessness and of having no value. Who was I anyway? I came literally from somewhere, out of nowhere. I existed right now, at this time, making this retreat in a foreign country. How did I ever come into existence and in this place and this time frame? As I mentioned before, the congregation had all German-speaking sisters. There were a few sisters from other European countries as well as Africa. How could I talk to these people who did not know my background? I was so ashamed of my background, the fact that I could not tell anyone I had no family. I had always said my parents were dead, and after all, they were dead to me! I could never ever talk to anyone. Why was I like this? I don't know. In later years, I had heard from the orphanage girls that the nuns used to say to us, "You are children of sin." They would also say very negative expressions about us and to us. My school friends in Belfast would relate all kinds of things that happened in the orphanage and were said over and over again. I myself had little or no recollection of ever hearing any of these disparaging remarks or of the nuns trying to belittle us. So if this is how it was, we collectively picked up and stored this in our subconscious minds. I do know that none of us ever dared tell anyone where we came from. We were ashamed. So to go and talk to a priest scared me. I had left the orphanage, I guess, when I was too young to remember anything that was done or said.

The retreat was halfway through, and I knew the sooner it was over, the better I'd feel. I'd soon be rushing on the hospital floors and once again there would be no time to think of myself. Some things the retreat master said did bother me. For example, one of his talks was different from the usual spiritual talks. He would say over and over, "Sisters, if you have never received love, you cannot give it." This shook me to the core. What was I doing all these years? I identified so much with what he said, but I wondered what I had been doing all these years of self-sacrifice and service. I thought all along that I had shown love to the mothers and babies, and this is what kept me going. What was he talking about? The remark just blew me away, and I kept mulling it over in my mind.

Being so emotionally drained affected me really hard. Was working in the hospital and giving of my very best to the patients not really showing or giving love! What was I doing anyway? This just shattered my world. It was my whole world to me and to be able to help people. I questioned myself over and over and tried to figure it all out. Was I not going about things in the right way? Did I really not have the right stuff for love? I began to look up *love* in the dictionary. I took it personally. This was definitely meant for me. I would never be able to give love. The dictionary said something about caring and compassion. Was I not doing this very thing, even though I had never received love . . . ? I argued it in my head. What was wrong with me? Sure, I had not ever been kissed in my life before or had I ever been given a hug by anyone (except the official welcome into the convent when I entered and all the nuns gathered to welcome us). The more I thought about it, the more I wondered. Because I had not ever received any physical expression of love, did that mean I was incapable of giving any kind of care? I did not agree with it, but my head kept swirling round and round. What do I do now? Deprived of affection in childhood, not receiving love was the cause of my world falling apart! It was almost as if I was living a lie not true to who I really was. I began to have thoughts of being in the wrong place. Being in the religious garb was probably not really genuine for me. It was not really me. Inside, I was full of turmoil, and outside I just kept my decorum to the best of my ability. One of the last days of the retreat, I plucked up the courage to go and talk to the retreat master. When it was my appointed time, I was trembling and shaking and wondered if I ought to be doing this, i.e., going in to talk to the priest. I walked in the door and to my surprise, the retreat master came toward me with his arms extended as if to embrace me. I got such a big hug from him, and as he hugged me, he said, "My dear, I've been waiting for you." I was in shock but it sure did feel so good to get a big bear hug for the first time in my life from any human being. Though I did like getting the hug from him, it did not seem right. I had never seen a priest hugging anyone up to that particular time. I wondered about it and felt very guilty. My conscience pricked me, and at the end of the retreat when it came time to go to confession, I wondered how I was going to confess to the very same priest who gave me the hug. So I was in a dilemma! The greatest shock came when he began to unzip his pants, and I feared trouble for myself. For the first time in my life when I had been a nurse and learned what sex was about, I was scared. This was the first time I was ever, in my life, so openly exposed to it. I tried to fight him off but he kept saying, "This is God's creation, this is love. Love surrounds you, come give me a hug." I was so gullible and wondered afterward if I was being such a prude? I tried to convince myself because he was a Frenchman, that was "his way" and I should not judge him. I went to the hospital wards after the retreat was finished and was beginning to feel I was needed and useful again. I kept all these happenings into the deepest recesses of my mind. Somehow, I was energized and felt happy. Out of the blue, I was called to the superior's office and was questioned about my interview with the priest. There had been serious reports from some of the other sisters, and I was one of the sisters called for an interview with him and as I appeared so very happy, so I was questioned. The conclusion was I must have experienced something or known something. I refused to say anything about him at that time. I would not then have given him away. All I could muster was that he helped me. And the big thing was it was pretty obvious that I was in an awful, emotional state during the retreat. So I was a suspicious subject! In those days, one did not speak of sexual matters anyway. The word *sex* was never mentioned as it is today, like a part of everyday vocabulary. Even if sex was talked about in the outside world, as it is today, it certainly was not ever, ever talked about in the convent. I was happy and ready for a good start and even just to get another hug. It would have been wonderful, as it felt so good to get that hug from Father. Now, I realized this priest was going to be reported. This was a serious offense. I felt very bad for him; but at that time and to that particular superior, who questioned some of us, I certainly was not going to let the priest down. That was in the 1970s, when anything like that was kept a hidden secret. I had not ever heard of anything like this happening, and it was a first for me. I went about my duties as a nurse and pondered over what had happened and tried to come to understand what caused him to act this way. I came to the conclusion that I was to blame, and that I was the cause of it in the first place because I was so emotionally downcast on my return from Ireland.

Looking back now, about thirty years or so later, I realized I was very vulnerable at the time. This priest may have been lonely. Whatever his problem was, he gave me a great big bear hug, my first and it did feel so good.

Chapter 47

Back to Hospital Life Again

Life went on in the hospital as usual, sometimes it was like a rat race, and we were rushing and always in a hurry. The work was never ending. Besides the nursing, we would have to do the autoclaving of the sets that were used for deliveries and Cesarean sections. All the instruments were washed and boiled in those days. Nowadays, the hospitals have the sterilized packs brought in from the companies, all ready to be set up when needed. We were trained not to waste any time. When there was a quiet spell in the hospital, there was always work to be done; and we would be sent to the kitchen, the laundry, or any division of the hospital that needed some help. I generally worked in the labor wards or on the hospital floors, but seldom in the nursery. In those days, the mothers had their babies brought out to them only at the scheduled feeding times. Everything in the nursery was timed not like the unpredictability of the labor wards, where the patients arrived, having labor pains, we would leave what we were doing and attend to the new arrival, while going in between times to attend to the other mothers in labor. I often felt I was in all places at all times and just had to keep going, going, going.

Years of working like this, at top speed, was great while I was young and energetic, but it really took its toll on me physically. All I knew was work at top speed and here I was feeling tired and longing for rest, just a little nap, or just to sit down for a few minutes! It seemed the early morning time in the chapel, before I began the day's work in the hospital, was spent dozing off. I had heard God loves me even while sleeping in the chapel. Would he love me when I was not able to give my very best working in the hospital? Gradually, I began to feel depressed. The old feeling of worthlessness and having no value just spiraled downward, and I was not functioning at all. My energy was not there to push me anymore. I was just going along with the flow like a mechanical robot. No one would know I was not giving of my best. Though there was nothing outwardly to show I was not feeling good, I felt totally out of control when I began crying and crying and there was no way I could stop crying. This was not me! What could I do to help myself? I was too ashamed to go to the superior and ask for some respite.

One day, I was having such pain that I was doubled over and hardly able to move. The superior took me to the doctor. It felt already better that I was getting some attention. Diagnosis was endometriosis. I was put on hormonal tablets and given an injection initially. I was then doing much easier work of folding and sorting out clothes in the convent, setting the tables in the refectory for the sisters, doing small chores, and helping when necessary wherever I was needed. When I returned to the hospital duties, I was assigned to the nursery on the top floor of the hospital. It was much quieter up on that floor than on the ground floor where the labor wards were situated and also the front office where admissions and discharges took place. Generally, there was more activity on the ground floor. So life was more quiet and predictable. While I was working in the nursery, we received word that a black baby had been left at the front steps of the hospital. The priest found the baby on his way to say Mass in the morning. To my surprise, we had what we called a boarder. He was a black baby among all the white babies up on our floor. As I was in charge of the nursery then and my name was Sister Mary Peter, the baby was given the name "Peter." The baby had the largest, sad, brown eyes you ever saw. I loved this baby from the start. Unfortunately, his head was always bandaged. He had been so badly bruised and beaten up; his head was covered with bruises from some obvious beatings. I attended to his dressings and kept his head bandaged. One of the patients, a mother who had a very sick baby in the incubator, came in one day, and while taking photos of her baby, took one of me while holding Peter. I treasured this photo and kept it for myself. In those days, we sisters had to have permission to have a photo taken. I still have that photo holding Peter to this day. Of course, I have wondered if Peter eventually found a good home and loving parents. Often, while cuddling and caring for him, I felt as if he belonged to me. I became so attached to the baby. I was eventually sent back to work in the labor wards and would use every chance I got to go up and see Peter in the nursery. Peter stayed a long time. Working in maternity wards gave me an education in itself. Just observing new mothers with their babies and also husbands with their wives, how many loving hugs and kisses were given. I observed the same caring and loving attention in almost every room that I walked into. After caring for a totally strange baby, I understood what love the mothers actually had for their own babies. They were their own flesh and blood. Naturally, working for years in maternity homes brought it very much home to me of the contrast of my own life compared to these patients.

The question that arose often in my mind was how was I, who never knew a mother's or father's love, never had a home, was actually qualified to be in a place like this? It certainly awakened feelings in me that I never knew I had. How I wished I had a husband who would love me and care for me and vice versa. How I wished I had my very own children. I was aware it was natural for me to feel that way and would try to put it into a spiritual perspective. I reasoned that I once gave this all up to enter the convent and dedicate my life to God! When I would have these natural feelings for love and affection, I would think I was offending God and taking back what I once offered to him, my whole life! I questioned myself many times. Was I really aware and did I understand what I was doing at the time when I entered the convent and dedicated my life to him? I only received and acquired all this knowledge after the fact, when I got all the new experience in my nursing career. Did I know what sexual intercourse was back then? Did I know why men and women fall in love and get married? This was a natural course of events after one started to grow and mature. Back then, did I know where babies come from? I could only answer a very definite no to all these questions. In my first job after leaving the orphanage, when the lady of the house had a baby, I thought that the nurse had brought her. The mother herself was tall and very thin, and she never once spoke to me that a baby was on the way. Many times when I told this story to someone or others, the reply I got was, "Didn't you know she was pregnant?" At that time, I certainly never heard that word *pregnant* in my experience, and she carried it well being tall and slim.

When I held the job of caring for Father Lynch's mother in Belfast, I also had to take the clothes of the Lynch family and the big things up to the laundry every Saturday in the Good Shepherd Convent, which was 3next to us, the Lynch's house. The girls in the Good Shepherd Convent were called "bad" girls who had got into trouble and were living in a section of the convent, doing penance for their sins. This Good Shepherd Convent was right across from the orphanage that I grew up in, and we often saw the bad girls from our classroom windows, these "bad" girls as we called them, were walking back and forth in single file with light black veils over their heads so that they would not be recognized. These "bad" girls did most of the domestic chores, and I would get a peep through the slit of the laundry room door at some of them. I felt so very sad at all these girls stuck in a place like this, but now I realize, it was a shelter for them if they were "bad" girls! Whatever that meant! Around the time I worked for the Lynch family, it so happened that one of our orphanage girls was put in there. I often wondered why she was there. Later, when I was in Belfast for the first time, I heard that she was pregnant and she was put in the Good Shepherd Convent 'til she delivered her baby. I wonder what happened to her, as I wondered what happened to many of them and what road their lives had taken after they left the orphanage.

I mentioned earlier in my memoirs, when I was in Africa, the Good Shepherd nuns housed pregnant girls and brought them in to our private hospital for the delivery of their babies. Was this why the girls were doing penance back in the 1940s in the Good Shepherd convent across from the orphanage in Belfast? We all knew in the orphanage these "bad" girls were in there to atone and do penance for their sins. The place scared me and I would drop off the Lynch's soiled clothes to the laundry door every Saturday and run off as fast as I could. I generally had Lynch's bicycle to carry the clothes in a basket attached to the front of my bicycle.

It was during these years in the '70s while I worked in the maternity hospital that a second chance came round again for me to go home to Ireland. We were allowed home every ten years. I thought about it and wondered if it was worth going as my first experience left me so down and depressed. My turn for going home was due in 1980. Some German sisters requested they would go home in 1980 in time for their parents' wedding anniversaries. Some of their parents had fifty-year anniversaries. So with me, it didn't matter when I could go. I decided I would go, if for no other reason, but to give myself, once more, a chance of trying to find my mother. It would also be a well-deserved respite from the hectic hospital life. I would be traveling to London, and then on to Belfast, Northern Ireland. It was the year 1978. On my return, I was to travel to London and then on to Rome, Italy. I was thrilled I was given a chance to see another country. As our sisters had a convent in Rome, I would be staying there. So I was delighted and availed myself of the offer and of the opportunity.

I duly arrived in Belfast, and stayed with one of my orphanage friends. This was the same family that rescued me from the house I originally stayed at on my first trip to Ireland. Mary and Paddy were great sports and they drove me out to Newcastle in northern Ireland where they had a summer house and where I worked in Father Lynch's home for a year before I entered the convent. It was good to relive that time again and look once more at the Mountains of Mourne in Newcastle. After Father Lynch's dad passed away, the family moved back to Belfast and I went with them. I visited the Lynch's house in Belfast also, the same house where I left over twenty years ago to enter the convent. I stopped there on the way back from Newcastle. We, of course, passed the orphanage and Mary said, "You know Maud, there's a social worker, who works entirely for the girls and boys' orphanage. They are grown adults, coming back to find their parents or relatives. There have been so many returning from all over the world that the social workers, employed full time, were trying to help them locate their relatives, if it was at all possible." My heart jumped to my throat on hearing those words. My God, I thought, am I glad I made the decision to return to Ireland. I wanted to get in touch with the social worker right away. I eventually was able to make an appointment to see the social worker and had a long talk with her. She promised to help me if she could. Even the very thought of someone being interested in helping me sent me soaring high. Meantime, I made some phone calls to people in the phone books who had my last name. But the last name on my birth certificate "Friars" was not the correct spelling. I found this out later. I had been positively sure I would find someone, because now I knew what my real name was. It was the one on my birth certificate. The social worker had a hard time locating anyone, but the very last day before I was to return to South Africa, London and then Italy, I received a phone call from the social worker. She had located a man with a similar name to mine, slightly different spelling, and he drove from Portadown all the way down to Belfast to visit me.

Mary and her husband Paddy welcomed him and as for me, I couldn't take my eyes from him. Even I myself saw a resemblance to myself. Paddy remarked when I was out of sight, "If that's not a relative of Maud's, then I'll eat my hat." He said he was no relation at all. The social worker called him because of his similar last name of "Friar." He was kind enough to take me for a drive to Portadown. He had done some research, he said, and would show me where he thought I was born. Some years later, friends told me he had this knowledge of my family all along, but I didn't really know if that was true. It did make me question as to how he came up with so much information in such a short notice. While on the way to Portadown to visit the place where I was born, an elderly couple were getting ready to go on an outing on their bicycles with their knapsacks all packed. They did stop to help us and directed us to the Fryers' (wrong spelling) plot. I found out that "Fryers" was my real name, but the hospital where I was born had made a mistake and spelled the last name as "Friars" and this was the name on my birth certificate. The people in the two houses living at the end of the wee lane were not at home at the time of our arrivals. They were vacationing out of the country. This was the same street name on my birth certificate of where I had lived. I was shown the linen factory in the distance where my mother, together with the rest of the family, had worked. The Irish cottages, there had been two of them, and they had been pulled down to build the two houses that now stood there. If only someone in those houses would come out and speak to me. As I walked back down the wee lane that led to the main street, I was too overwhelmed to speak. I could feel I would erupt if I tried to talk. I pictured my mother walking down this lane. The very thought of it gave me goose bumps. I was trembling! I wanted to remain in that wee lane and stay there with my thoughts. Imagining my mother once walked along this road, along these very steps that I was now walking. "Oh God, hold me up," was the only prayer I could muster. Mr. Friars who drove me around was very patient, I couldn't utter a word to him. I was too full emotionally and unable to cry or speak. We drove a short distance to the only graveyard in the area of Portadown. He said, "We are not sure if your mother is buried here or not but it seems according to the records she is buried in an unmarked grave." "So she's dead?" I sputtered. He nodded his head and took me to the unmarked grave. I was speechless and did not believe what I just heard. I stood for the longest time, looking down at the grave with not a single sign to show who was really buried there. It was wrenching for me as I stood there with my thoughts. My mother is down there in this very spot where I am standing!!? I was not going to leave this spot; someone will have to carry me out of here. I wanted to stay there and not move. I could easily get a shovel and dig for as long as it took me, to see if that was my mother. Mr. Friars had no idea of how or when she died, but he would send me more information after more research.

Mr. Friars drove me back to Belfast, passing the hospital in Lurgan where the records had shown I was born in that hospital. This is where my name was spelt wrong on the birth certificate. This happened to many people back in those days. It seemed I wasn't "Maud" but Sarah on the birth certificate. The real surname was "Fryers." This was the way I spelt my name in the orphanage. I had looked for my mother under both last names, many times before. I wondered why I was called Maud in the orphanage. Mr. Friars drove me back to Belfast and after spending a little time with Mary, Paddy, and myself, he promised to keep in touch and write. Actually I really didn't have to worry about what my name was. I was now Sister Mary Peter again and was leaving the very next day for London. Time was far too short for me to take in all that had happened. Now, I was a little more hopeful, having had some information to go on. I still kept thinking if that was really my mother that was buried in that unmarked grave, not actually a grave but flat grassland with no numbers or names.

I was now in my forties, and I figured my mother would be getting old, that is, if she was still alive. I wanted to take care of her and would have got permission to do just that, leave the convent on a temporary leave, and be there for her. Now, there was no chance of doing that. I was determined to find out if my mother really died and was buried in that unmarked grave. I found it hard to accept or really believe it to be true.

No need to say where my mind and thoughts were on the journey back to Africa. I tried to keep it all straight in my mind. I arrived in London to find there was some kind of a strike on, and I was on standby. Fortunately, I boarded the plane for Rome that same evening and was feeling good that we had a convent in Rome and that I would be picked up by the sisters. I had their telephone number with me. I arrived about 2:00 AM in Rome. I didn't want to disturb the sleep of the sisters. I was trying to make this persistent person, who approached me wearing a Roman collar, to understand what I was trying to say but he insisted on me giving him money and he would give me the tokens used only for phone calls. I eventually, very politely, tried to wave him away; and I won in the end. I wished then that I could speak a little Italian. I continued standing in line to go through customs and while standing in line, I thought maybe the religious man was trying to help me get through the customs faster because I was a nun. Maybe he was sent to the airport by the nuns at our convent. He didn't have their address or their telephone number, so I became suspicious. I was becoming wise in the ways of the world. So I waited in line, at the airport like everyone else, and was enjoying the fact that here I was in Rome, the Mother City, and I was going to take in every minute of this city, starting with the airport.

After moving up the line very slowly, and I being one of the last in line, I eventually reached the customs officers. They all had officer-like uniforms, and they were all men. It looked like they took their duties very seriously and seemed strict. I was just a little intimidated by them. I produced my papers and when they asked me for my visa, I was flabbergasted. I told them I did not have a visa. They told me I could obtain a visa somewhere in the vicinity of the airport, but I would have to pay for it. As I moved away and tried to think of what to do next, I could not see a single person around except the few officers at the top desks. I went to look for a seat. There were not many, not like at the other airports where one could always find a seat. Toward the exit of the airport, I found a place to sit and stayed in the same place 'til I got my thoughts together. I already had my suitcases. While I sat at the airport, I saw many flights coming and going. I was sitting, just watching the officers go in to a side room probably for breaks. I walked around now and then, not really concerned as I would be able to call the sisters in the morning and tell them that I'm stuck at the airport because I had no visa. It was weird to hear my own solitary footsteps echoing on the marble floors. I imagined someone jumping out at me anytime. There was not a soul to be seen. It was dead quiet. I sat down again; and it was on the spur of the moment, more fear of being all alone at the airport, that I got up, took my suitcases, and walked out the exit. Outside were so many taxis, and I had been previously warned as to what color of a taxi I was to take. I had written the color in my small address book and had looked this up before I went outside. I didn't waste any time, and I made a beeline for that yellow-colored taxi. Off I went in the taxi, almost 4:00 AM, and I wondered if I would get there in one piece. On arrival at the convent, I couldn't see any door anywhere. I kept saying to the driver of the taxi, "Where is the door?" Anyone who has been in Rome will have had the same question. There was no doorbell either. I wouldn't have really worried, but I had to get one of the sisters up and out in order to pay the money to the taxi man. The taxi driver had to get his money and so he began hollering at the top of his voice. I was afraid of him waking up the people round about. Everything and everyone seemed closed in and surrounded by a strong fortress. I didn't think we would ever arouse anyone. At long last, a voice called from the very top window. "Who is it?" she called down. I tried to shout back up there that I was Sister Peter. "Are you from Australia?" "No," I shouted back, "from Africa." "Where are you coming from?" the voice asked. "I just arrived at the airport and I made my way here." "Who are you, are you from Australia?" By this time, I did not want to shout anymore. I called up. "Please come down, I'm from Africa." "What is your name?" the voice asked. "I'm Sister Peter." Finally I was relieved to see the unrecognizable door open and happy and relieved that someone came to pay the taxi man eventually.

I spent ten wonderful days in Rome apart from the terrible creek in my neck that I got from continuously looking up at the wonderful art in all the churches. I was determined to see as much as I could see and not miss anything. The sisters were wonderful and would take me to see certain places of interest, and were very knowledgeable about Rome, having spent many years in Rome and had learnt the Italian language. I wanted to see Castel Gondolfo, this is where the pope goes for his summer vacation and was vacationing there at this time. I went on my own this particular Sunday. I met an American nun on the bus ride to Castel Gondolfo and was she pleased to connect with someone who spoke English.

We took care of each other's purses when visiting the bathrooms and finding something to eat, etc. Usually, the pope held an audience outside, and he would preach and welcome the audience from a balcony. As it was beginning to rain slightly, we were ushered into a large hall. We were both as close as we could be to the pope when he arrived out on the inner balcony. He was Pope Paul VI. He looked very ill, but in spite of that, he talked in eleven different languages. His voice seemed so strong. Three days later after that, his last audience, he passed away. Rome was mourning his death. After the audience, we went back and made our way to the Vatican. The American nun had already seen the Vatican and so we both just wanted to get one more ice cream near the Vatican. It was, we were told, the best ice cream in the world. It tasted so good, maybe because it was the month of August and we were both parched from the heavy depressing heat of August. While we were at the pope's holiday house, we wondered why on earth the pope came to this place, full of big high gray walls surrounding the inner quadrangle. One of the guards, when we asked him, opened a tiny window in the wall and showed the two of us the outside, which was a most magnificent scenery, all man-made. What a surprise! We were satisfied.

The sisters tried to get me booked for the return flight to South Africa. The reason why I had spent so long in Rome was there was a ground strike on at the airport. I left to go to the airport about 2:00 PM, to catch a plane at 7:00 PM. The sisters left me off early as they were going on a retreat somewhere. The convent was to be closed up for a few weeks. So I was dropped off, and to my horror, there was no water anywhere. Then I found out it was because of the ground strike at the airport, nothing was functioning. So for the night, just like everyone else was doing, we lay on the floor with our suitcases cushioning our heads. There were no seats at the airport. There were no planes coming in or going out. I could not phone the convent as there was no one there. I felt confident I would be able to get through the customs as it was easier getting out of the country than coming in to the country. I had my return ticket to South Africa anyway. Never mind not having a visa. Well, we lay all night near our suitcases and dare not move for fear our suitcases would disappear in our absence. About 6:00 AM the next day, a plane was waiting for Australia and one for South Africa. I was so relieved to know there was a plane leaving for South Africa.

The officers were working fast to get us out of the airport and on the plane. When it came to my turn in line he said, "Visa!" I had the habit on and I guess he thought I was all right. I didn't say a word! I just gesticulated with my hands like the Italians do, and so he waved his hands as if to say go on quickly, get out. I took off, as fast as my tired legs would carry me, after such a night at the airport. I don't know why they had to get us on the plane so quickly. It seemed like we had all walked or ran straight through. I was happy to sit in my place on the plane and wait for some water, which was all I wanted. What a stroke of luck that was that I got through the customs. Thank God for the strike, that is what saved me. We sisters later talked about me not having a visa when I was traveling. The reason was that the German sisters did not need one, so no one thought of me being Irish or a South African citizen, and would need one. I was back safely and that was all that mattered.

The pilot announced over the loudspeaker that usually the planes left in the evenings, not morning, and he told us to look out of the window because the view was something we would probably not see too often. The sunrise over the Alps! It was too beautiful for me to describe. It's a scene I've often tried to recapture in my mind. I was spellbound, as we all were.

Chapter 48

Big Changes in the Convent

Soon after my return to South Africa, I was back on the wards again, physically present but my spirit and thoughts were at the graveside of my mother. It was all like a bad dream. Too fast for me, and too much had happened in that one day. Here, back at the old routine, I had a difficult time focusing on my work. Work, which was usually my salvation, did not seem that important in my life anymore. I moved along mechanically to get through the motions, but my heart was not in the work. I knew I could not continue in this way. I did not have the energy that I once had. The work in the hospital was continuous, a lot of responsibility; I made some heroic efforts along the way to keep going, but I feared for myself. After Pope John opened the windows, as the expression went, things did start to change in the convent, slow changes in the beginning. Mainly, the changes were outward changes, simplifying the habit and the veil that we wore. These changes were humongous changes for some sisters, especially the older members. I was fine with the habit changes that were simplified, just so happy to get rid of the excess material that we carried around. It was when things got to a more personal level, and we were having group sessions to discuss where we were on a personal and spiritual level. We were encouraged to be open to one another. This was all new for us, and as for me, I could not just do this. We had never had anything like this in the convent before. I was definitely all for any change, but please do not ask me to join those groups.

Somewhere along the way in the convent, certain external and once important issues and rituals fell by the wayside. The weekly Chapter of Faults was done away with. This was too good to be true. I loathed that session and always thought it was so dumb, petty, and totally unnecessary. "Thank God," is what I said over and over again.

It was shortly after I got back from Ireland that I plucked up the courage to ask to go for psychiatric nursing training. Underneath my reasoning, I figured I would get some help for myself. I could not remain in the convent either and show the sisters who I really was by sharing in groups; I did not want to be exposed or questioned. I knew I would not be able to handle it. In the recesses of my mind, I recalled reading something and I don't know where I read it, as we had only two books that we lived our lives by. One was *The Rule of St. Augustine* and the Constitutions of our own Congregation. Maybe there was another book. What bothered me was what I had read, when I was in the novitiate, as a novice, something in one of these books that the Order did not accept any person who was illegitimate. Well, that stuck with me, and it was one of the reasons that really upset me from the beginning. It remained in my mind, and for want of a better expression, "it stuck with me like a sore thumb that never healed." I would always stick out. I tried to think it over in my mind but at that time, long ago I was only guessing that I was born out of wedlock. When I was already finally professed and was leaving for Africa, it was then I got the birth certificate and this document proved it. What was I to do? Just stay put? I could not leave now as I had taken my final vows for life. It was just like marriage vows. After all the years in the convent and keeping so much of this to myself, I was not ready to be exposed. Maybe this is not the way it was going to be, but I was not ready or prepared for the changes now taking place. Intellectually I could agree with the changes and the newly formed group sessions, but I did not want any part of it. Maybe, I was afraid of the sisters finding out who I really was and this was very frightening. I, no doubt, had very poor self-esteem. That word "self esteem" was not part of the vocabulary in those days. I should have known about all these papers that were needed when I entered. I certainly did not know at that time, back then, that one had to have all these papers, especially a birth certificate.

I was accepted for the psychiatric nursing training. Once again, I had to face the authorities and produce all my nursing certificates, midwifery, and my inatriculation certificate from England, and all my essential papers that were asked for, including my birth certificate. Once I would get through the initial requirements for being accepted, I would be fine, but I was afraid I would not be accepted because of my birth certificate. I thought, maybe the authorities would think I would be very unstable when they saw the birth certificate. I was always expecting the worst and kept dragging myself down as I was used to doing, from as long as I could remember. Maybe the psychiatric nursing will straighten me out somehow, and I will get some help along the way by studying the subject of psychiatry if I'm accepted.

I was finally all set and ready to go. I discovered that the place called the nurses' home was situated far from the college quarters and hospital where I would be working. I had to make a fast decision to get transportation. We would all be going to college at the same time, so I could perhaps get a ride in someone's car. In the meantime, one of the nurses suggested that I get a moped, a 50cc or 75cc moped. Most students were using them in Pietermaritzburg, in the province of Natal, at that time. There were parking spaces marked out for motorbikes and mopeds in every parking lot. It was great! I was also given permission to wear regular clothes instead of the nun's habit. Such freedom I was not used to but I could easily get used to it. It was wonderful altogether. I learned how to fill up the gas and handle the cash money. I spent the money very sparingly and kept a record for the convent of the little money that I did spend. I passed the test to be able to ride the moped and felt I had made great strides. I was all set and ready. In college, the students gave me the nickname of the Flying Nun. We had so much fun. Life was great for me, and there was no rush for anything. I was more relaxed. I had more time than I ever knew but I knew that I needed it for study. I was delighted when I was given permission from my superior to buy a 50cc moped, and a helmet. I was now independent and did not have to rely on riding with other nurses. Besides riding it for college classes and for work afterward, I would go for a little ride now and again and enjoy the thrill of the wind blowing and the freedom that I felt in doing it!

Just as general nursing opened up a whole new world for me, so did the psychiatric nursing course. The study of how the mind worked and how it affected the physical body of a person appealed so much to me. I gradually learned the whys and wherefores of my own behavior. It was like a prolonged moment for me when I began to understand why I behaved the way I did and the cause and effect of it all. Wow! Learning to spell words *psychosomatic*, etc. was a challenge, like many of the other words relating to the psychiatric training. I enjoyed every moment of that course, and it was a very happy time and very worthwhile time I spent in the psychiatric wards. There was enough staff and camaraderie that we all felt supported while working on the wards. It was a one-year course. I often thought I could bring back some of what I learned when I returned to the convent. When the course was finished, I remained for one year, working in the same psychiatric hospital, just to apply what I had learned. I was delighted to be able to stay on for another year and continue to work with people who had taken the course with me, and I felt I could just be "me."

I do not want to give the impression it was altogether a utopian situation. For me, it could be called that, compared to the situations that I was used to in our own hospitals. The mere fact I had some free time, in itself, was great. I had not had freedom before, and I wasn't used to it. I was working in a relaxed atmosphere, generally, and there was not the superhectic activity that I was accustomed to in our own hospitals. It was a pleasant change for me in every way. I had my time and days off which I had never had before. So that is why I called it a utopian situation for me.

At the beginning of the psychiatric course, the head tutor had warned us some of us would go through difficult times. "It is not going to be easy for you, this is a course that may affect you personally. Be forewarned!" She also said there was a psychologist on the staff and if we needed help anytime during this year, to make ourselves available to go and talk to him. All the tutors on the staff would be available for us also. We were certainly going to be taken care of in every way possible. I did wonder how this course was going to be so different from the general registered nursing and the midwifery course that I passed in the 1960s. Somehow, I was so cocksure of myself, telling myself if I already made it through the other nursing training and the convent discipline, etc., that I would definitely not have any difficulties. At least, I would be able to cope with whatever came my way! If I had made it through very tough times already in our own convent hospitals, then I would make it here. It was a good change.

I sailed through the first six months fairly well 'til the midterm college classes began. We sat through videos after videos and had to discuss afterward what we observed. (This was the first time I had ever seen or heard of videos.) I had not ever seen TV either, so this was an entirely new experience for me. I was doing fine up to a point; many of the nurses could be seen wiping tears here and there. Then, the following day or two, videos were shown of children who had been abandoned by their parents or taken away from them and placed in foster homes. A video was shown of an orphanage, and we were to observe the children's facial expressions. They were dull, lifeless, and some of them would sit in corners away from the main body of children, just staring at everyone that passed them by and looking longingly for maybe some kind of attention. They appeared to be just lost in their own world. The psychologist came in to the class to discuss the videos on the children. I was too overwhelmed at seeing the tapes that I couldn't speak. I hoped I wasn't looking conspicuous. I broke down eventually and sobbed my heart out outside the classroom. I couldn't keep control any longer. My whole childhood appeared before me as if to condemn me, and I feared I would not be allowed to continue the psychiatric course. The fact I was brought up in an orphanage and did not know my parents or relatives was, I thought, sufficient reason to disqualify me from continuing the course. I could not help while watching the children on the videos from breaking down and crying because I had so deeply identified with them. It was the first time in my life I was so exposed to this. It was too vivid a memory for me. The psychologist gently came over and asked me to come to his office afterward. That, in itself, caused me to tremble even more. By the time I reached his office, I was in a state of panic. A monitor was placed on my finger, and I did some relaxation and breathing exercises. I was on the monitor for about thirty minutes and felt I had calmed down enough to leave and ride my moped back to the nurses' home. I had been so emotionally distraught that I couldn't even mutter any word to the psychologist. I had some emotional upheavals after that initial emotional scene in the classroom, but I persevered through them all. In my head, I knew it would have been better to talk to someone, but I would pull myself together again and get on with my studies. I rode the moped around and around that evening to help me feel better before I returned to the nurses' home. It gave me a real sense of freedom and some fresh air. I was in shock myself that I lost control of my emotions, and I was determined to keep a stiff upper lip and not disgrace myself again. I was more upset over the fact that I did not have better control of my emotions. What would the students think? The fact I was also a nun didn't help. The very fact that I was a nun made me feel even worse because more control was expected of nuns. I truly felt I was in disgrace. Feelings didn't count. I was familiar with those words, but I knew for sure after this experience that feelings did hurt! They really did hurt!

Being back on the hospital wards was just wonderful. As students, we didn't have the full responsibility because we worked under qualified staff. We were still learning. So I could take life a little easier, not having the sole responsibility. I studied very hard before the final exams, and I was delighted when we got the news that the entire group had passed. It was the end of a great and wonderful year.

We had a big celebration when we graduated at the end of the year. The medical superintendent greeted us all individually and had a few words with each of us. It was a fun day and a relief that all of us had passed the exam. I had not seen too much of the medical superintendent while I was a student but now I saw her regularly, making her rounds in the hospital. I was given permission to remain on at the same hospital for some practical experience. I was delighted about this. I just felt that life, in general, was going at a much slower pace than what we experienced at our own hospital. I saw it certainly made a difference when we were completely staffed. We had enough support as well.

It felt so good to be working on the floors in the Psychiatric Hospital. Having completed my studies and exams, I could now give my full attention to the patients and learn as much as I could on the wards. One afternoon, the medical superintendent visited my ward while she was on her rounds. I had heard she was loved by everyone. "Hello, Sister, how are you getting along on the wards?" she asked. I said, "Fine, Doctor, I'm enjoying it now that my studies are finished." We had a short conversation, then she said, "Where are you from, you don't sound South African?" I replied, "No, I'm from Ireland." She was startled at my reply. "Good gracious, you're from Ireland." She was delighted to hear I was from Ireland and she said, "I don't believe that at long last I have met someone from the old sod, in South Africa! You are the first student nurse I've met from Ireland, and I don't meet too many people from overseas anyway. So tell me, what part of Ireland?" I replied, "Belfast." "Oh no, you don't mean to tell me!" She grabbed my arm and pulled me into an empty room nearby. So began a long friendship that I still have to this day. She invited me out for dinner the following night. This was the first time I had ever, in my life since I entered the convent, gone out to eat. I did feel kind of nervous, but not for long. I was afraid the doctor would ask me just whereabouts in Belfast I was from. It so happened, she herself in the course of the conversation, said, "You know I must tell you 'the story of my childhood', it's kind of interesting." My ears must have cocked up especially when I heard her mention the very name of the street where the orphanage was located. Wow! She, the doctor, Joan McDaughter, had lived and was brought up on the same street as I! The story from the doctor was that her mother was very ill. Before her mother passed away, and during that period, her father was able to get a girl from the orphanage nearby to take care of the two children, the lady doctor was the younger of the two sisters. This girl from the orphanage was the only mother that she knew or remembered. She said, "She was a wonderful mother and a wonderful woman. Those girls in the orphanage were well brought up, and I got to know everybody up there at the orphanage." I did not believe what I heard nor did I interrupt her 'til she had finished talking. We went outside and continued our conversation because the place (restaurant) was closing up for the evening. I said to the doctor, "You are really not going to believe what

I have to tell you. I was brought up in that same orphanage!" And as they say in Ireland, "We could have talked 'til the cows came home." I would take my break for lunch and go and visit her. We had such good times and many good laughs. "It's a small world after all" This was the first time that I was able to talk about the orphanage without feeling ashamed of being brought up there or of the stigma attached to it.

After I completed my psychiatric training and had a follow up experience of one year in the hospital, I then returned to the convent. I was assigned to be in charge of the infirmary at the Mother House. The work experience in the infirmary here was very different from the hospital experience, or the fast pace in our hospitals. I was glad about that. I knew I would have to give myself time to adjust to the new surroundings and daily routine. After giving myself time to assess the situation, I hoped I would be able to incorporate some of my skills of letting the sisters talk and be heard, and be free to be themselves and feel comfortable with me in charge. I hoped the sisters would know I was available for them and also approachable. I tried to keep a happy atmosphere so that all would feel relaxed and that there was no one there looking over their shoulders at all times. I would be there for them. So my ideals were high. I thought the aged sisters in the infirmary were due for this kind of atmosphere after living a life of strict discipline of obeying rules and regulations all their lives. It was their time to relax and enjoy life as much as possible, in spite of their aches and whatever else ailed them. But change did not come easy for the elderly sisters who had given their whole lives to service and were themselves so disciplined and so hardened to any change.

At this time, changes were also taking place in most other Orders of Nuns. Change began with external rules and regulations. There was now a whole new trend taking place within our own convent. First, the habit that we wore was changed. I laugh now, when I look back and recall the comments that were made by some of the sisters when the new regulation was in: the habit was to be two inches above our ankles. That did not go down too well by many in the infirmary where the older nuns lived, or even by those younger sisters in the convent. We thought we would welcome the change and then came the veil. I remember when we changed from the starch to cellophane wrapped around our faces and heads. We thought this was great not to have to starch the headpieces anymore. Now we were to wear a simple veil and do away with all the starchy stiff pieces and cellophane. I was delighted with any change, and it made me feel so much freer and alive. When we wore the starch and cellophane on our heads, I remember one of the doctors asking a group of us sisters in the hospital what the reason was for us to be wearing, what he called, the "buckets" on our heads. This time of change was a very difficult time for most of the sisters, but especially for the infirmary sisters. So I had my work cut out for me, dealing with so much recalcitrant behavior. So much change was taking place at one time. Some of the sisters were already wearing their new simple veils and of course, showing some hair. This fact seemed to show a kind of defiance, according to some of the older sisters . . . "they gave all that worldly appearance up when they took their vows and now they are taking it all back again." I understood how difficult it was, for many of the sisters, never having had any change in their whole lives. It was a drastic experience for most of them. I remember the superior actually calling me aside to talk to me about my hair showing, I was showing too much. What hair I was exposing was what grew on the side of my temples. It meant I would have to cover my forehead with my veil and have it just over my eyebrows in order to cover all my hair. What really shook me to the core was the question she asked me, "Where did you get all that black hair from?" It was not a sincere question she asked me, but she appeared to be so angry at all the hair I had and it was still raven black. I was stunned with the question! When she continued with her unpleasant remarks, I was becoming so shaken up that she actually asked me such a question that didn't need to be asked. I angrily responded, "For goodness sake, where do you think I got it from, you have to ask God!" It took a long time for any kind of change to be accepted. The decision was made for the older sisters to remain with the old familiar habit, but they were to try and tolerate the sisters who were willing to change. Gradually, over time, many more changed to a more "modern" habit.

I really did enjoy my time in the infirmary with the older sisters. On the whole, it was a good experience for me to watch these older folks with a vast, rich experience behind them and good, down-to-earth common sense. So many of them appeared to be just so close to God. I recall a little old Irish nun saying to me one day, after I had finished cutting her toenails and had cut her hair and generally perked her up a little. She said, "Sister Peter, the man who missed you missed a lot!" We laughed so heartily in that little cell of hers. Every time I would drop in on her, I found that most of the time she was praying. She would say she was talking to God. What a vital lesson I learned from her and from many others. Most times, she would be knitting or reading while praying or talking to God as she would say. What a life of simplicity and joy. What I recall above all was a beautiful radiant smile on her face. She showed this radiant smile always, in spite of the crippling arthritis that she had. No wonder that I can't forget those people, who were so much part of my life for so many years. This life in the infirmary was my kind of life with wheelchairs, walkers, walking sticks, sisters shuffling along, many doubled over, and crippled. I really cared for these sisters, and I felt I was needed. I never felt I was needed in our hospitals. Oh yes, I was needed for the work, and so long as I could keep going at top speed, I was needed.

I was happy doing my work in the infirmary, but after my two years of experience outside, working in the Psychiatric Hospital, I missed the camaraderie and the constant learning and keeping up with the trend. The convent seemed so archaic in comparison. I saw change happening but it was confined to changes within the convent and which, also appeared to be so petty. Changes that should have taken place long ago, though the changes seemed, at the time, monumental to the sisters. I was happy, but felt I wanted to break the boundaries, and just get away and get out to see something different, instead of the same never-changing monotonous routine every day.

Although the workload at the Mother House Infirmary was much lighter, there was plenty of it. There was not the hectic pace of running our feet off as it was in our own hospitals . . . It was still hard to fit in everything that I was supposed to accomplish. Besides the sisters in the infirmary, I had to attend to those sisters living in the Mother House who were admitted to the infirmary with various symptoms and illnesses. In those days, there were many sisters, about one hundred who were either teaching or nursing or doing domestic work, e.g., working in the bakeries, the gardens, kitchens, etc. Many of these sisters could only come after teaching or at the end of their workday. The evenings were often as busy for me as during the day. Many of the resident infirmary sisters were dependent on me to assist them with their baths, etc. In the evening, it was difficult for me to coordinate it all, without friction arising, which sometimes did and then I was not very popular. Often when I should have been in the chapel for some prescribed services, I just could not make it. I was the only person in charge with a few African girls helping me. Many times, I was so tired; I didn't know how I was going to make it through. From being so overtired, I would go to my cell at night and sob my heart out. At 5:00 AM, I was to be up and greet the dawn of a new day with a smiling face. During my psychiatric training, I got enough insight myself to know that work was not who I was nor was what I did that identified me as a person. I realized now that all along, my religious life I had tried to work to show who I was without consciously knowing what I was doing to myself. Now that I felt I couldn't work with the same energy as before, I felt my whole world was falling apart. Maybe my turning the big fifty midlife crisis had something to do with it also!

After my training as a psychiatric nurse, I realized fully what I had been doing. I now knew that I had worked a lot harder in order to be accepted because I had not received the love and assurance as a child. The expressions like "midlife crisis" or "inferiority complex" did not exist then and did not enter my vocabulary before. Now it was all so clear to me in theory. In spite of thinking I knew most of the answers to my problems, I was still not functioning to my fullest potential and it was because I did not have the energy to keep going as I used to. As a religious, living such a strict religious life, crying was not very acceptable, and I myself thought it was showing weakness. I was supposed to be a strong person, and I felt the sisters would now see how weak I was. I was too proud to let them see that I was even having any problems. I would find a quiet space to go where I could cry when I really needed to cry. I would try hard to look all right again and assume my work. The fear of doing anything wrong had kind of dropped out of my system. I just did the best I could, but with all the changes, I was now worried about people seeing me as I really am; and my biggest fear of all was having anyone find out who I really was. This fear just cramped me in my daily activities. I felt such a terrible anxiety about the groups that were formed that the real me would already be out there for all to see. Why I had this crippling fear, I don't know, but it took over my life. I was not allowed to cry in the orphanage, I made up for it in later years. The psychologist had said, "Sister, you don't allow yourself to cry!"

Added to all that was happening in my life, more changes were taking place. Group sessions eventually were divided into smaller groups. There were so many issues and discussions pertaining mainly to the changes in religious life. Many of us did not like this kind of change, where we were to talk about ourselves. I found it to be too big a jump for all of us who were only used to a silent regimental life all laid out for us. I was not in a frame of mind to talk on a spiritual plane when so many practical problems needed to be addressed and dealt with. Though I certainly wanted change and was enthusiastic about it, I backed out of the small groups. One of the first groups was being run by a priest, and we had a whole day to ourselves, a kind of retreat that was a change from the old retreats where we just listened with no participation.

The Gospel reading that was chosen for the day just hit me and touched me to the core. The words, "Should a mother forget her child, and if she should forget, yet will I not forget you." I probably had heard that part of the Gospel many times; I was so stoic then and I didn't let it get to me, but now I was sobbing uncontrollably. The only safest thing I could do was to take flight. I know and I made myself so conspicuous, but I could not face the following group session. I walked and walked in the grounds outside for relief. Sister T, who was on the same retreat, approached me later and wanted to help me but I was too emotional to speak.

One Sunday, I was back at work in the infirmary after the retreat, when I received a message that one of our young sisters from the mission hospital had died. It was about twenty minutes' drive from the Mother House. I was in shock. We so desperately needed nurses especially young ones to swell our ranks. I had previously worked on night duty with this same sister, and though I wondered what actually happened, I was suspicious because sister had been discharged home from the hospital the previous night Saturday and was very upbeat. She had been admitted to the Psychiatric Hospital and was there for approximately two weeks. Diagnosis was manic depression or bipolar disease. I was present the previous night when she came home from the hospital, and we had a welcome celebration for her. It was good to see her home, and we all hoped for another nurse to help us. I recalled one of our tutors at the Psychiatric Hospital where I worked and trained, saying, "Look out, when the depression lifts and they begin to feel good, this is the very time when these people plan things." These words often stayed with me and made sense. Here her words rang true. This sister committed suicide in the early hours of the morning. We were in total shock. It was difficult for all the sisters to understand why she did such a thing, but one had to try to understand the mental anguish that this sister and any person with this diagnosis go through. Most of the older sisters were shaken up and failed to understand this dreadful episode, and after this happening, I was trying to explain to the older sisters in the infirmary why this happened. Some understood but some would not be convinced. The latter were saying this was an unforgivable mortal sin. I had been asked to go to the hospital and lay her out for burial, but by the time I got someone to drive me up there, two of the sisters had already done the good deed and laid her out for burial. In those days, it was customary for the nurses to lay out the patients who had died.

The fact a sister had committed suicide was such a shock that I don't think we ever got over it. Even though I had experienced these episodes in the hospital and knew the whys and wherefores of this disease, at least, as much as I could know as a nurse, it remained a shock for all of us. She had used a large kitchen knife to slash her throat! What a mental state she must have been in.

Chapter 49

Off to California

It so happened that a new regional superior was appointed for the convents in South Africa. One day, I made an appointment to see her. I could not explain or talk to her of what was really going on, but I gave her sufficient information through writing to let her know I needed some kind of help. A course of studies was offered to me, but I told her I needed more help for myself not more studies. So in due course, I was told I would be sent on a program but I would have to wait for an opening. I was pleased I had actually spoken to the superior, and something was being done. I was very grateful for that. It made me feel good that I had asserted myself. I got the urge that I had, definitely, to do something for myself.

The House of Affirmation, the international therapeutic center for clergy and religious, was at the service of all the religious orders. It was a residential center for people, clergy, and religious who wished to reassess their vocational and spiritual life in the light of their emotional problems. There were quite a number of these houses in the States, one was in England, and I think there was one in Australia. I was eventually sent to California where there was a House of Affirmation. I did not go there directly but stayed at one of our own convents nearby in California. It was an old-age home run by our own sisters, and I worked in the nursing home 'til I was called. Meanwhile, while waiting my acceptance to the House of Affirmation, I had to travel back and forth and be thoroughly evaluated. I did many psychological tests while waiting, and in October of 1982, I was sent to St. Louis, Missouri, where there was a House of Affirmation. Little did I know then that St. Louis would be my final destination. I am still in St. Louis, twenty-six years later, sitting at my typewriter, writing my memoirs. The one question I have been frequently asked is "How did you get to St. Louis?" I'm glad they didn't ask me, "What high school did you go to?" I believe that question is a frequently asked question, here in St. Louis, Missouri.

I felt very welcome at the House of Affirmation and well received in this residential community. I was as ready as I could be for any kind of help. Besides all the sessions we had to attend, I began to feel better and more rested. I also knew that I was being kind of selfish having this time away for myself, but I often heard the response when I would mention it, "You are worth it!"

Gradually, as I attended the individual and group sessions, it dawned on me that all my religious life I had tried and was trained to bury self, self didn't count. Now it was self that was sort of coming out and begging for help. My problems were buried for so long under the guise of a happy person on the surface. Now here, in this program, I could be "me." I discovered this person they call "me" was quite unique, and "being" was important, just as much as the works I did, even if they were good works. Up to this time, I had relied very much on my work and on what I could accomplish as my self-identification through hard work. My religious education stressed so much that "self" didn't count, it made sense to me back then because we were so full of zeal to be good religious and to give only our very best, and there was to be no lukewarm religious. During this period that I spent at the House of Affirmation, I tried to use up the time well to learn all that I could. With the help of the therapies, I tried to resolve, to some extent, the psychological conflicts rooted in my childhood. As best as I could, I tried to get some insight into my grief and childhood losses, and not just "get over them." This would help me to understand and lift the depression that I had been going through for so long. This was a time for "me" to reassess my vocational and spiritual life. Over the nine-month period at the House of Affirmation, and having had a thorough evaluation of my progress, I finally made the decision to leave the convent. I felt at peace with the decision and did what my heart told me, that I had to be true to myself. This time, away at the House of Affirmation, was a very fruitful time for me. There was help from the residents and staff any time I needed it, and people were there for me. I, of course, was not used to having so much focus on "me," but it was my turn! Being a community, we all helped each other and consoled one another when difficult times arose. Naturally, there were difficulties mostly arising from an underlying immaturity, which resulted from a lack of affirmation in our lives and especially going back to childhood days where some of us did not receive any love or affirmation of any kind. We were all professional and well-grounded in our spiritual lives as well. Most of the religious priest, when they had finished the course at the House of Affirmation, went back to their parishes. Most of the religious women also returned to their convents. I felt it very much when I left the House of Affirmation, I was leaving a little cocoon of very supportive people and stepping out into an unknown world in a new country. Fortunately, I had a fairly good start of being with all American people at the House of Affirmation and where I had learned a lot of neat English expressions; only in America, did I hear there were different words and different meanings in the English language.

I would often get mixed up, and I still do, with the simple things in the language like "Jell-O" and "jelly." In England and South Africa, the language Enlish was the same, so, after thirty-three years, it was just not easy to pick up the terminologies that I had never heard before, until I came to America. My English wasn't the best as I was listening to German sisters speaking English all day and the patients speaking Afrikaans and the Africans speaking Zulu, etc. It felt good to only have to concentrate on the English language, but I needed to brush it up as well. "Jelly" to me meant the "Jell-O" that shakes. I never heard of "Jell-O." "Jelly" in America meant "jam" in South Africa and England. It was always a joke among the residents when they heard me speak and repeat after me, "I'll do it 'straight away' instead of 'right away.'"

Chapter 50

Exclaustration while Living in America

When I left the House of Affirmation to emerge into the outside world of America, I had to deal with so much that was different but I was determined to understand and master the language. What really puzzled me so much was the terminology referring to the baseball games. I had never heard of baseball in Africa. Expressions like "The ball is in your court," "Step up to the plate," etc. I got my first exposure to baseball when the Cardinals was on in 1982, the year I arrived in St. Louis.

The first time I walked into a grocery store, it was a novelty for me. There was so much to see in the department store aisles. I would go there just to see what I could see and watch the people shopping. I had never been in a shop or a grocery store before; it was all like Christmas to me. It all seemed too much and how did the people know what to choose. I would look at the Jell-O and try to find the jam and see what it was called in America. I would write down some names that I saw and try to ask when I got back what they meant. I was aghast at the amount of food in the stores and the aisles full and chocker block of anything you needed or wanted.

Someone from the House of Affirmation had helped me to find lodging, a room in a lady's house, not far from the House of Affirmation. This was great because I could go back to visit the people I knew. Some of these priests would give me a ride to town when I needed a ride. They were there to give me support, if I needed support, and I certainly did need it. The superior from my congregation in California came to visit me, and she offered to help pay the rent for me 'til I got a job. After I talked with the superior (I had previously written to her, telling her I wanted to be out and free for a while), she was very understanding and supportive. I eventually received a letter from Rome, the Apostolic Delegate, who gave me leave to be on exclaustration for two years. These two years would give me ample time to decide which way I wanted my life to go. It was a very difficult decision for me to make. It was not in my nature to let people down like this. I cried when the superior left to go back to California. It felt like I was walking away from all that I ever knew and had. It hit me so hard to see her go, and it hurt me to do this to her. What was I doing anyway? I went back and forth on the decision that I had made for some time. I thought of all the sisters that I had left behind, and I cried some more. It was just like a kind of turmoil in my mind . . . "How could I do this to them?"

The first thing I had to do was to try and get a green card so that I could get work. I could only get my student permit leave extended. For this, I had to go downtown and the people at the House of Affirmation were very helpful in giving me rides when I needed them. It was tough dealing with the immigration office. Each time I would get down to the office, I would be given another paper to fill out. It became a long drawn-out business. I went down by bus one time with another sister, and we decided to make an outing for ourselves at the same time but the line happened to be too long. I filled out a couple more sheets of paper but then I had to go back to the bottom of the line again, so this was taking up a full day. It was a very frustrating time because I was not getting anywhere fast. The whole process was lengthy and complicated. Trying to call on the phone was next to impossible. Sometimes, when I thought, I had it all put together, I would be given more legal papers, and told to take them to another government building downtown. At times, I would become really frustrated with the system and I fully understood why some people sneak into the country illegally. It took a long time for me to get the extended leave. I was trying to follow the rules. I was fortunate to continue having help with filling out the papers and having people drive me to town. It was difficult for me to understand the various contradictory instructions on the papers. How did those foreigners who could not speak English manage? I eventually got my green card, and in due course, my permanent residence. I was more than grateful to the House of Affirmation people who helped me with the paperwork and helped with their cars. They gave me so much of their time willingly, and without them, I would not have made it. I was advised to stay in the States if I was going to leave the convent. There were so many riots and uprisings in South Africa that it would not be safe for me to go back, especially if I was starting life, outside again, in South Africa. It was a time, looking back on it now, that was very challenging. Obtaining my permanent residence, or the time leading up to that time, was very, very hard indeed; and many times, I just wanted to forget the whole thing and go back to Africa. I was still holding my return ticket to South Africa and a ticket to Ireland. I was advised not to go to Ireland because I would not have a chance of getting a job as a nurse over there. Ireland, the place of my dreams, I had to put out of my mind. Eventually, I mailed both my tickets, which I was holding, back to South Africa and my return ticket to Ireland back to the convent in California. When the sister from California had come to visit me, I returned my ring as I was no longer living as a sister. The whole picture was parallel to going through a divorce. In my mind, I went back and forth with the pros and cons of religious life, and how could I let go of such a good life that I had lived well for thirty-three years. In the convent, we had to maintain silence, be passive and submissive, and obey our superiors and those in charge of us. Food was placed on the table every day without us ever entering the kitchen. We didn't handle money. We had no responsibility except to the immediate task of nursing or teaching or domestic work. So how would I manage the outside world?

So many legal hurdles had to be met with during this time. The cultural adjustment was just as tough, and I would feel so stupid for not knowing things that those living here took for granted and never gave another thought. Later, I was trying to measure up to my nurse coworkers, when I got the nursing job and be on top of things, at least as much as I could be. The president of the House of Affirmation was very helpful in assisting me in whatever I had to do. She showed me how to go about getting a savings account, what to do and say when I went to the bank. As this was going to be my first time ever to step into a bank, I was terrified! I was to open a savings account. The very word "open" threw me. Was that the correct word to say? I checked what I had written on a piece of paper. I knew I had to do this sooner or later. I was in the line at the bank and when my turn came, I walked up and acted as if I knew what I was doing. "I would like to open a savings account." The teller said, "I would like some identification? Have you opened an account with us before?" I replied, "No." "May I see your driver's license?" the teller asked. Of course, I had no driver's license but I told her I was taking driving school lessons. Now, I can laugh about it, but back then, it was very humiliating. I went back to the House of Affirmation, and I explained what happened. The response was just roars of laughter. One of the resident sisters at the House then tried to explain to me what I was to do, but we were still laughing so much that I wasn't taking in what she said to me; I was trying to do so many things at one time. Also, learning how to

drive a car was one very scary time. When the driving instructor drove up
and told me to get in on the driver's side, I point-blank refused. I told him
I would only get in if I could sit on the passenger side, at least 'til I got used
to being in a car. I also said, "The car is too big!" So it was like a tug-of-war
to see who won. I asked him if, for the first lesson only, he would let me
just sit in the driver's seat and not drive and just become familiar with the
gadgets that were in front of me, and just hold the wheel! I emphasized I
needed to be familiar with everything before I could go on the road. I told
him that if he let me drive on the roadway, it would be dangerous and I was
afraid something would happen to him. I was frightened beyond words. I
don't recall the rest of the lesson but the instructor probably never forgot
this little gray-haired foreign lady. I did continue with my driving, and I did
pass the tests. Was I happy? That was a big achievement! My next big thing
on my to-do list was to write my State Boards Nursing Examinations. That
took four days of tests. Again the guys, priests at the House of Affirmation,
drove me down to the center where I would be writing the exams. I got
the results about six weeks later that I had passed. Just wonderful! I was so
happy I had, prior to that, met the standard requirements to enable me to
write the State Boards without having to do any further college studies. My
transcripts and scores from South Africa were accepted in the States.

About this time, my green card arrived. It was like giving me the green
light to go ahead, get started. As I didn't have a car then, I asked about the
nearest hospital or nursing home so I would be able to get a job as a nurse
and be able to walk to work. I needed to get work fast and make money to
live on. Up to this time, I had no money. My rent was being paid by the
convent in California. It was sent directly to the lady who owned the house.
While I was waiting for a job in a hospital, I got a private job to take care of
an elderly man in his nineties. He belonged to the same church as I did and
that is how I got the job. I had an old bicycle from the House of Affirmation,
and it was lent to me so I could get to work. The elderly man lived with
his daughter. As I didn't have my green card yet while I worked for them, I
could only be paid cash and very little at that. Usually, when I arrived, the
daughter would take the opportunity to go out someplace and leave me
with him. The daughter usually left a "high ball" in front of him before she
left. No sooner had she closed the door behind her than he would begin to
holler at me. "Come here, young lady, bring me a decent high ball!" I had
no clue what he was trying to mutter at me. I did understand what a high
ball was eventually, but I naturally thought it had something to do with a
ball that he wanted to throw around. I looked around for a ball. I told him

I couldn't find one. "Well, look in the garage, there might be some there," he said. I did wonder what kind of a ball he was talking about. I knew it was to be probably thrown high, but how? I found a ball, but somehow I figured he would not be satisfied with whatever I brought him. "Woman," he yelled at me, "don't you know what a high ball is?" I nervously said, "No, I don't." I had to help him get out of his armchair and into the wheelchair so that he could help himself to get a decent high ball. I learned a few phrases from him such as, "How stupid women were!"

When I had accomplished most of what I had set out to do to make a new life in America, I passed my driver's test, passed my State Boards, received my green card in the mail, I was ready to go for an interview for my first post in a nursing home within walking distance. I had set up an appointment ahead of time with the superintendent of the nursing home.

All went well at my first interview and a date was settled as to when I would start on the wards. The superintendent was finished with the interview, when I realized I had forgotten to ask her when I would be able to take my vacation. I needed to write down the dates, and could I settle that with her sometime? I saw her expression change to one of shock and total disbelief that I, who was not even on the wards yet, had dared to ask for any holidays. Her response was, "My goodness, you needn't expect a vacation in this place 'til you have built it up. I can't believe you had the audacity to ask such a request, when you haven't set foot in the hospital yet."

I tried to explain that everyone in South Africa had to take a thirty-day vacation, it was mandatory, and we had to plan way ahead of time. She responded, "No wonder, they have no money over there." Here I was starting off definitely on the wrong foot and that was before I even got my foot in the door.

I thought about a car and it would be great to drive myself to work. It would be a straight run to work, so I wouldn't have any problem with directions. A friend of mine accompanied me from the House of Affirmation to check the price of used or secondhand cars. I was a jump ahead, thinking it would be no problem to look at the cars, shop around because that is what I had heard people do. One looks around and shops. I also thought in between my driving lessons, I could have my own car to practice in. The car dealer came out and saw me peering in the window. He said, "Do you like this one? Would you like to drive it around?" I looked at my friend and said, "You take it for a ride, I'll wait here." The car dealer was puzzled and asked, "Who's buying the car?" I said, "I am." "Don't you want to get in and take it for a ride yourself?" the dealer asked. I had to explain I was thinking of buying a car for later. He managed to bring me inside while my friend drove the car around. It was then that he found out I was just taking driving lessons and that I did not have a license to drive right now. Twenty years later, I met this same friend at a restaurant just by chance and she related the story of me about my going to buy my first car. Everyone was enjoying that story, and I did too. People were looking over to see where the shrieks of laughter were coming from, but it brought back memories of how anxious I was not to waste any time because I needed to get things moving quickly.

During this time, after I got my green card, I was now a resident alien. I had also gone through the proper channels to go on leave from the convent. After all the necessary paperwork was completed, I wrote to the superior in South Africa. She had to contact the bishop in South Africa who was in contact with the superiors over there and in California and then on to Rome, Italy. The letter only arrived from the Apostolic Delegate in Rome, stating I was now on exclaustration for a period of two years, during which time I would be dispensed from my vows and religious life.

It was the actual finality of it all that got to me, even though I knew I already had two years to make up my mind. At this time, I was dealing with so much and I realized what was life for me took precedence over vocational or religious life. I was going to live this life, which I never really had before I entered the convent.

"What is life for me precedes what is a vocational life." I read this somewhere in a book and thought it definitely applied to me. Of course, there were many times when I would go back and forth about the decision I had made. It was a big step for me. Many times, I would question myself as to what on earth I was doing. At other times, I was so exhilarated about the freedom I had. It really struck me that, in fact, this decision was the first major decision I had ever made on my own; and it was indeed very frightening. I was truly grateful for all the help that was given me up to this present time. I tried to convince myself that after all, it is not permanent, it is temporary, and I still have two years to think things over. "Exclaustration," what a horrible word. It sounded like I was banished forever or cut off from everyone.

In the orphanage, my name was Maud. In the convent, I was Sister Mary Peter. When I was in the process of going through all the necessary paperwork here in America, I just mentioned green card, interviews, etc., I had to remember to sign my name as "Sarah." This was the name on my birth certificate. I had to go by my legal name on the birth certificate. As this was the first time I called myself Sarah, I would keep saying to myself,

"Remember, I am Sarah." I would say Sarah over and over to get it into my head. After all, it was a much better name than "Maud." I liked Sarah. It felt like being christened with a new name and here I was, starting off a new life in America.

It was a good chance for me to have attended the House of Affirmation. It was like a period where I was able to assimilate a little of the American culture and learn from those people at the House of Affirmation. It was like a listening and learning session as well as a healing and therapy session. I could ask questions if I didn't understand. In other words, it was like a stepping-stone for me to branch off out into the unknown world of America.

Gradually, the people at the House of Affirmation were leaving and others would be arriving. It was an ongoing shifting of the people until I did not know anybody there anymore except the staff, and many of the staff I knew were changed.

The old bicycle was holding up well and it got me to work back and forth on a straight run, but one day, the bicycle broke down and I had no way of getting it fixed. I could have taken it to a bicycle shop, which was on my way to work, but I had no money at that time, so I walked to work and back. It was a little scary walking home after eleven o'clock at night. My shift was three to eleven in the evening. I was fortunate enough to get a ride occasionally from any nurse who was going my way.

Everything was going more or less well for me. Like a foreigner feels in any new place or job, I did feel stupid and lost at times. I longed to find someone whom I could talk to and hoped to make some friends. I actually prayed that God would send someone along my path. One day on the wards, I was in the process of giving the prescribed medicines out to my patients, when this person approached me and said, "Hello, are you Sarah?" I said, "Yes," but hesitant to say anymore. "Are you from Ireland? I hear that you have worked in South Africa but are actually from Ireland." She continued to welcome me and told me she was leaving for Ireland the following day. How I wished I was going with her. When she introduced herself as "Mary," I knew she would be a good friend. Time did not permit us to talk much more but Mary said, "I'll see you when I get back." Meantime, while she had gone to Ireland, I got another job through a nursing friend of mine who had done the House of Affirmation program with me. I was able to get an apartment right next to the new job in the hospital and nursing home where I was working. I could walk to work.

The superior in California sent me money to buy a car. I was thrilled and offered to repay the loan when I started to bring home a check. It was like having a check come in and wondering how I could possibly save any money. I had hoped to save so as to be able to go to Ireland. At the same time, I was paying my rent and utilities, and paying back so much every month to California for the car loan.

I could certainly not afford to buy anything I would have liked or wanted. I gradually was able to go to church sales and buy a few clothes. I thought of sending the loan for the car back to California; I had an apartment right next to my work now so why did I need a car? The apartment was not kept up as it should have been. The doors and windows had to be all duck-taped to keep the draughts out and so I went back and forth in my mind with the same question: should I buy the car and move out of the apartment that was so dilapidated and not maintained? I could live in a car very easily as I had no property or anything else. My possessions would all fit in a brown paper bag. Today, it is plastic bags. I thought of asking the convent nuns, who owned the hospital where I was working, if they would allow me to park in their hospital parking grounds and live in the car. Of course, I got no permission for that. I was able to go to the bank at this time where I had opened my savings account. The directress at the House of Affirmation had asked me if I had a checking account opened yet. She told me to go to the savings and loan place where I already had the little savings account and open the checking account. She told me that probably I would be required to put a minimum of $100. At that time, I thought that was a lot of money and would I be ever able to get that kind of money together. I worked toward getting it and eventually got my own checking account. I was so delighted to be able to manage what I did, so the first chance I had to get to the House of Affirmation, I showed my checking account to the directress of the house. While spending some time socializing with those resident people still there at the House of Affirmation, the directress looked over my checking account to show me how I was to write in the checks that I deposited and those I would withdraw when paying bills like utilities, etc. I asked her what she meant by the word utilities, of gas, electricity, water and so on. I was horrified that I also had to pay for all that besides paying for the rent. I told her I don't think I could afford to live in an apartment. So that was what made me decide to live in my car. As the directress was looking at the checking book, she said, in a shocked voice, "My God, what have you done?" I looked in amazement at her facial expression. "Don't ever do that. You have signed all your checks, do you know what that means?" the directress asked. Of course, I had no idea. I was just being my usual self of being ahead of the game. I thought I was being organized and up to date with everything.

Today, I recall that incident so well, and I chuckle at my innocence or rather ignorance about the ways of the world. Thanks to all those people who came into my life back then, I wouldn't have made it without them.

I was constantly learning and discovering new things in my new country of America. I had to catch up on so much. I was debating in my mind if I ought to buy a car so I could live in it and then move out of the apartment. I also tried to figure which was the best way to save my money. The weather decided for me. When the heat arrived that summer, I knew I couldn't live in the car. So I remained in my apartment and eventually bought my car. The superior in California sent the money for the down payment for my car and with the advice of the people around me at work; I was made to realize I would need a car in St. Louis as there was very little public transport that would be available or accessible.

I settled down in my new job, right next to my apartment. I thought a car was a car and wondered why one had to shop around. I wasn't aware there were all the different kinds and makes of cars. My goodness, how could anyone keep up with it all? I was advised by the superior in California to buy a new car because being a woman, it would save a lot of repairs. I had the money for the down payment, and she advised me to take out a loan for the car. Sometimes, I became very despondent when I would think of all the money I would be spending and the loans I would have to pay back. It was too overwhelming. My wish was that I could save up enough money to be able to go to Ireland was *put on the back burner* (another English American expression I had learned). Practically speaking, I was just living one day and one hour at a time, just trying to cope. The term "down payment" and taking out a loan from the bank was all new to me. How could I take a loan out at the bank, when I didn't know what that meant and I had a savings account in a savings and loan? Was that the same as a bank? The directress at the House of Affirmation came to my rescue again. Though I had help, it all remained overwhelming!

When the superior from California came to visit me at the House of Affirmation, she talked to me concerning my reasons for leaving. She was very understanding and supportive. One of the remarks she made to another resident was, "I would make a wonderful wife for some widower." "I was known to be a great worker." The directress had responded to her, saying, "I was an eternal optimist." All these remarks gave me some hope that, in spite of everything and in spite of all that I was dealing with, I would make it!

It was very time consuming but necessary to go through all the business that I had to deal with and still keep going to the immigration and naturalization office downtown. As I was having some problems dealing with the naturalization and immigration office, I was given five names of people to make a choice for one of these people to help me. All of them were attorneys except the person who had worked for many years in the immigration office. I chose the latter because it was people from the immigration who could help me to file all the papers that were necessary. He told me I had already done most of the work myself but at least, I had someone now with expertise in this field. How fortunate I was to find this person. With his help, I filed an application form. I was a resident alien at this time, and I was applying to become a permanent resident. I had my physical, my fingerprints, and necessary photographs all taken care of and given instruction on the laws of the country. If I obtained my permanent residence to be admitted in to the country, then I was informed I would have to remain or reside in the United States for at least five years after I was admitted. My one thought was that "my trip to Ireland would have to remain on the back burner!" Shall I also say the "luck of the Irish" was with me? I was told the deadline or the fixed date for people from the North of Ireland to get in to the country, of the United States, was October. I was delighted to have been able to get in to meet that quota for the North of Ireland people. So I was admitted for permanent residence after appearing before the judge in court for final hearing. All the investigations for fitness and for citizenship were completed. I was finally in the country lawfully. I felt a certain kind of freedom now that it was all behind me. I felt I could just hug everyone I met and tell them the good news!

The lady, who introduced herself when I had just started in my first job in the nursing home, had contacted me after returning from Ireland. I also visited her in her home. Her name, as I mentioned, was Mary. Mary said to me on one of those visits to her, "You know, there's a lady I know, who would love to meet you, her name is Maureen Kelly. She just lives round the corner from me. I'll introduce her to you one of these days."

I had never kept a journal in my life. I had not heard of people writing in their journals before. It so happened I needed to keep track of all the business as well as immigration business. I had to write in some important data for my own information and memory. So now when I looked up in my book, I noticed July 26 was a significant date for me. I had not thought of that date before. I arrived in South Africa, July 26, 1955. I arrived in the USA on July 26, 1982. It was July 26, 1990, when I became a citizen. I had studied the manual for citizenship and passed. I ought to keep that day as a celebration day. The reason I took so long to go for my citizenship, long after I obtained my permanent residence, was that I did not want to go through all the hassle that I went through before. Of course, it was not as bad as I expected. I only had to obtain the history book from the immigration office and study it on my own. I guess I had a fear of ever seeing the office of immigration again.

It was also on the 26 of July 1984 when I was introduced by Mary to Maureen Kelly. She had been a widow since 1982 and since then had lived by herself. I was very happy to meet her as she was born in the North of Ireland, and in the conversation that followed, we both discovered I knew people that she mentioned and also some places where she had been. Her house had pictures of Ireland and Irish memorabilia. I was intrigued with all the Irish collectibles, and I just felt so much at home in her house. Having been in Africa for twenty-seven years, it was good to experience a touch of home. It certainly made me long to see Ireland once more and see all the girls from the orphanage again. Maybe some of them would still be in Ireland, and some had maybe traveled to faraway places like I had traveled. I had hopes and dreams for myself, now, especially, as I was free of seeing more of the girls next time and of course, I would be free to look up my family, and have more time to do it in than when I previously was in Ireland as a nun.

When Maureen Kelly saw the condition of the apartment I was living in, she eventually asked me if I would consider moving in with her. I was reluctant to move to her house, for the simple reason I wanted to be able to be responsible and capable of handling my own life. This was a first time for me to be on my own, and though it was a bit scary when I was living on my own, it was good for me not to be too dependent on anyone. I wanted to prove to myself that I could do it. So I was hesitant to move in with Maureen Kelly.

I continued working in the same nursing home. It gave me some stability to be in the same job and to earn some money. Life might have been somewhat easier, if I had come directly from Ireland or England, but I was from another totally different world. The culture was very different in Africa. I have been in the convent for thirty-three years and twenty-seven of those years were in Africa. It certainly was culture shock for me. It was also déjà vu for me, like being on my own in the world after I left the orphanage, to go out into the unknown world again. The only difference was I had more experience now than back then in Belfast. I was about twelve or thirteen years of age back then, and now I was fifty-four years of age. I did not have the experience that I ought to have had. I did not know how to handle money. I would sit in my apartment and try to figure out the small change or coinage. I would bring some small change to work and had them taped to a piece of paper with their names next to them. I tried to remember which one they called a nickel and when one was called a dime. The paper money was easy. I became familiar with going to the bank, writing checks, and keeping tabs on my money. It was not easy at this time, trying to save as I had to pay back my loans. It was a struggle of trying to keep a balance of $100 in the bank. I learned about social security and pension and discovered if I worked at least for ten years, I would be eligible for a pension and social security when I retire. I was hopeful about the future, and if health permitted, I would be able to work longer than ten years. Many times, when I felt so stupid about ordinary things and bereft of any intelligence, like most foreigners I think experienced, I was still full of hope and determined to keep on going. I was very happy with the people I worked with and generally upbeat with the way things were turning out. I was making a new life for myself.

After I had spent two years on exclaustration from the convent and vows, the final papers arrived from Rome. I had previously gone through all the proper channels before I reached this step. Though I had left or was leaving the convent of my own free will and had done all the soul-searching while I was living at the House of Affirmation, I was still, in a way, very frightened of the step that I was taking. This was it—my fate was sealed. The deed was done!

I was genuinely frightened at the direction my life was taking. I was aware I was at a major crossroads in my life. I was trying to be connected with my friends at work, while feeling disconnected. I tried to feel I belonged, while really, I was not belonging anywhere. To go to work was my saving grace. I was not thinking of my own problems then, but I was so caught up in the work of the moment, and I was trying to acquire as much knowledge as I could. I knew I was an achiever and a survivor.

Once on my own, alone in my apartment, I would find myself sliding back into myself and was again trying to cope with the thoughts of my unworthiness. I wanted so much to rise above the deprecating thoughts and show a good face. Being alone seemed to be a problem for me as my thoughts would wreck havoc. Working lifted me above all this. I tried to help myself and find out why I felt so awful when I was alone, and after much thought, I realized I was my true, real self once I was out of the public eye. I could be who I really was with all my hang-ups. I couldn't help thinking I lived my early years in the orphanage, with hundreds of children, and after entering the convent, I was again with hundreds of sisters, so being "alone" was also new to me. So I figured, I had never been alone before and I would have to conquer this as well. I was still carrying a lot of unresolved questions and emotional baggage.

My new expression, "on the back burner," for a while, would be my one and longed-for wish, and that was to see Ireland again and find out if I had some relatives over there. The nurses, as well as people out working, go home to their families or parents at the end of the day. I go home to myself. To be an orphan, in this world, is not easy. I know, I will have to carry forever the loss of not only a mother and father (I tend to forget there was a father in the picture), but a permanent loss of ever knowing a family. At this age that I am now, there is the potential loss of ever hoping for a family of my own. Sometimes, when I thought along these lines, it would be depressing. I learned this fact was going to be an ongoing process in my life of dealing with this loss on an everyday basis. Trying to hold on to God as my anchor was my last resort. I had a hard time praying or saying prayers. My prayer would take on the same form of just questions to God. "Oh God, you said somewhere in the Bible, it is not good for man to be alone. Why was I alone in this world?" And here I was, voluntarily choosing this lonely life.

When I had been working at the nursing home for about two years and after the final papers arrived from Rome, I was now free. I was determined to keep going and be happy in the work I was presently doing. It was not actually a nursing home; it was an infirmary of retired sisters, something I was familiar with. It was more like the situation I had left behind in Africa. Many of these sisters were professional people. It was here I learned so much. I learned about baseball and some of the terminologies used in baseball. There was a sister in her nineties who would listen to the baseball games on the radio and give us all the news of what was happening. I gradually learned what it meant to "step up to the plate" and all the other baseball expressions, and Mark McGwire's home runs! Life was becoming more interesting, and I was becoming more familiar with everyday happenings.

Chapter 51

"Nurse Becomes a Patient"

After being on the job for two years, I was busy on the infirmary unit one day when I went in to answer a call from one of the sister's rooms. A nurse aide had been helping the sister and was trying to hold her up to prevent her from falling. As I entered the room, I was just in time to catch the sister from keeling over. I myself was bent over immediately and I couldn't get up straight. My back had the most excruciating pain, and I could feel the nerves in my legs and feet were on fire. I had sharp jagging pains in different parts of my legs. I was unable to move from the bent-over position I had fallen into while helping the sister. I was put in a wheelchair and wheeled over to my apartment. I thought I could help myself to get on my feet, and literally, it was very difficult and very painful to move. I felt pain throughout my entire body even when I used my hands to hold on to the back of a chair or place my hand on a table. It was painful. The pain radiated down both legs, and I was totally incapacitated.

A nurse from the nursing home brought me some pain medication to relieve the pain, but it didn't help at all. I managed, with help from the nurse, to lie on the bed and I stayed there for a few days. Every movement was like an electric shock going through me. It took me a long time to move from the bed to the bathroom and back to the bed. Every little twinge was a worry and a foreboding sign. After a few days of this terrible pain and unexpected spasms, I had suddenly fallen to the floor in a bath of perspiration. It took me some time to even move from the position that I was in on the floor to call for help. The nurse assistant, who lived next door to me, came home from her shift about 3:00 PM. I had been on the floor all night, hoping for someone to come in the morning, but it took all day before. I got help and that was by managing to throw something at the wall that divided our apartments that I got some help. I heard the door opening and closing so I knew there was someone there. I was so relieved to see a human face, and when she appeared, I immediately asked her to phone my friend Mary. I had made short movements to try to reach the phone, but I couldn't reach it. The intense pain prevented me from moving even in the slightest way.

I recall Mary arriving but can't seem to recall much more. I have faint memories of lying on the gurney and being wheeled in to the operating room. The medication helped the awful sharp pains, and I recall being in the waiting room ready for surgery. Even then, I vaguely recall the fact I had lost everything and was not in control of what was happening to me. I prayed short prayers. "Please God, take me now, I will not be missed by anyone, and I am not leaving any family or relatives behind." Hope seemed lost! I thought of many things, as I lay there, recovering from the back surgery. I was confined for nine days in the hospital. Severe pain would catch me at every move that I tried to make. I wished I could be suspended from the ceiling and left to hang there so that no one could touch me. When I wanted to change my position, I couldn't do it because when I tried to put my hand on the side rail of the bed, just this one little move would cause terrible pain. I then, just had to let go and let whatever happened happen. It was a case of just staying in the same position, even just trying to raise my head was causing pain all over. My mind wanted to move but my body couldn't, not even the slightest wee bit. I certainly remember my friend Mary arriving at the hospital one morning, and she brought Maureen Kelly with her. Together, they had the nurse bring me an injection for the pain, and as they waited for the shot to take effect, they were preparing basins and towels in the room. I was given a bed bath and my position was changed. It felt so good; it was like having angels administering to me. I was just experiencing a ray of hope again! Oh, what a relief it was, just to have someone in my life that cared enough to do this kind deed for me.

On discharge from the hospital, I was taken down in a wheelchair but was still very weak and helpless. I was taken to Maureen Kelly's house instead of taking me back to my apartment. Here, I was taken care of by this very kind and gentle lady. I fully realized how blessed and privileged I was to have her at this downtime in my life. Though I fully realized all this, I was not used to being cared for. I was used to taking care of other people all my life, so I did find it hard to be in this position. I recovered enough to be able to leave the house and go for my follow-up visit to the surgeon who operated on me. He was amazed at my recovery. He had previously told me I had a fifty-fifty chance of recovery. My diagnosis was multiple level lumbar decompression.

I was told by the doctor to walk and walk, and if I am looking for something to do, just get out and walk and walk and walk some more. It took just about three months for me to recover enough to think of getting out from the house and walk outside. It was as though I was a child, seeing the outside world again as if for the first time. It gave me new reasons for hope and a new appreciation of life.

A very frightening thought for me was the loss of wages and absence of work. I had been worried about it all and especially the medical bills that would start coming in soon. My recovery was approximately three months, a long recovery time for anyone who had no money coming in, and already had loans to pay back.

I got a job at the nearest hospital on the psychiatric unit. I started working two nights a week. Sometime later, the unit I worked on closed down and the head nurse on the maternity ward heard I had been a midwife in South Africa, and she came up to see me on the unit where I was working. Arrangements were made for me to start full time as soon as I could on the maternity ward. I was delighted to have a real full-time job, but more than ever, to work at a job I was trained in and accustomed to.

Chapter 52

In 1950s Technology Stepped In

Of course, I had many new things to learn. Technology was not in the picture when I was doing midwifery. I worked using my own intuition and experience, and besides taking blood pressure and temperatures, we used a handheld fetal stethoscope for listening to the baby's heart rate. I recalled, when I had last worked in the maternity hospital in Johannesburg, the doctors gradually started bringing in these huge cumbersome boxes. They were kept in a side room and no one was to touch them. The first doctor that had one, explained to me it was ordered from Scotland. In fact, we would not enter that particular room where these big boxes were kept unless a doctor was with us. It was set up in a room eventually, alongside the patient's bed. It was the first fetal monitor I ever saw. It could be wheeled into any room and connected to the patient, but usually just prior to delivery time and only in the last phase of labor. We nurses would look at this big box, more like a TV set looks today and marvel at the wonders it could do, while being scared to touch it. I often thought of that first monitor, and here I was in America years later, watching the nurses read it like a book, and I was so fascinated to see a fetal monitor in each room. The difference was the nurses here were watching the monitor all the time and were more familiar and knowledgeable than some of the doctors were, especially because they were familiar with their use on an everyday basis. How times have changed! Those of us nurses who were new, of course, had to learn the fetal monitor, but I think I was so intrigued and amazed at this new wonder of a machine and the multiple things I could read on the screen. This was so exciting for me after using the handheld fetal stethoscope all those past twenty years. As much as I was enthralled by all the new technology, I was just as every bit amazed at being able to keep up with my full-time job. I did a lot of walking in the wards, which no doubt was a great way to get my walking exercises in, while earning a paycheck at the same time.

I continued at the same job, in the same hospital, for eleven years. There were a few nurses who worked on our unit with me, on different shifts, and who were all in their sixties. After eleven years, a letter went out from the hospital authorities to all the older nurses. It stated in words to this effect that we were to think about retirement. It would be an optional retirement, where we would receive certain benefits and a severance pay. We were all very surprised, especially receiving a letter of this kind at a time where there was so much publicity about the severe shortage of nurses. Though the letter stated retirement was optional, it was also saying that if we did not take this offer now, then we would regret it later. I was not happy about this arrangement. I gave it some thought and finally decided to go with the offer of retirement now. I was afraid that if I didn't retire now, that down the road, if I remained on the job, I would be jeopardized in some way or form. The not-knowing-what-was-in-the-future kind of made me feel scared. The letter was kind of final.

During the years that I worked in my last job in nursing, I was able to save some money and fly to Ireland; I went with a friend of mine who lived in New York and had worked there for twenty-seven years. She also had been in the same orphanage, and like me and many other girls, had entered the convent. As far as I know, I think that I was one of the girls who remained in the convent the longest. I often heard that children of alcoholics often marry alcoholics. I couldn't help thinking that maybe that was why we girls converged toward the convents to spend the rest of our lives in the safe comfortable zone that we were familiar with, following the same pattern that we were used to, and didn't know any better at that time. The girl from New York traveled with me to Ireland. I remember arriving at the airport in New York and seeing the large sign above where the bags were checked. It was Belfast. The very name of Belfast lifted my spirits. We would be flying directly to Belfast. Previously, when I traveled, I had flown in to Shannon Airport and visited our friends in the south of Ireland, and then from the south, we made our way up north. This way left very little time for me to spend in Belfast. This time, I met more of our orphanage girls than I did on my previous visits to Ireland, and I also spent more time in Belfast.

Chapter 53

Back to Visit the Orphanage in Belfast

One of the first pieces of good news, which I heard from our girls from the orphanage, was that we were allowed to go inside the orphanage to look in the "big black book." That book was there; open for any of us to look up information on ourselves. It was a large thick book with a lot of information in it concerning us all. I was both excited and angry. I couldn't help thinking of my teen years of trying and begging the nuns to tell us something about ourselves. I had asked the sisters when I went to the orphanage on my first visit back if they had a book where all our information was written such as when we were placed in the orphanage. I thought on my first visit to Ireland that since I had become a nun that I would get that extra privilege. No such luck. It was all strictly private. Now I spoke to the social worker of the orphanage who was taking on that particular duty at this time, and she said that she would certainly do what she could. There had been so many of the orphanage girls returning to Belfast just for the same quest as I was. Because of the number of girls coming or returning like myself, a social worker was appointed by the bishop just for the orphanage girls.

When I saw the black book (jokingly called the "Doomsday Book!"), I thought that at long last, sixty years later, I get to see what was written about me. The only information they had was from the day I was admitted to the orphanage, the day that I was baptized, confirmed, and the day I left school to go out to work. I already knew from my birth certificate that I was from Portadown in Ireland, and that my name was Sarah. Here in the black book, they had me written in as "Maud." I was really disappointed that there was not any pertinent information about me. I don't recall any dates that were written in the black book. I had not been looking for that kind of information, so I was not interested any further. I hoped that the social worker would be able to help as she had promised. I had not gone to the orphanage by myself, a group of us planned to go together. We had so much fun and laughter as we walked around and recalled so many things that happened while we grew up there. Every turn and corner had a story to tell. It was a large building that was now standing empty. No more children, no more elderly in the old-age home. I wonder where all those many hundred of children were today. The orphanage was one hundred years old, and it was to be demolished! Though we have a great gathering and so much fun that day, it was the end of an era then end of a century, it spanned a lifetime for many of the sisters as well. The place was full of memories as we walked around and recalled old times. This was the place that housed us and gave us a safe haven. This is the place where we were schooled and disciplined, and this was the only world that we ever knew. I couldn't help recalling the song that we were taught in the orphanage, and I think that we all still remembered it because automatically we all broke out in song, before we left the orphanage for the last time. We sang in unison as we made our way through the orphanage grounds. One of our girls wrote a parody to the song titled "The Old House," meaning the orphanage. The original song was "Lonely I Wander through Scenes of My Childhood."

> The old house was a song
> We learned in our childhood.
> It brings back fond memories,
> Of happy days of yore.
> Gone are the young folk,
> The playground is silent.
> The shouts and the laughter,
> Are heard there no more.
>
> 'Twas here we played games
> Like net-ball and tennis,
> Hide and go seek behind those great trees
> And when autumn came round,
> We would gather the chestnuts,
> Searching and wading through
> All those green-colored leaves.

But the saddest of all,
Was the loss of our chapel,
Where we sang in the choir,
From our earliest years.

Still today, I can hear
The sound of the organ
And it takes a great effort,
To hold back the tears.

It's hard to let go
Of the scenes of one's childhood.
But we are so grateful
To have shared them so long.

We're thankful to "ALL"
Who shared in our childhood,
But as the song says,
It is time to move on.

—Kitty McCoy

It was wonderful to have met and spent time with everyone up at the orphanage, to get to know them all again, and to hear their stories of how everything had turned out for them. I wished that we were all closer geographically. I wished that I didn't have to move on, as it said in the song.

It was time to board the plane back to St. Louis, USA, and back to work to earn my living once again. I returned to Maureen Kelly's house, and we both sat and talked. I, of course, had visited her relatives, her first cousins, and was able to give her firsthand information about them. At one time, I said to Maureen Kelly, "Next time, when I go to Ireland, you will come with me." She replied, "I have wonderful memories of my last visit, and it won't be the same again, all my friends and cousins over there are growing old and I don't want to burden them." Maureen herself, naturally, was beginning to lose her hearing and also her eyesight, and I thought that in the month that I had gone she appeared feebler. It was good to come home to her; she was like the mother that I never knew. In the first two years that I lived with Maureen Kelly, I was reticent about talking to her, but gradually my story unfolded; and once I was able to talk openly with her, we had great conversations. We would sit on the patio and reminisce: she would love to talk about Ireland and her family back then, and I would tell her stories of Africa and of course, about the orphanage where I was as a child. There were numerous coincidences in our lives. To start with, we had a substitute teacher in the orphanage, and her name was Maureen Hennessy. When I moved back with Father Lynch from Newcastle to Belfast, the Lynches had bought the house from the Hennessys. The Hennessy children were Maureen and Kelly's first cousins. I had been working at the Lynches in that same house where her cousins had lived! Small world!

In another incident, I told her that as I stood at the bus stop in Belfast, waiting to go out for the evening, a man approached me with a slab of chocolate. He came across from a confectioner's shop nearby. He told me not to let anyone see it, just eat it up, and enjoy it. I had never seen chocolate before. He said, "You know, I can't sell it in the shop, we haven't been given permission to sell it yet." This was just after WWII was over and the chocolate was coming back in to the shops for the first time. I put it in my coat pocket and as soon as I found an out-of-the-way place, I pulled the chocolate out to eat it. It had started to melt and the paper wrap and chocolate were melted together. This man was Maureen Kelly's relative. Maureen said, when I was telling her the story, "That was my uncle, he owned that shop." It was the only shop on that street.

Maureen Kelly, when she lived in Ireland as a child, went to school just down the avenue from Lynches. I used to slip in to that same school and get on the swings in the playground, and hoped that I wouldn't be caught trespassing.

There was a church situated alongside the end of the orphanage grounds, outside the high wall surrounding the orphanage. It was the Holy Rosary Church. This is where I was taken at eight years of age to be baptized, and Maureen Kelly was christened in the same church.

After I had returned from Ireland and things had settled down for me, Maureen Kelly thought that it would be a good idea if I became a citizen of the United States. It was she who rekindled the love of Ireland in me and at the same time taught me what America stood for. I obtained the history book and together we studied. Maureen would ask me questions about the history, and if I didn't know the answers, she would just say, "Look it up." It reminded me of when I was training to be a nurse in South Africa, and our French teachers gave as the same kind of responses it we asked any questions. "It's in your books!" they would say. So in June 1991, I became a citizen of the United States.

It was just a short time after I returned from Ireland that I received a letter from the social worker in Belfast. In it, she stated that this affidavit had been found in the archives of the orphanage. It was handwritten.

> I, Ethel Fryers, of Knockamuckley, Portadown, hereby declare that I wish my little girl, Maud, aged about six, to be taken into the Nazareth House, Ballyfaneigh, Belfast. I wish her to be brought up a Catholic and cared for by the nuns. I will not claim her back again.
>
> Signed in the presence of the undersigned witnesses this 21st of February, 1936 at Portadown.
>
> > Canon McDonald
> > Margaret Creaney

There was a third signature, which I couldn't make out; it was difficult to decipher the handwriting.

I was standing in the light of the kitchen window next to Maureen Kelly, when I first read the affidavit. My eyes were glued to the sheet of paper. "Was I really holding a piece of paper in my hand with my mother's handwriting? This was the first time ever that I had some firsthand information of my mother. My mother wrote this declaration?! Did she?" I was trying to hold back the tears and be my casual stoic self, but I was unable to speak. Maureen Kelly was with me, and she noticed that I was looking at this sheet of paper, I just handed it to her, and we both stood and cried. I just sobbed my heart out and the words that choked me up were "my little girl" and "I will not claim her back." Oh, God! How could she have done this? A gentle reminder from Maureen, "You'll be late for work!" She followed me 'til I got into the car, and she asked me to give her a call when I got there. She was afraid of me driving while in such an emotional state. I tried to show a brisk stoic manner, and I was able to get through the evening shift.

Driving home that night, I had to be extra careful because so many questions were going through my mind. I, of course, read and reread the letter over and over, 'til I knew it by heart. The contents of the letter were sad, but I was in shock by the fact that I was actually touching and holding something that my mother wrote! I had often been told that I had a good memory, but it bothered me that at the age of six, I was put in the orphanage, and why can I not remember any of those years? At age six, I should remember some things. This confirmed the fact that I was not placed in there as a baby, as I had always thought. Now at sixty-nine years of age, I feel that I'm still that six-year-old girl, still looking for her mother. My school friend, who traveled with me on my trips to Ireland, was of a different mind as were many of the other orphanage girls. Their attitude was, "They didn't care for you, why should you care?" I did care, and I wanted answers! I was too far away to make an attempt, or to even know where to begin. I was late in starting my search, whereas most of our girls had never left Ireland. Consequently, over time, they found out about their families and had married and had their own families. I think the majority of them certainly felt fulfilled.

So many people have a consuming passion to go all out to find their ancestors. I had met people from America who were over in Ireland, looking in churches for information, just basic questions about parents or grandparents, and their ancestors. Many visited graveyards, looking for names of relatives. As an Irishman, a friend of mine, once said, "You know, so many people spend so much money and time doing that sort of thing. For goodness sake, they're all dead!" As the conversation continued, he said, "You know, they just want to find out more about themselves, that's what it boils down to." I thought how true that statement was. I was only looking for my mother, and I had such a curiosity about myself. Did I look like her or my father? I wanted to solve the mystery of where I came from and who I was.

When I was in Ireland in the last few years, one thing puzzled me. I often heard our girls talking about "the girls" coming back from Australia. It puzzled me but eventually I asked the question, "What do we know about girls living in Australia? What is all this talk about Australia?" The reply was, "Surely, you must remember when so many of the girls from the orphanage went to Australia!" I could not understand how I had no recollection whatsoever of any of the girls leaving for Australia. I was puzzled! I said, "You know it must have been before my time."

The more I thought about it, I did wonder why some girls whose names I remembered were living in Australia. I thought that perhaps they had married Australians. Father Lynch had given me some of their addresses. It seemed to be the fact that the orphanages had so many children to take care of, especially so many WWII orphans. So not only the orphanage that I grew up in, but many other organizations and establishments sent children to Australia. So there was a big exodus from time to time. Orphan girls and boys were shipped off somewhere. I missed that last *exodus* to Australia in the late forties because I was, as one girl said, a "situation girl" back then.

My friend, Patricia Kelly, no relation to Maureen Kelly, was in the orphanage with me and had lived in New York for twenty-seven years. In 2002, she died and her ashes were flown to Ireland for a memorial service. Pat, as she was known, had entered the convent one year after I had entered, but because of ill health, she was sent away. As I mentioned before, when I traveled to Ireland, we always went together. It was sad to be going to Ireland by myself, and also that I was going for the memorial service of Pat Kelly. The memorial service was held in a nursing home that was a brand-new home. The orphanage was demolished, and this home was where all the elderly people from the orphanage were being transferred. I've known that over the years, no name was better known among the girls than Pat Kelly's. Pat was the girl that opened her apartment and her heart to every one of the girls who landed on her doorstep in the 1940s. She remained the same generous girl all of her life.

I held up pretty well at the service until I had to throw the clay on her remains and then I wept. I couldn't help but notice that all those present at the service and at the graveside were the orphanage girls who shared so much over the span of seventy years.

During the homily at the memorial service, the priest said that it was so unique to have a group come together like this one. We were all from the orphanage and some of the men who were present were from the boy's orphanage. The presiding priest was very overwhelmed to see a group come together, many from far, just for one of their own. He spoke of loyalty, ties of friendship, and genuine affection that knit us together over the years throughout our lives. This friendship will not unravel with death. The years will move on and some will die, but I will always have the surety of seeing the same group of girls, though diminished, still keeping in touch with one another. We have all been shaped by the unique history we have lived during our formative years. We orphan girls were shaped by a very different time and grew up in a very different place in the world. Most of our girls have married and had families of their own. It was good to see the children of some of these girls helping in whatever way they could to enhance the celebration of one of their own. We are like one large family who share the core experiences and values of sisters and brothers who grew up in the WWII era in an orphanage.

The orphanage itself has been demolished to make room for more modern buildings, and I am happy to have been given a video of it before and after it was demolished. Our memories, of course, will always be with us.

When Pat Kelly and I visited Belfast throughout the past years, we always used the house of Bobby and Imelda McKnight as our base. Bobby McKnight died a few years before Pat Kelly. Imelda and her family had Pat Kelly's remains placed in their family's grave. I was very impressed by this ultimate and complete sign of friendship of one of our own girls.

I have not forgotten the lady that I lived with all these past years, from 1986 'til 2002, Maureen Kelly. Pat Kelly had visited her here in St. Louis, and they became good friends, called each other on the phone, and Pat never missed sending Maureen a Christmas card and St. Patrick's Day card. Now they are both gone to a happier abode up above.

Pat Kelly was truly my sister and Maureen Kelly as I mentioned became the mother that I never had. Maureen saw me through so many problems and difficulties when I was not only new in the country but right up to her death. There were so many things that happened to me, scary but funny in hindsight while I was living with Maureen Kelly. Just to relate one incident that happened to me this one year, I came home from buying my car stickers at the license bureau, and I was scraping off the previous stickers from the car while it was in the driveway. I couldn't find the current year's stickers; they had been blown away with the wind, while I had been scraping off the old ones. I went to work that night. I was on night duty at the hospital. The next morning, a scared Maureen Kelly approached me, and in a soft voice said, "You have to phone the police station, the police called last night." She was so frightened that I had been in trouble. I guess that she wondered what kind of a person she had living with her. The police had not told her what happened. I immediately called the police office, and I was told to come down. What a relief to hear that they had found the stickers. While the police were patrolling the grounds of the nearby mall, they found my shiny license tickets glittering in their car headlights! It was 2:00 AM when they found them, stuck in the bushes.

Another occasion, which scared her was when I first started to drive to work after my back surgery. The first few days back at work were just fine; I arrived safely. Maureen had driven me back and forth a few times so that I would know the way. About the third day, Maureen got a call from the hospital, saying that I did not turn up for work, where was I? I had inadvertently driven on the highway. I had never been on a highway before; I was so scared. I apparently had driven on to the highway cloverleaf, and I couldn't get off it! I circled and circled and circled. Each time that I would get off the ramp, I could see big signs and billboards marked Kansas, Tulsa, etc. I would go back again on to the first exit and go circling round and round again. A few times, I stopped, hoping that if no one else stopped at least I will eventually see a policeman. I did at last get off on the road again and off at the first ramp. I don't know where I landed. I saw a group of about ten or twelve men standing around. They were, I supposed, going home after work. I was happy to finally see some people, and I approached the group. I must have looked like a damsel in distress because one of the men said, "Don't worry, I'm going in your direction," and he drove his car right into the hospital parking lot where I worked.

I thought I would be reprimanded for being about four hours late for work. But it was good to be on familiar ground. Maureen was waiting up for me that night as she usually was, and she was anxious to know what on earth had happened to me. In the beginning of my stay with Maureen Kelly, I did a stupid thing. I signed each check in my checkbook as previously mentioned, so as to be prepared and as I thought, organized. I had done this signing ahead of time before, when I just acquired a checking account, but I learned a lesson from Maureen then that she could write as much money as she wanted because I signed the check first before I wrote it out. She jokingly said, "I know that you don't have any money to talk about, so the check wouldn't be worth anything!"

When I arrived at Maureen's house the first time after my back surgery, among my belongings was a teddy bear. Maureen Kelly did not understand why I had a teddy at this age of my life. This teddy bear was bought to give to me during my stay at the House of Affirmation. I was not used to having a toy of any kind; this was the first teddy bear that I had ever received. Maureen was in the process of gathering up stuff and collecting for some charity group, and my teddy bear went out with the stuff that she had collected. "You are passed that stage, for having teddy bears. You didn't have that in the convent, did you?" I didn't get upset about it. I kept telling myself that I was really behaving as a child by keeping the teddy bear.

On the other hand, having done the House of Affirmation, I learned to treat myself to fun things. I learned the valuable lesson that a therapist quoted out of the blue. I had been complaining of someone I knew back in Africa who used to act like a child and sang only childish songs and so on, and how it annoyed me. The therapist replied, "That seems to be something that really bothers you a lot. There seems to be a pattern here." Then the therapist said, "Your problem is clear, you were never a child!" I will never forget that remark. It hit me like a bolt from the blue. So I tried to recall those words of the therapist. It has helped me to put things in perspective for myself. Hence, the reason for my teddy bear.

After I had lived with Maureen Kelly for maybe two or more years, I gradually unfolded my story to her. Maureen was strict with herself and of course with me as well. I was comfortable with it as that was what I was used to in the convent, some strict superiors. All of whom were good people from the good old stock way back when. Maureen stated to someone that if she had known about me before I came, she would have treated me differently. This strictness was what I was just comfortable with all my life, and I needed it at that particular time 'til I became adjusted to my new country in America. The difference was that Maureen was concerned about me and she was, as I already mentioned, the true mother that I never had; it was good for me to feel like a child in her presence at times. I told her so often that I missed a lot, but I more than gained it back during my years of living with her. When I got a little more information on my mother, I showed Maureen the paper from Ireland. "Look," I said, "this is the biggest coincidence ever, you are the same age as my mother would have been, she was born in the same year, 1906."

Maureen's daughter lived in Detroit, and one day as she was down visiting her mother, she told me that her mother talked to her on the phone one day, and said, "I have another teenager living in the house!" That was me!

Maureen developed macular degeneration in her late years, but her peripheral vision was good, and she could get around the house. I would read the headlines in the paper and anything else worth reading to her. It was Maureen Kelly who said to me one day, "Your life has been so different, you ought to write your story." After some time and thought, I decided to write my memoirs. When I retired from work, I had more time on my hands and so I speeded up with my story. I would read what I had written to her from time to time. She would say, when I would read the newspaper to her, "Put the paper away, and bring out your story." I was afraid that I would not have the story finished before she died, but she already knew it all before I put it on paper. When she died, she took a big chunk of me with her. She would occasionally say to me, "I don't know why God is keeping me here." I would reply with same response, "God sent you another 'child', albeit a teenager, to take care of you in your old age." Maureen enriched and blessed my life in so many ways. She died at the good old age of ninety-six. The person whom I met on my first day at work in the States was Mary, and I am grateful to her for introducing me to Maureen Kelly, who just lived around the corner from her. I have not mentioned Mary so much; she has been my friend since that first day and is still today. I can only say that

God works in mysterious ways and he certainly worked on me in sending me a sister and a mother and the whole Kelly clan as well.

One day, I said to Maureen Kelly, "Maybe you'll see my mother before I will." She already had a ministroke, and while being cared for by her daughter, she did mention to her that she was going to see my mother. She had not forgotten. I was pleased to know that she remembered her promise. Once, when we were talking about all the people that she is going to see up in heaven, all her relatives that went before her, she added, "I will see your mother, and I'm going to tell her what a wonderful girl you are." She would call me her angel from time to time, and by the way, she replaced my teddy bear with a most beautiful angel doll. It is the only doll that I've ever possessed, and it has a place of honor at home in my living room.

In 1949, when I was a novice in religious life, the superior general had said to me "Your mother could have aborted you!" Now, having lived over three scores of my life, in spite of all its emotional ups and downs, I look back at this amazing life that I had and the fact that I existed. Mom, I didn't know you, but I THANK YOU.

All dressed in our Sunday best for the arrival of the bishop, Father Lynch took the photo.

All the orphanage girls now out working. Fr. Lynch gave us a day's outing by the sea. He took all the photos.

Father Geoffrey Peter Lynch

S Friars photo taken 1945

S Friars as Sr. Peter 1975

As nurse in African Hospital

Printed in the United States
215843BV00001B/70/P